ENVIRONMENT AND SOCIETY

The Enduring Conflict

ENVIRONMENT AND SOCIETY

The Enduring Conflict

ALLAN SCHNAIBERG
Northwestern University

KENNETH ALAN GOULD
St. Lawrence University

St. Martin's Press
NEW YORK

This book is dedicated to the memory of
Chico Mendez, Karen Silkwood, and Cesar Chavez,
ordinary people who rose to the challenge
of extraordinary circumstance.

Their struggles continue.

Editor: Louise H. Waller
Managing editor: Patricia Mansfield-Phelan
Project editor: Suzanne Holt
Production supervisor: Alan Fischer
Art director: Sheree Goodman
Cover design: Sheree Goodman
Cover photo: © Telegraph Colour Library / FPG

Library of Congress Catalog Card Number: 92-63066
Manufactured in the United States of America.
8 7 6 5 4
f e d c b a

For information, write:
St. Martin's Press, Inc.
175 Fifth Avenue
New York, NY 10010

ISBN: 0-312-09128-1 (paperback)
       0-312-10266-6 (cloth)

Preface

Environment and Society emphatically rejects these environmental myths:

- Environmental problems are being solved.
- Economic growth is compatible with protecting our environment.
- Recycling is the key to solving environmental problems.
- Everyone is concerned with ensuring a safe environment.
- Global problems can be addressed by local solutions.
- Better science will solve our environmental crises.
- We should educate our leaders, rather than politically confronting them.

We decided to write this book precisely because so many of our students have entered our classes believing these myths and because so many of our social scientific colleagues have left these myths unchallenged. This work has integrated our analytic skills and our social concerns, with regard both to the domestic and global inequalities in the hazards arising from ecological degradation and to the worldwide quality of daily life.

All industrial societies are built on a central belief that they can progress by conquering nature and expanding production. We accept this idea as a genuine social belief, but we challenge its premise, from both an environmental and a social perspective. Social tenacity in clinging to this belief in economic growth has permitted a particular form of political-economic system to emerge in modern industrial societies, especially the United States. In recent decades this modern system, which we view as a *treadmill of production,* has continued to erode environmental systems and to impoverish increasingly larger numbers of people. Indeed, in this book we argue that the inherent logic of this political-economic system is in fundamental and enduring conflict with the realities of both the global environment and social justice within and between societies.

v

At an early stage in the modern United States concern with environmental pollution and depletion, many scientists thought that a new environmental science would lead to a modern form of environmental enlightenment. They predicted (or at least fondly hoped) that this knowledge would introduce a new era of environmental stewardship in which nature would be preserved for the utility of human and other species. Despite the creation of environmental protection legislation in the three decades of modern environmental concern, however, many processes of natural destruction have actually accelerated. This is true despite the United Nations environmental conferences in Stockholm in 1972 and Rio de Janeiro in 1992, and despite the rise in both capitalist and formerly socialist countries of an expanded environmental movement, challenging both governments and industries to stop this destruction.

At this writing, industrial organizations have simultaneously created global environmental problems and new global poverty. Ozone depletion, which permits increased ultraviolet radiation on earth, and probably a global warming, which will affect our climate, agricultural production, and the habitability of coastal settlements, have emerged despite scientific anticipation and warnings about these problems. Although some preventative steps have been taken, they have been timid and inadequate to deal with these global problems. Other national and regional problems such as desertification and human-induced water shortages have already created international social poverty, death, and despair in the intervening decades. Especially in the 1980s, poverty, disease, and disillusionment have increased dramatically among the poor, working classes and even among large elements of the middle class in both industrial and less developed societies, while the treadmill has redistributed its benefits upward in the social hierarchy.

This book seeks to explain why the treadmill of production generates an *enduring conflict* with the natural environment. We trace the core logic of industrial systems, ranging from the logic of the firm to the logic of global capital markets, which continue to dismiss most environmental concerns. Equally important, however, we show that our institutional and individual commitments to this treadmill are quite widespread.

In effect, our argument challenges the widely diffused environmental action mantra of modern movements, *"Think globally and act locally."* The treadmill of production, we argue, is neither a global nor a local institution; rather, it is a network of regional, national, and, increasingly, multinational economic organizations. These organizations are coupled to regional and national government agencies, providing them with economic resources and cultural approval. Finally, this network impacts directly on regional, national, and international ecological systems as well as on human populations and social classes, all of which are acted upon by these treadmill institutions and have the potential to react to them.

This book, then, is first an analysis of the enduring conflict between environment and society. It examines how the economic institutions of the treadmill of production were formed, protected, and supported within our societies. We note that, in general, those social interest groups that derive the greatest economic benefits from the treadmill are able to pass on the environmental hazards and other costs to less powerful groups, both within and across nations.

From this perspective, it is clear that no environmental consciousness-raising effort can in itself alter the treadmill. Instead, we offer a range of options for challenging the treadmill, all of which require us to engage in social and political conflicts with the logic of the interests that are most supportive of this economic system. Included in this discussion are our internal conflicts between our desires to obtain more of the material goods and services that the treadmill offers and our desires to avoid the environmental and antisocial damages that this system produces.

Through this perspective we refute other analyses that suggest that human nature or Western culture has endangered our planet's systems. In contrast, we point to a historical crafting of the modern treadmill, which has emerged from coordinated social, political, and economic decisions. We explore the ways in which these decisions *may* be changed and the ways in which they ideally *must* be changed, if our social systems are to preserve some modicum of social justice. As pervasive as the modern treadmill is, we argue that it is a product of social decisions. As such it may be changed through the purposive mobilization of the disempowered, who must be prepared to engage in political conflicts and confrontations with established social, economic, and political hierarchies. Although the outcomes of these conflicts are by no means assured, the result of the failure to engage in them is clear. Failure to challenge the treadmill of production will most assuredly produce ever-increasing ecological destruction and social inequality.

ACKNOWLEDGMENTS

This shared endeavor is a product of our many years of intellectual interaction. Each of us has had important intellectual and socioemotional support from our colleagues and families during our creative and bureaucratic adventures with this manuscript. Our insights have benefited from sustained interactions with our colleagues in the Environment and Technology section of the American Sociological Association, although not all share our particular reading of the evidence for the enduring nature of environmental protection conflicts.

This book also grew out of our teaching experiences and the frustrations both of us have experienced in finding materials that our undergraduate students could assimilate. From these students at St. Lawrence University and Northwestern University, we have learned that even painful truths can be incorporated if they are presented clearly and cogently. We hope that their feedback to us over our years of teaching has resulted in a clearer and more persuasive argument in this book.

At St. Martin's Press, Louise Waller has been a strong and supportive shepherd of this project. Suzanne Holt has been patient, highly competent, and good-humored as project editor dealing with impatient scholars.

Finally, we acknowledge the enduring contributions of our friend, colleague, and student—Adam S. Weinberg—whose caring and critical commentary throughout the process of generating this manuscript has been a vital intellectual and emotional resource to both of us. His generous giving of his time and thought have been invaluable, and we look forward to an even more active engagement with him in future work.

Allan Schnaiberg
Kenneth A. Gould

Contents

Epilogue:
International Words and Deeds **225**

"Happy is the man that findeth wisdom, and the man that getteth understanding."

—Proverbs 3:13, King James Bible.

"And should they see a fragment of the heaven falling down, they would say, 'It is only a dense cloud'."

—The Koran [XLIV] Sura LII—The Mountain, verse 44.

"For in much wisdom is grief: and he that increaseth knowledge increaseth sorrow."

—Ecclesiastes 1:18, King James Bible.

Part I

Why Should We Be Concerned?

1. Social and Environmental Health: Risks and Vulnerabilities of Global Pollution and Depletion

ENVIRONMENTAL UNSUSTAINABILITY: WITHDRAWALS AND ADDITIONS

In recent years, the idea of sustainable development has emerged on the world's policy stage. Essentially, this model argues that countries need to integrate the interdependency of social and natural systems into the planning of their economies. We can regard the two faces of this interdependency as the *ecological sustainability issue* and the *economic developmental issue*. The interdependency of these two systems incorporates two assumptions:

1. Societal functioning requires us to maintain some features of environmental systems.
2. In order to preserve these features, environmental functioning requires us to restrict some of our social uses of these systems.

In many ways, these elegantly simple principles provide a central focus for this chapter and for this book. As we will point out, however, certain social factors make it unlikely that either our own society or the global society will readily adopt these principles in the future.

Sustained development is a goal, and in many ways it is a utopian one inasmuch as it implies a congruence between ecological and economic goals. Interestingly, this concept has been proposed in a number of earlier historical periods, ranging from the turn of the century with the rise of the utilitarian-conservation movements to 1973, when E. F. Schumacher presented his intermediate technology proposals (see Chapters 6 and 7). In each historical period, some temporary coalescence of social interests around this type of goal was almost immediately overwhelmed by other social interests with different economic goals. Typically, the sustained development principle was found to pose obstacles to powerful interest groups.

Thus espousing sustained development as a goal is insufficient to set in motion the societal processes that will lead to its dominance over competing goals. Even the globalism of the modern concept of sustained development is not new. Schumacher's "Buddhist economics" goal for intermediate technology was "to obtain the maximum of well-being with the minimum of consumption" (1973: 61). He first delineated this strategy in 1973 and his message was reinforced by the energy crisis of the later 1970s. It, too, had an initial following, but it met the resistance of powerful economic interests in both the underdeveloped and developed countries. Although Schumacher's strategy led to important rethinking about sustainability and to new social movement organizations and even some applied projects in a number of countries, at no point in its history did it dominate the economic agenda of any society.

The social resistance is captured in the phrases "Buddhist economics" and "energy crisis." These phrases direct our attention to two distinct types of issues that have dominated environmental conflicts over the past several decades:

1. What parts of the natural systems do "we" have to maintain?
2. Who among us has to act?

These dual conflicts have raged across the intellectual, political, and moral planes of modern industrial societies and were among the most contentious issues raised at the United Nations Conference on Environment and Development held in Rio de Janeiro, Brazil, in June 1992. In this chapter, we begin to answer the first question. Although it is primarily an ecological question, we address it from a societal perspective. (Chapter 2 moves on to the second question.) Essentially, these two questions can be phrased more specifically as:

• Why do we have to sustain parts of environmental systems?
• How do we decide on which parts to sustain?

Global environmental degradation presents a major challenge, but it is subject to many conflicting and competing interpretations, even within the natural and social scientific community. These conflicting perspectives increase in number and in intensity as we move from basic sciences to their application in political and economic institutions devoted to making and implementing economic development policies (see Chapters 3–5).

Let us start out with a brief ecological primer, which at its broadest level encompasses the following generally accepted scientific principles about ecosystems and society's role in disrupting them. Two sets of initial organizational principles affect every part of the global environment. The first set of these principles is stated by the first law of thermodynamics, which affirms that matter cannot be created or destroyed: essentially, matter cycles through the global environment. While any form of matter can be chemically or physically transformed, all the original materials are preserved in either the new or the original form. The social impact of this law cannot be overestimated. Many modern problems of local pollution, waste disposal, toxic waste hazards, and international and global problems of desertification, ozone depletion, and global warming are a direct testimonial to the differences between ecological-thermodynamic principles and our socioeconomic perspectives. The principle that perhaps best illuminates the social perspective is: "out of sight, out of mind." As producers or consumers we "dispose" of materials, but these materials merely cycle through ecological systems, disrupting them. In our starting social analysis, we refer to this cluster as problems associated with *additions* to ecosystems. Generally, these are pollution-type problems, but at the broader global level, they are also part of a newer cycle of depletion issues, because they involve chemical reactions or physical transformations of the ecosphere, which includes the earth and its atmospheric envelope.

The second principle of ecological organization is stated by the second law of thermodynamics which affirms that, as energy is transformed from its potential energy form (e.g., coal or radioactive nuclear materials) to more socially useful forms of kinetic energy (e.g., combustion to drive turbines or radiation to heat water to drive turbines), a loss of organization, or an increase in entropy occurs. Essentially, this points to degradation of energy in its social applications. Energy gets reduced from organized chemical forms into randomized heat, which is less readily usable in social production. These processes thus lead to *withdrawals* from ecosystems.

For example, in a nuclear power plant, concentrated chemical energy in the form of radioactive core elements (of uranium) is easier to move around and to incorporate in power plants. It also poses enormous risks to humans and the surrounding environmental systems, if the elements are discharged into the atmosphere, as at Chernobyl or Three Mile Island. In contrast, the "waste heat" produced by the unused energy in the turbine-propelling superheated and piped steam/water is difficult to use, and it is generally dissipated into water or air. There it represents an addition, which may create an environmental problem, inasmuch as it disrupts local fish or bird populations by changing their ecosystems through the added heat. Generally, the second law of thermodynamics points us more toward problems of depletion, especially of food and inanimate energy sources. Here the central feature is loss of potential energy, and hence loss of social utility. For this reason these processes are said to involve withdrawals from the socioeconomic potential of an ecosystem.

Although these two principles of ecological organization are clear, their applications in the real world of societal-environmental interaction are much more complex and hence subject to considerable conflicts. Specifically, while we may focus on either the cycling or the degradation processes involved in any economic activity, the reality is that both additions and withdrawals, or both cycling and degradation, occur simultaneously in most economic activities (and most social activities as well). For example, we have recently become more enamored of recycling as a solution to landfill and incineration problems with waste disposal. But to actually recycle wastes, we expend considerable energy (and human power) to collect and package them for shipment, and we expend yet more energy to remanufacture them for social uses. In this remanufacturing process we often create new forms of pollution (e.g., inks from remanufacturing using recycled newsprint). Thus, we started with a problem of additions to land/water from landfills, or to air from incineration, generating local pollution. But the problems of recycling-remanufacturing entail other potential ecological disorganization, for they require new withdrawals to make this re-production happen in our socioeconomic systems. They may also generate dispersed pollution. Factories hundreds of miles away from the community that is recycling are actually spewing pollutants into water or air or land portions of ecosystems near their remanufacturing factories.

In closing this section, let us reiterate that the two laws of thermodynamics are the basic organizing principles for the natural environment. As we will stress in Chapter 2, however, these are not the organizing principles for the economies of our societies. Indeed, modern industrial societies operate on economic principles that directly oppose the thermodynamic laws. This opposition is at the core of this book, since it is the source of "the enduring conflict."

FROM LOCAL PROBLEMS TO GLOBAL PROBLEMS

These two ecological organizing principles shape most features of our natural environment. At the local level, the environment is organized into ecosystems. These ecosystems represent an arrangement of living species, residing in a matrix of nutrients and spatial locations (territories or "homes"). Species of living elements exist in a food chain, wherein each level of a food chain pyramid eats species below it, and in turn is eaten by species above it in the food chain or "pecking order." Sociologically, we can view such a food chain as an occupational structure: each species has an occupational role or niche that determines its relationship to other species and to the nutrient base. Ecosystems have a production structure, although most of the biological production is directly related to reproduction, and its primary product is biomass (the accumulation of biological matter of species in the ecosystem).

Food chains are pyramidal because of the second law of thermodynamics: each specie has lower biomass than the species it feeds on, because some of the potential energy of the eaten specie is lost in being eaten and incorporated into the eater specie. Thus, the biomass of humans, who lie at the top of many food chains, is much lower than the biomass of the species they eat. These losses of potential energy are substantially lower for vegetarians than for the meat-eating members of our species. When domesticated animals eat vegetation or other species, there is a great loss of energy or an increase in entropy, the "degradation" of energy forms. Vegetarianism can thus be seen as ecologically more efficient than raising herds of cows, sheep, pigs, goats, or chickens to fill our plates; the former involves losses of energy only from plants to people, while the latter involves losses from plants to domesticated animals, and then from such animals to people. Yet even small-scale and "primitive" vegetarian populations produce some forms of withdrawals and additions: they use local water for themselves and the plants they gather (or plant), and they contribute human wastes to the local ecosystem. This can affect the local mix of living species, as well as the nature of local nutrients. If these human populations compete for natural plants that are also sustenance for animal species, they may reduce the local populations of these animal species as well.

Even without considering human populations, however, local ecosystems may be changing or stable, depending on the natural history of an area. Stable ecosystems are in equilibrium, with a relatively unchanging proportion of each specie and a relatively unchanging mixture of nutrients. Even without human intervention, natural processes can also lead to irreversible changes in ecosystems. For example, a pond or swamp or other form of wetland will gradually become "eutrophied": that is, water will slowly be absorbed, and new earth will eventually supplant the water. This absorption of water and growth of plant species that is associated with a gradual filling-in process depends on the presence of sufficient nutrients in the pond to support plant growth. Long-term processes of heating and cooling of the earth, the rise and fall of active volcanoes, and earthquake and tornado occurrences are all natural processes related to atmospheric changes, gravitational forces, and the shifting of geological plates on the surface of the earth. Thus, even in the absence of humans, earth's "good old days" are not entirely recoverable, because of irreversible natural changes, especially those involving the movements of geological plates.

Between these poles of equilibrium and irreversible ecosystem changes, there is a third type of ecosystem dynamic, the temporary disruption. Ecological systems have a kind of "shock absorber" feature, which protects the system from becoming permanently disorganized. In the broadest sense, we can refer to this feature as the generalized carrying capacity of the system, although this is actually a more specific ecological concept. This capacity protects the basic structure of the ecosystem, despite changes stemming from weather fluctuations, some natural disasters, or plant and animal diseases. Generally, as with other types of systems, ecological systems are buffered against permanent disruption (which we will call disorganization below) according to their redundancy and, some ecologists believe, according to their complexity. Redundancy and complexity offer both qualitative and quantitative kinds of buffers. For example, if a species of animal can survive by eating a variety of different plants or other animals, it may withstand changes in the availability of a single species of subsistence. Similarly, if the population of a species is small, it may also withstand the shrinkage of its food supply. However, we should note that even natural temporary disruptions may lead to the starvation and death of animals, for the population of a species may be forced to shrink under conditions of limited subsistence. Thus, "temporary" is not synonymous with "gentle" or "benign." One normal mechanism of adapting to external shocks that ecosystems experience is population reduction. The difference between a temporary reduction and disorganization is that disorganization entails the elimination of a species, while a temporary reduction entails only a population reduction.

So far, we have focused on the natural dynamics of ecosystems. However, especially at the local level of ecosystems, human interventions have increasingly caused disequilibria in ecosystems, producing more temporary disruptions. While some disruption has occurred throughout human history, the degree and form of such ecosystem disequilibria have changed in recent decades. Almost any human habitation will disrupt a local ecosystem somewhat. Dwellings displace plant and animal species; hunting and gathering food to support local human occupants further disorganizes the ecosystem. When human populations were small and relatively immobile, this disorganization was quite limited (see Chapter 2). It was localized, it affected few species, and local ecosystems often recovered most of their functions, mix of species, and level of nutrients.

With settled agriculture and especially with all forms of industrialization, the impact of human interventions on ecosystems changed in two ways: (1) more ecosystems were affected by human withdrawals and additions, and (2) the effects were more harmful and more enduring. These changes frequently are more intensive and extensive than the historical disruptions, creating more permanent ecosystem disorganization. Such disorganization involves a permanent change in the plant and animal species of an area, often associated with a change in ecosystem nutrients. Pollutants that are not chemically broken down by ecosystem species may interfere with the absorption of nutrients, or more simply kill off some populations of species. But even those pollutants that are (biodegradable) may overload the capacity of the system to absorb and decompose these chemicals, leaving the remainder of pollutants to alter the contexts for species. Thus, when phosphates from detergents were routinely passed into bodies of water, they promoted the rapid growth of algae and depleted the oxygen content of such bodies, often reducing the fish population and accelerating the natural eutrophication process.

The most powerful of these disorganizations occur in international or global sinks, including the oceans and the atmosphere. We have now entered a new stage of ecological disorganization in which we seem to have created the first documented human-made, enduring, harmful global impact, by creating an ozone "hole." Through the diffusion of synthetic industrial chlorofluorocarbons into the upper atmosphere, we have reduced the ozone at that level, thereby permitting higher rates of ultraviolet (UV) radiation to penetrate to the surface of the earth. Among the harmful effects of the ozone hole are increased skin and eye burning in animals and humans, reduced crop yields, and elevated risks of skin cancer through unprotected exposure to the UV rays from the sun. The evidence for these changes appears fairly clear after much scientific debate in the past decade (Roan 1989).

Scientists are somewhat more uncertain about the net atmospheric increase of carbon dioxide caused by the widespread human combustion of fuels and reduction of trees, which absorb carbon dioxide. Global warming, or the so-called greenhouse effect, is said to have risen because carbon dioxide reflects more of its heat back to earth. It is predicted that this global increase in average temperature will change the climate in many agricultural areas, alter coastal water levels because of partial melting of polar ice caps, and produce other dislocations of ecological and economic activity. This assertion has been subject to much more disagreement among scientists, although evidence increasingly seems to substantiate this global impact. In the cases of both the ozone and the increased carbon dioxide, policy debates and some agreements have been initiated to slow these forms of global ecological disorganization. In both cases, however, further changes in global systems will continue to take place because of past economic activities. In both situations, too, political-economic resistance to these meliorative policies is much in evidence because improvements mean greater costs for powerful economic interests.

Human activities have produced a variety of ecological disorganization impacts at both the local and global levels. These include desertification in tropical rainforests, sub-Saharan Africa, and elsewhere, owing in part to human activities ranging from cutting trees for firewood to plantation agriculture and multinational mining, all of which reduce vegetation in tropical climates. In turn, reduction of vegetation facilitates the removal of the thin topsoil of such ecosystems, making the land hard and unsupportive of small-holding subsistence agriculture and leading to permanent losses of trees and other ground cover. While the natural processes of drought also occur in the African continent in particular, the loss of topsoil and the declining fertility of soils, especially laterite soils, derives partly from human factors as well. Other "routine" disorganization occurs in wide swathes of countries including South America (Rudel & Horowitz 1993).

Another arena of multinational ecological disorganization includes the diffused pollution of the oceans, along with the substantial elimination of many species of large aquatic mammals and fish such as whales. Species extinction is more dramatic with these larger animals and with large trees such as old-growth redwoods, but species extinction is a routine feature of most industrial and many industrializing societies. Some of these losses are due to direct withdrawals—of habitat, nutrients, and food supplies—in the extractive or primary economic activity. Other losses are due to the additions of pollutants, which interfere with the reproduction and survival of living species.

Thus, at every ecological level, human activities have disrupted natural systems. In recent decades, these disruptions have become more diffused, larger, more central to ecosystem functioning, and long-lasting or nonreversible. What does this imply for the sustainability of development?

THE SOCIAL IMPLICATIONS OF
ECOLOGICAL DISORGANIZATION

Let us return to the start of this chapter. The environmental policy objective has recently begun to shift toward the ecological sustainability of economic development. Generally, each form of ecological disorganization noted above has one of three logical outcomes: (1) it may decrease the sustainability of development, (2) it may have no impact on the sustainability of development, or (3) it may increase the sustainability of development. This uncertainty as to outcome raises the need to clarify what is meant by sustainability, by which we mean ecological sustainability.

It should not come as a surprise that this clarification is not quite as simple as the policy words imply. Some features of ecosystems will support some forms of economic development, at some level of growth, for some time into the future. At the turn of the twentieth century, a scientifically based conservation movement arose which struggled with many of these same issues. The criterion of that period was a vague sort of utilitarianism. Each ecosystem, it was believed, would be organized so as to produce "the greatest good for the greatest number," presumably the greatest number of citizens. This in turn devolved into a concern with generating a sustained yield, a concept that is actually quite close to the modern notion of sustained development (see Chapters 7 and 9).

This earlier struggle focused mainly on "rationalizing" production in agricultural and extractive (mining, forestry, irrigation) industries. Today, the task is more formidable: we want to find a more rational, enduring form of production that also takes into account manufacturing, trade, services, and even consumption, in addition to agriculture and extraction. The earlier period frequently generated an interesting form of socioeconomic and political conflict, for the U.S. and state governments often wound up defending the expansion of large-scale enterprises at the expense of local small producers. It was argued that these small producers could not design their production in ways that would contribute to a sustained yield, and could not show scientifically how their operations would sustain the yield. A third, and more cynical, political assessment is that unlike the powerful corporations that were beginning to emerge in the agribusiness sector, such small entrepreneurs could not mount the financial resources to hire lawyers and influence politicians to fight for their interests.

While this scientific conservation movement marked a substantial step forward in understanding some of the ecological realities of western United States, its ecological focus was very limited. Biological scientists were interested largely in conserving a single element of an ecosystem, whose yield they wanted to sustain. The remainder of the ecosystem was not an object to be preserved. The major exception to this narrow objective is the case of the U.S. national parks, whose preservation was designed from a more wholistic basis. Even this issue is subject to much contemporary argument about the actual boundaries of parks. Expansions of national parks often crossed ecosystems and were often piecemeal additions to existing parks, decided more on the basis of politics and economics than on ecological system integrity. Thus, the fight over extending the Redwoods National Park in recent decades hearkens back to this earlier decision-making process. Similar conflicts exist concerning all types of natural preserves, ranging from the Redwoods to the Indiana Dunes to the Everglades and many other national and state natural areas. Even within each park, especially in densely visited parks such as Yosemite and Yellowstone, debates arose in succeeding decades over how much to weigh the comfort and convenience of visitors (and profits of concessionaires) as against strictly preserving the natural features of parks. As we have seen, then, ecological factors have been in tension and conflict with socioeconomic and political factors, from the earliest form of conservationism through the rise of modern environmentalism, and continuing into the sustainable development movement. This conflict is likely to endure indefinitely, regardless of any changes in economic and social policies we adopt. However, we believe that the intensity and outcome of conflicts can differ markedly for different segments of the population, depending on how the ecological policy-making process is shaped. Although this chapter emphasizes ecological realities and the societal problems associated with the pollution and depletion of the ecosystem, policy-making also has implications for population subgroups depending on particular environmental protection policies (see Chapter 9 especially and also Chapters 6–8).

Next, let us summarize the issue of the social implications of environmental disorganization. When large volumes of natural resources are either withdrawn from or added to ecosystems, the ecosystems begin to suffer permanent disorganization. The societal implications of this damage cannot be precisely estimated, but they tend to emerge along the following lines. Withdrawals of natural resources increase the likelihood that we will simply run out of these resources. Such depletion has already occurred for many resources and in many countries. For example, fossil fuels such as oil are no longer in large supply within the continental United States; as a result, we are drilling for oil in the waters of the outer continental shelf, posing new costs and the ecological problems of oil spillages and water pollution. We are also moving petroleum drilling to other, less developed countries, including most recently the socialist bloc countries, such as China, and the formerly socialist bloc, such as the Commonwealth of Independent States.

Other ecosystem resources have likewise been exhausted; examples are tin in Malaysia, water in large parts of the western United States, and topsoil in many regions of Latin America and Africa (from deforestation). Some cases of depletion are the result of direct extraction of this particular resource, whereas others, as in the case of topsoil, are the indirect effects of our use of other resources. For example, desertification occurs in Africa not because the topsoil is extracted but because either the trees are removed as a resource, or the trees and plant crops are removed in areas with marginal rainful levels. In rainforests, topsoil is lost because of too much rainfall (i.e., soil washes away). Paradoxically, loss of topsoil in sub-Saharan Africa is attributed to too little rainfall (i.e., the topsoil blows away, much as it did during the "dustbowl" era of the Plains states in the United States). Similarly, water or soil itself is not extracted as a withdrawal but becomes socially unusable because of the additions of pollutants.

This social usability or utility of ecosystem elements is a central issue. Sustained development can occur alongside declining social utility. A manufacturing organization (see Chapter 3) can still use polluted water for cooling in its production operations and may continue to use bodies of water as a "sink" for dumping production byproducts (polluting types of additions). At the same time, local citizen groups cannot use these bodies of water for drinking or recreational uses (swimming, boating, fishing); and other producers (fishing companies) may have their livelihoods eliminated or reduced through the reduction of aquatic species. Thus, the original polluting industry may sustain its future development, while other producers and citizen groups will thereby lose their future developmental possibilities. Chapter 9 explores the social and political dimensions of this issue; what concerns us here are the ecological dimensions of sustainability.

From the standpoint of an uncertain future course of societal development, then, the issue of ecological sustainability becomes much more unclear. We may now have a good sense of which elements of ecosystems are vital for particular forms of production, but whether other elements will become important for the current production processes in the future is unclear. Fuzziness also surrounds the issue of the sustainability of future production forms that have not yet been discovered or attempted at the pilot plant level of testing. Ecologists argue that we cannot distinguish between resources and unneeded elements of ecosystems, since today's necessity may be the future's waste and today's waste product may become the future's necessity. This lesson is illustrated by the situation on Native American reservations in the United States, where economically valueless "wastelands" were provided for native populations in the nineteenth century, but proved to be essential sources of energy minerals (coal and uranium) in the late twentieth century (Gould 1990). Similarly, in the quest for economically valuable radium, uranium was discarded as waste material. Today, some of the richest uranium ore in North America sits at the bottom of Lake Ontario, where it was dumped as slag, and now contributes to fresh water contamination (Gould 1991).

Other historical examples abound. When water power was important for milling and other early industries, local streams were an important ecological resource and coal was an unnoticed feature of ecosystems. Later, when steam power arose, the streams were abandoned and coal became an important resource. Still later, other fossil fuels, such as petroleum products, which were previously ignored (sometimes as they seeped up into bodies of water, "polluting" these bodies), became valued resources. Electrical machinery permitted a variety of ecological inputs ranging from coal to oil to nuclear fuels. Thus, other features of a manufacturing site could be ignored, and only the materials relevant for the electric utility's operations were a valued resource. If at some point in the future wind or solar power should become important sources of industrial energy, then certain geographic or ecological features of plant siting, which are currently ignored, will become important. The location of manufacturing facilities relative to wind forces (average speed, stability, gusting, etc.) or to solar incidence (regularity of sunlight, intensity of light) will become very important. Conversely, in the face of ozone depletion caused by chlorofluorocarbon emissions, solar radiation today is in effect polluted by the withdrawal of ultraviolet screening, permitting harmful UV radiation to affect human, plant, and animal health. Rather than being only a resource, then, solar radiation is also a hazard. A reduction of the ozone hole would lessen the threatening features of solar radiation and increase the resourceful features.

This example also indicates the complex relationship between the two organizing laws of the ecosystem, the two thermodynamic laws. In a root sense, all energy on earth (certainly all nonnuclear energy) derives from the sun. Fossil fuels were living plants at one time, and all living plant and animal species depend for their existence on sunlight, or food sources that are themselves dependent on sunlight. Thus, on the one hand, earth exists as part of an open system, continuously deriving new kinetic and potential energy that is radiated by the sun. This solar process counters the terrestrial effects of entropy from the second law of thermodynamics. On the other hand, though, for each social use of some terrestrial source of potential energy, entropy laws still apply to this transaction in two ways. First, there is the energy loss associated with the extraction process itself (mining, damming, or harnessing in some way). Second, there is the entropic loss involved in the conversion from potential to kinetic energy (through turbines, flows, or other dynamic conversion processes). Moreover, each entropic outcome is also associated with changes stemming from the first law of thermodynamics: materials are withdrawn from ecosystems (depletion) and waste products of extraction and conversion are added to ecosystems (pollution).

When coal was the primary fuel for generating electricity, its sulfur component produced sulfur dioxide emissions from the combustion of coal. During the early period of modern environmental concerns in the 1960s and early 1970s, attention was paid primarily to sulfur dioxide which was considered hazardous to both humans and agricultural production. Accordingly, three responses were made to reduce the social problem caused by ecological disruption: (1) conduct an increased search for low-sulfur coal, especially in the western United States; (2) remove sulfur dioxide from smoke stacks through the use of "scrubbers" of various types in order to transform airborne sulfur dioxide into a more manageable "sludge"; and (3) use much higher smoke stacks to disperse sulfur dioxide away from population centers (where environmental groups and government agencies attended to this air pollution problem).

These proposed solutions ignored the realities of ecological organization, however. The first solution created massive disruption of western U.S. ecosystems, causing local pollution and depletion of the countryside, which threatened both agriculture and tourism. On this ecological and social account, electricity consumers benefited by reduced sulfur dioxide emissions, while western producers, consumers, and tourists faced reduced profits and pleasures from less pristine ecosystems. The second solution produced a similar reduction in air pollution. But the sludge thereby produced was highly toxic (including much sulfuric acid), and landfills and ponds where this sludge was dumped produced land and water pollution, which affected the drinking water and some forms of aquaculture and agriculture. Thus, the ecosystems and social decisions transformed a local air pollution problem into a local water and land pollution problem. Finally, the third solution transferred local air pollution problems into long-distance air and water pollution, which destroyed forests and polluted streams hundreds of miles away. Water mixed with sulfur dioxide in upper airstreams reappeared as polluted water ("acid rain") that was carried by these streams into distant ecosystems. This rainfall produced a loss of trees, reducing forestry industry production, profits, and employment in the eastern United States and Canada. It also reduced fish yields as well as the recreational use of forests, lakes, and streams in this area.

This ecological example finds parallels in all other forms of electricity production. Oil-fueled power stations help induce oil spills far away, in oceans and rivers, as well as various forms of air pollution around refineries and the power plants themselves. Nuclear hazards include the hazards of mining, manufacturing, and transporting control rods for power plants, as well as more dramatic hazards at plants such as Chernobyl and Three Mile Island, where plant disasters ended in the dramatic shutdowns of operating nuclear plants.

Even "renewable" energy sources are not without problems. The equipment needed for windmills and solar power have their own ecological costs, as they do in their operations, by affecting wind patterns, noise, and solar radiation patterns, especially when used in large numbers. Geothermal energy, wave energy, and other "free" sources of power also pose problems. The point is not that there is no ecological solution, but rather that all energy production systems produce some ecological disruptions. We need a broad form of ecological impact analysis, and not a narrow form that sustains a specific type of development. When we look at the power plant example, we see that the ecological and concomitant social problems that have been underassessed or simply ignored were a result of *nonecological* analysis.

The rubric of sustained development, therefore, is a rather weak guide for hard thinking about ecological realities. Too often this concept, or its historical precedent, suggests another social utopia, a recurring fantasy of a "free lunch," as Barry Commoner (1972: 45) used to put it. Every previous source of energy, at one point in its history, made a similar promise of a free lunch and each fell far short of fulfilling such a promise. In the light of the two laws of thermodynamics we should be skeptical of any future promises. The Latin philosophical expression *ex nihilo nihil fit* ("out of nothing comes nothing") may apply to ecological realities. The "something" that we draw from ecosystems, for every type of energy use, thus becomes an enduring "thing" that will be added to some ecosystems and withdrawn from others. It will not disappear, though it may be transformed chemically or physically, and it may be dispersed widely or narrowly. Similarly, finding new sources of energy, even more ecologically benign "renewable" sources such as wind and solar radiation, raises questions about the "somethings" to which these new energy resources are applied. New energy resources would permit us to create wider forms of pollution and depletion, including energy-intensive strategies such as mining the ocean floors or creating space stations for manufacturing (which pose unprecedented global hazards along the lines of ozone depletion). As we note above, many of these transformations and dispersions of energy and materials may create new societal problems emerging from disorganization of different ecosystems, even while they apparently solve the initial social problems arising from the initial local or regional ecosystems (Commoner 1990).

WHY SHOULD WE PROTECT THE ENVIRONMENT? COMPETING VIEWS AND VALUES

Most of the answers to the question posed in this section have already been alluded to above. Here we attempt to summarize the major types of societal impacts of ecological disruption and especially of ecological disorganization. To shape this overview, we can think of societal impacts as falling along two dimensions: (1) humans as a biological species versus humans as social actors organized in a society, engaged in producing and consuming goods and services; and (2) current needs and capacities of humans/societies versus future needs and capacities of humans/societies. These dimensions generate four categories of concern about ecological disruption: health, mortality, and nutrition; reproduction and survival; quality of life; and future economic opportunity (see Table 1.1).

Table 1.1 shows why some social scientists believe it is imperative that they play a role in dealing with environmental problems. From a conventional social science perspective, environmental disorganization has the potential to change:

1. The dynamics of population growth through changes in the incidence of illness, death, and live births.
2. The average levels of living of individual social actors, as well as the average resources their social and economic institutions will have available.
3. The distribution of resources and risks among more and less powerful groups within the society.
4. The political mobilization of various parts of the society to engage in controlling this distribution.

All four of these issues are characteristic features of social science in general and sociology in particular. They correspond, respectively, to

TABLE 1.1 Dimensions of Social Concern about Environmental Decay

		Time Dimension	
		PRESENT	FUTURE
Activity Dimension	BIOLOGICAL	1. Health, mortality, and nutrition	2. Reproduction and survival
	SOCIOECONOMIC	3. Quality of life	4. Future economic opportunity

(1) demography and population studies, (2) industrialization and modernization, (3) social stratification and inequality processes, and (4) political sociology.

As this chapter suggests, we have strong motivations to act both individually and collectively in order to protect ourselves from the effects of present and future ecological disorganization. In this book, we take no moral stance on the values of preserving the natural environment, apart from a concern for preserving and enhancing the quality of social life. We are unabashedly and unashamedly anthropocentric; that is, this book is oriented to the needs of human society. We have taken this position for several reasons, and most notably because there is no social scientific justification for any particular ecological value, apart from the somewhat utilitarian position we have stated. One's preferences for protecting any particular ecosystem or any particular plant or animal species within it, or for maintaining a particular body of water and ignoring additions to another adjacent body—all of these remain individual preferences. Even the modern movement to preserve animal rights should be treated in a similar fashion of individual or group preferences. Why? Because the choice of protecting laboratory animals or fighting euthanasia in animal shelters is just that—a choice based on each member's own preferences and values—and there is no *societal* implication of these preferences that we can integrate into our perspective.

As in virtually all scientific writing, certain value preferences undergird this book and its arguments. We value the following: life over death, wellness over illness, individual choice over individual constraint, greater equalization of opportunity that a particular society and world economy can generate through its use of ecosystems, and greater empowerment of the unempowered through reorganizing the extraction of resources from ecosystems. Therefore, this analysis is built around our values and preferences for public policies. The reader should note this important point, particularly in prescriptive sections where we discuss what *ought* to be done to change our social structure (especially Chapters 9–10). While these preferences also affect which relationships between societal structure and ecosystem structure we have chosen to focus on, they are less signifi-

THE OZONE CRISIS:
TOO LITTLE TOO LATE?

In 1974 two chemists at the University of California–Irvine discovered that chlorofluorocarbons (CFCs) had the potential to deplete the earth's protective ozone layer. Although their research was confirmed in 1976, powerful CFC producers such as Du Pont (see ecostration for Chapter 5) ignored this evidence and encouraged political actors to do the same. The first step toward eliminating CFCs was not taken until 1978, when use of CFC in spray cans was banned in the United States. However, with the inauguration of the Reagan administration in 1981, the ozone issue was taken off the American political agenda. Anne Burford, the new EPA administrator, rejected ozone depletion as a sensational scare issue. Progress on addressing ozone depletion was stalled in the United States until 1985, when scientists discovered that nearly half the ozone over Antarctica had disappeared. Unfortunately, CFC manufacturers failed to respond to this new information.

Two years later, in September 1987 in Montreal, representatives of 43 nations developed and signed an agreement for phasing out CFC production. The Montreal Protocol called for a freeze on CFC production at 1986 levels by 1990; a 20 percent reduction by 1994; and an additional 30 percent reduction by 1999. An extension of the phase-out was granted to developing nations in recognition of both the difficulty in replacing CFCs in poorer nations and the limited contribution of these nations to the creation of the problem. Although the Montreal Protocol was an important step forward in coordinated international environmental action, many viewed the agreement as inadequate. Some scientists believed that an 85 percent reduction in 5 years was needed. Others noted that, with the exemptions included in the protocol, only a 35 percent reduction would be achieved by 1990. Meanwhile, CFC producers had failed to respond to ecological warnings for 14 years.

Since Montreal, scientists have discovered that the ozone layer is eroding much faster than previously predicted. Ozone depletion in the Northern Hemisphere is depleting two to three times faster than expected, and the ozone over Europe has depleted 8 percent in the last decade, twice as fast as in the previous decade. This accelerated depletion has led some nations to act unilaterally to phase out CFCs sooner. For example, Germany will ban CFC production by 1995, and Canada will phase out production by 1997. In addition, calls for renegotiating the Montreal Protocol have been widespread.

Nevertheless, we are already experiencing a 4 to 5 percent ozone thinning globally, which was not predicted to occur until 2025. This thinning could allow as much as 6 percent more ultraviolet (UV) radiation to reach the earth's surface. Exposure to UV radiation has been linked to cataracts and blindness, skin cancers, immune deficiencies, reduced crop yields, and impairment of phytoplankton growth (essential to the marine food chain). As many as 12 million additional cases of skin cancer are expected in the United States alone in the next 50 years as a result of increased UV exposure.

> For each 1 percent loss of ozone, the incidence of nonmelanoma skin cancers is expected to rise 5 to 6 percent. And since CFCs last in the atmosphere for decades, even with an accelerated phase-out, peak UV levels will not occur until 2010 or 2020.

cant for the descriptive analyses of how societal and ecological systems actually relate to each other.

Both Table 1.1 and this issue of values suggest which dimensions of ecological disorganization we have chosen to downplay. Generally, the table highlights the distribution of risks to the citizenry arising from ecological withdrawals and additions. It deemphasizes issues of national economic and political power, and of economic growth; it places much less stress on growth in the gross national product and average profit rates. All of these topics are discussed in various chapters, but these issues are not our paramount social and political issues. Thus, this book does not directly address topics such as national security or optimal investment paths in the face of environmental disorganization; other books address some of these issues. We have neither the desire nor the capacity to deal with those topics, although, they will be treated in passing within our extensive treatments of our main concerns. Note that we do not consider these issues irrelevant or unimportant, but our focus derives from our social values and scientific skills.

The title of this book is also germane to this discussion. Our analysis is based in part on our prior professional research experiences in the area of environmental protection conflicts. Upon reflection on these issues, we have concluded that the *enduring conflict* surrounding natural resource use is closely related to these differences in values. Those values (economic growth and national security) that we underemphasize here have historically been in conflict with the values that we do stress in this book (health and the empowerment of citizens). Moreover, the analysis of environmental problems is itself dominated by the values of economic growth and related concerns of powerful social actors, even in sustainable development concerns. We seek to redress this imbalance by emphasizing "ecological use with a human face" in this book. Our questions about both ecological disorganization and environmental protection are aimed at laying bare the realities of how less powerful groups in our society and others suffer as a result of both ecological disorganization and the economic burdens associated with environmental protection. Put simply, while we analyze the powers and values of "Wall Street," our social concern is with the impacts on "Main Street" of both ecological and economic realities. Furthermore, our policy suggestions are designed to empower Main Street in its "enduring conflict" *with* Wall Street.

MOTIVES FOR STUDYING SOCIAL-ENVIRONMENTAL RELATIONSHIPS

Our objectives in this book are somewhat broad. At one extreme, this book can be used as preparation for a political career in fighting for *environmental justice*, which we define as environmental protection aimed at equalizing social opportunity. At a less intensive political and social level, our analysis and arguments can serve as a guide to what a concerned citizen should do in her or his voting behavior, and perhaps also in joining some "mainstream" environmental groups such as the Sierra Club. Next, this book can be regarded as a kind of ecological farmer's almanac, which predicts some of the ecological and political "weather" that is likely to occur in coming decades. This may help the reader think about a career in institutions in view of likely ecological changes, on the one hand, and political and economic responses to them, on the other. That is, we offer some guidance in predicting future environments—ecological and social, economic, and political ones. Finally, this book is about viewing the implications of environmental change and policy-making in terms of our everyday private lives. Thus, this book also covers issues touching on the reader's own sense of self-worth, relationships to peers and relatives, role as partner and parent, and broader relationships with different generations within the reader's own family.

A cautionary note: the arguments in this book will often make you uncomfortable. That's a necessary part of our task, which is to challenge existing social models. We seek to help the reader understand this problem by providing some stimulation, some new linkages of everyday life and everyday assumptions about our social and economic institutions, and insight into our own personal and familial coping styles. Such stimulation may be uncomfortable at first, but our task is to empower the reader to understand and help shape this *enduring conflict*.

SELECTED REFERENCES

AYRES, ROBERT U.
  1989 "Industrial metabolism and global change: Reconciling the sociosphere and the biosphere—global change, industrial metabolism, sustainable development, vulnerability." *International Social Science Journal* 41 (3): 363–374.
BLUMBERG, PAUL
  1980 *Inequality in an Age of Decline.* New York: Oxford University Press.
BROWN, PHIL & E. J. MIKKELSON
  1990 *Toxic Waste, Leukemia, and Community Action.* Berkeley: University of California Press.

BULLARD, ROBERT D.
1990   *Dumping in Dixie: Race, Class and Environmental Quality.* Boulder, CO: Westview Press.
BUNKER, STEPHEN G.
1985   *Underdeveloping the Amazon: Extraction, Unequal Exchange, and the Failure of the Modern State.* Urbana: University of Illinois Press.
CATTON, WILLIAM R., JR.
1980   *Overshoot: The Ecological Basis of Revolutionary Change.* Urbana, IL: University of Illinois Press.
COMMONER, BARRY
1972   *The Closing Circle: Nature, Man and Technology.* New York: Alfred A. Knopf.
1990   *Making Peace with the Planet.* New York: Pantheon Books.
COURT, THIJS DE LA
1990   *Beyond Brundtland: Green Development in the 1990s.* London: Zed Books.
EVERNDEN, NEIL
1985   *The Natural Alien.* Toronto: University of Toronto Press.
GOULD, KENNETH A.
1990   "Environment, extraction, and development: How has uranium extraction constrained the future on the Laguna-Pueblo Reservation?" Paper presented at the Midwest Sociological Society meetings, Chicago, April.
1991   "The sweet smell of money: Economic dependency and local environmental political mobilization." *Society and Natural Resources* 4: 133–150.
HAWKINS, KEITH
1984   *Environment and Enforcement: Regulation and the Social Definition of Pollution.* Oxford, England: Clarendon Press.
LYMAN, FRANCESCA
1991   "As the ozone thins, the plot thickens." *Amicus Journal,* 13 (3): Summer.
MORRIS, DAVID
1992   "The four stages of environmentalism." *Utne Reader,* March/April, 157, 159.
REDCLIFT, MICHAEL
1987   *Sustainable Development: Exploring the Contradictions.* New York: Methuen.
ROAN, SHARON L.
1989   *Ozone Crisis.* New York: John Wiley & Sons.
RUDEL, THOMAS K. & B. HOROWITZ
1993   *Tropical Deforestation: Small Farmers and Land Clearing in the Ecuadorian Amazon.* New York: Columbia University Press.
SCHNAIBERG, ALLAN
1980   *The Environment: From Surplus to Scarcity.* New York: Oxford University Press.
SCHUMACHER, E. F.
1973   *Small Is Beautiful: Economics As If People Mattered.* New York: Harper & Row.
STRETTON, HUGH
1976   *Capitalism, Socialism, and the Environment.* Cambridge, England: Cambridge University Press.
WORLD COMMISSION ON ENVIRONMENT & DEVELOPMENT
1987   *Our Common Future.* New York: Oxford University Press.
WORLD RESOURCES INSTITUTE
1992   *World Resources 1992-93.* New York: Oxford University Press.

2. Society as the Enemy of the Environment: Battle Plans for the Assault

LIVING WITHIN ECOLOGICAL LIMITS: A HISTORICAL IDEAL

When the emergence of the current environmental crisis is discussed, the disregard for ecological limits that typifies modern industrial societies is often contrasted with the alleged respect of preindustrial societies for ecosystems (Burch 1971). The reverence for nature that runs through the cosmogonies and religions of "native" peoples is often held up as an ideal from which Judeo-Christian and atheistic industrial societies have departed, with dire consequences for the natural world. Many preindustrial or nonindustrial societies have indeed managed their interaction with the environment in less destructive and more sustainable ways.

However, this historical sustainability of nations often encompassed a mixture of careful environmental balancing in some communities and significant economic expansion in others. Within these societies, certain areas produced ecological disorganization. On the one hand, therefore, much can be learned from nonindustrial societies' respect for nature, as well as contemporary variations in the ecological and economic behaviors of industrial societies (Stretton 1976). Yet it would be a mistake to romanticize this apparent harmony of society and environment, since all societies eventually face the necessity of deciding on some forms of ecological additions and withdrawals. It is important that we juxtapose the historical differences between places and periods of ecological stability and ecological disorganization.

Although the ecological changes made by many ancient societies are difficult to assess accurately, some basic notions as to the destructive potential of premodern economies are discernible. China, one of the world's earliest great civilizations, is still experiencing the negative consequences of some environmental withdrawals made in earlier centuries. Much of the ancient Chinese forests were extracted as much as 900 years ago to provide a variety of fuels, textiles, and building materials, and to clear the way for the expansion of agriculture. China thus remains a nation that suffers from severe levels of deforestation. The Yellow River, which is an extremely important feature of Chinese geography, ecology, history, and folklore, is so named because of the color of the sediments that the river carries away. Massive deforestation resulted in uncontrollable erosion of topsoil (World Resources Institute 1992). That topsoil is essential to a nation that must feed approximately 20 percent of the world's population from only 8 percent of the world's arable land. Modern Chinese efforts to reduce topsoil erosion have, therefore, been quite extensive.

Similarly, the fabled cedars of Lebanon were felled, along with most of the ancient forests of North Africa and the Middle East. Although the extent of the Sahara Desert in ancient times remains a mystery, it is clear that the sandy wasteland that now exists supported an abundance of biological diversity in ancient times. Although it may be impossible to determine the extent to which natural climate change caused the desert to expand, it is clear that human utilization of the local environment without regard for long-term sustainability contributed to the expansion of a much simplified and less productive environment. Thus, North Africa, which once served as the granary of the Roman Empire, must now struggle to provide domestic food supplies for its local populations (Brown 1992).

The great Mayan civilization of pre-Columbian America is believed to have declined largely as a result of exceeding the threshold of the ecological limits imposed by the natural ecosystems in which they lived and the technologies they had available to manipulate those ecosystems. Again, the extent to which ecological factors contributed to the decline of the Mayas remains unclear. But recent scientific evidence seems to indicate that population expansion, soil erosion, and deforestation increased the vulnerability of that society to disruptions of the status quo (Brown 1992). When societies move toward the edge of ecological limits, even small changes in economic, social, political, or ecological factors can have a major impact on the society's ability to survive.

Predating all these examples are the ancient inhabitants of North America who, ten to twenty thousand years ago, migrated with the woolly mammoths to insure a supply of food and textiles. It is argued that these ancients hunted the mammoths to extinction, since their rates of extraction exceeded the capacities of these enormous mammals to reproduce (Schnaiberg 1980: ch. I). The mammoths may have faced extinction from natural causes at some later date, as climatic conditions shifted (in patterns similar to those theorized about dinosaur extinction). Similarly, the preindustrial human conquest of many island ecosystems, which had developed in isolation from the species of the large continents, resulted in the extinction of a wide variety of relatively defenseless creatures. The giant Moas of New Zealand fell victim to the appetites of nonindustrial Polynesians, long before the arrival of Europeans initiated the extinction of a large number of island species in a worldwide pattern.

The noble respect for nature displayed by nonindustrial societies in the past, and in the present, often coexisted with domestic or international pressures to override these principles (Mumford 1963). Modern industrial societies would be well advised to examine and incorporate much of the socioenvironmental ethics espoused by pre- and nonindustrial peoples into their current systems of values. But they must also attend to the important historical disjunctures between ethical words and technical deeds, which were often initially built around military or political ambitions. If we are to achieve long-term socioenvironmental sustainability, all societies will either have to redefine their ethical relationship to the natural world or struggle to live up to the goals established by those cultural constructs.

The industrial revolution of Europe in the eighteenth and nineteenth centuries did not begin the damaging of fragile natural systems, but it greatly accelerated it both locally and globally. If we are to find viable solutions to current environmental crises, it is important that we not overly idealize some "golden past" in which all human societies lived in a stable, low-tech world in harmony with nature. This propensity to refer to a nonexistent golden past often leads to modern policy proposals that are equally mythic in their own assumptions (e.g., in appealing to self-regulation by a "community"). Certainly, many areas experienced such a social and ecological balance for long periods of time. Yet the conflict between human societies and natural systems is a perennial one, since the "average" experiences of citizens even in the premodern world were quite variable. Without question, the industrial revolution exponentially expanded the depth and breadth of this conflict. In effect, as a result this conflict became more central to the question of survival of more societies, and certainly of more people, at the end of the twentieth century than ever before.

EXCEEDING ECOLOGICAL LIMITS: FROM PREINDUSTRIAL TO POSTINDUSTRIAL PATTERNS

Despite the numerous examples of preindustrial environmental destruction, for most of history (and prehistory), human societies were forced by their relatively more limited technological capacities to live within the constraints imposed by ecological limits. Preindustrial societies depended on a clearly limited agricultural base for their survival. Ecological additions and withdrawals as well as population growth were kept in check by the fertility of the local ecosystem and its capacity to provide sufficient and reliable supplies of food. Those societies that exceeded the limited capacity of natural systems to provide food for their populations went into decline and ultimately collapsed. History is full of examples of agricultural societies which, through exceeding carrying capacities or experiencing extreme conditions of drought or blight, were destroyed by their inability to adapt to ecological limits (Volti 1992).

The Anasazi or "Ancient Ones" of the American Southwest serve as an example of a highly advanced civilization that collapsed under the pressures of the local ecology. Although the exact cause of their decline remains controversial, it is likely that the Anasazi abandoned their sophisticated settlements because the local environment was unable to provide the necessities for human survival. Whether their decline was a result of a shift in human techniques, populations, or ecological factors beyond their control, the ability of their local environment to sustain their system of ecological additions and withdrawals presented Anasazi society with clearly defined limits. The technological capacity to obscure the ecological limits to human activities would not emerge until long after the time of the Anasazi.

"OVERCOMING" LIMITS: SUCCESSIVE WAVES OF INDUSTRIAL REVOLUTIONS

Despite the apparent similarities in the potential for preindustrial and industrial societies to overshoot local ecological limits, there are important qualitative and quantitative differences in the ways in which these two types of societies degrade ecosystems. Preindustrial societies, when they did surpass ecological limits, did so primarily by exceeding the carrying capacity of their agricultural bases. Either their populations expanded beyond the capacity of local ecosystems to provide sufficient food crop supplies, or by overharvesting important natural resources such as trees or animal species. While these ecological errors had dramatic negative impacts on affected societies, they tended to produce less drastic long-term consequences for local ecosystemic organization and have little impact on the global biosphere.

In contrast, industrial societies may exceed ecological limits in more numerous and pernicious ways. Industrial societies have the capacity to exceed ecological limits through the introduction of greater quantities of additions than local (and global) ecosystems can absorb. Mass production of economic goods necessitates the mass production of environmental bads. And these additions often have a much more devastating impact on ecosystems, due to the synthetic nature of newly introduced toxic chemical compounds. The combination of increasing quantities of increasingly destructive additions allows industrial societies to create more wide-spread and long-lasting ecological disorganization.

Also, mass production necessitates the extraction of ever-increasing amounts of natural resources, both renewable and nonrenewable, from increasingly fragile ecosystems. Industrial societies also demand a wider variety of potentially more-dangerous natural resources, such as uranium. The technological capacity emerging from the technological revolution to create greater levels of more pernicious additions and greater levels of more pernicious resource extraction for exponentially expanding populations has meant that industrial societies can and do exceed ecological limits in ways that were and are impossible for pre- or nonindustrial societies. And industrial societies can, in addition, disrupt ecosystems in the old ways as well.

The emerging technologies of the industrial revolution freed human societies from the ecological limits that had constrained the expansion of agriculturally based economies. No longer dependent on the fertility of local ecosystems to provide the agricultural products necessary for human survival, industrial cash economies allowed for economic expansion which, at the time, appeared to be limited only by the ability of human ingenuity to take technological advantage of a seemingly infinite supply of natural resources. Once the countryside could effectively feed the cities, a massive expansion of urban industrial centers was possible.

The technologists of the industrial revolutions lived in a world with a cornucopia of resources to be extracted and manipulated to produce seemingly endless supplies of manufactured goods and wealth. Both Adam Smith, the father of modern capitalism, and Karl Marx, the father of modern communism, believed that the problem of production had finally been solved by the emergence of new technological innovations. No longer would human societies have to struggle to meet the basic needs of their populations. The crux of the political and socioeconomic debate in the industrial era would be centered on the *distribution* of the endless wealth made available to societies through modern technologies, not on the ability of modern technological complexes to provide all the goods that people demanded. No longer forced to live in the relative poverty of subsistence agriculture, and no longer dependent on a finite resource base for the provision of goods, politics in the industrial world turned its attention toward the distribution of infinite wealth and away from the question of human survival in an untamed natural world. However, it would not be long before ecological limits reemerged and reimposed themselves on human societies in the form of crises of resource depletion and environmental pollution.

The industrial revolution in Europe largely emerged in response to increased international trade with the societies of the East. New transportation technologies (primarily larger and more navigable ships) made it possible for the otherwise technologically backward societies of Europe to enter into trade with the more advanced societies of Asia. An increased volume of trade required an increase in manufacturing to produce goods that could be traded for the products of the East. In many ways, the socioeconomic and technological changes of the early European industrial revolution emerged from conditions similar to those the United States is experiencing today in regard to trade with a technologically and economically more advanced Asia. In order to gain the goods produced in the East, the West needed to increase the production of products to be traded. Failure to do so would result in a balance-of-trade deficit. Technologies of mass production were developed to expand European economies to keep pace with the importation of goods from the wealthier Asian societies.

The new technologies of mass production required reliable and harnessable supplies of *energy*. Early industrial technologies made use of natural hydrologic systems to provide this energy. Waterwheels were used to convert the energy of the solar-powered hydrologic cycle into a usable form. Thus, the earliest industrial facilities were located on reliable rivers and streams. Later developments would utilize the energy contained in combustible materials to turn water into steam, which would rise to turn turbines and generate power. Despite the assumption of rapid technological advancement, modern nuclear power plants simply use nuclear reactions to produce steam from water to generate electricity. In the industrial revolution, as today, water meant power, and power meant mass production.

The centrality of water in industrial technologies produced locational advantages for towns situated on rivers (and later, lakes), for these towns could insure a steady source of power and a reliable transportation system for shipping raw materials and manufactured goods. Water also provided a reliable industrial sewer to absorb the chemical byproducts of the new technologies. Towns that had such locational advantages became the manufacturing centers of the industrial revolution. Towns situated on natural ocean harbors emerged as the trading centers from which manufactured goods were sent and received. Other towns, which emerged and prospered on the basis of their agricultural fertility or centrality at crossroads of overland trading routes, went into decline. To this day, industry still tends to be located near water for cooling, energy, waste disposal, and transportation advantages. From Gary, Indiana, to Singapore, water is a key resource on which industrialism depends. This is why our dirtiest polluting industries remain located on our primary bodies of fresh water. The Great Lakes, which account for one-fifth of the world's total supply of fresh water, are host to the largest complexes of polluting industrial facilities in North America (Ashworth 1987).

In the early industrial revolution, it was believed that the planet could supply endless amounts of fresh water for industry, agriculture, and human consumption, while simultaneously absorbing an endless supply of industrial, agricultural, and human waste. It was not long, however, before the ecological limits of the earth's fresh water resources would once again reimpose themselves on human societies, first in the form of bacteriological epidemics and later in the form of chemical carcinogens. Cholera epidemics killed huge percentages of urban populations until sewage treatment or diversion was applied to reduce the negative health effects of using the same body of water as a toilet and a drinking fountain.

Industrialization began to run into ecological limits in other ways as well. As we have seen, mass production requires greater capital investments in the technologies of production. The introduction of new technologies alters the labor to capital ratios. Workers can no longer supply their own manufacturing technologies. Whereas preindustrial manufacturers owned their tools, looms, and mills, industrial workers must use the machines owned by others. Industrialization created a larger and more powerful role for capitalists in investing in centralized technological facilities. Industrial technologies required nonworker ownership of the means of production.

Investment in large and expensive centralized technologies resulted in the emergence of factories, where workers were brought together to operate these technological investments. Factory work emerged with many similarities to a military organization of labor. As in the military, a hierarchical chain of command was established. Workers became the foot soldiers of mass production. Capital investors became the captains or generals of industry. Supervisors or middle managers were created to oversee the production process. The geographic centralization of production required workers to "go to work" at the same times and in the same places as other workers. This represented an important social change from production in the home in an unregimented time frame. Limited transportation required that industrial workers live near the factories. As a result, the first company and industrial towns were established.

The increasing primacy of industry over agriculture caused a migration from rural to industrial centers. Advances in agriculture allowed fewer and fewer agriculturalists to provide food for greater and greater numbers of urban industrial workers. This was true in Europe in the industrial revolution, just as it is true today in the nations of the South. In this book "South" refers to those less industrialized nations that are more commonly referred to as the Third World; they are located primarily to the south of the industrialized nations, which are referred to as the "North." (A fuller discussion of the South and North is provided in Chapter 8.) This rural to urban migration alters the population distribution of societies and results in the emergence of mass urbanization, with all of the urban problems that are all too familiar to us today. In many ways societies become more complex as factory work takes people out of agriculture and throws them together in industrial cities. Family structures are also altered, as people begin to spend most of their waking hours engaged in work away from their homes and families. All these processes of early industrialization are still being played out in the South, where rural to urban migration in search of factory work draws people out of agriculture and away from their families.

Of course, all this centralization around industrial technologies produced intolerable local living environments. While managers did, and still do, live upwind of their factories, the workers live near and downwind from them. With industrialization came urban smog, overcrowding, and negative health consequences that continue to plague industrial cities. Centralized production meant centralized populations, which, in turn, meant the centralization and accumulation of industrial and human waste. In 1800 London reached a population of 1 million, the first European city to do so since the collapse of the Roman Empire. By 1856 London's population exceeded 2.5 million, and over half of Britain's population lived in cities and towns. Such rapid urban growth exceeded the ability of government and industry to plan for the expansion of urban services. The result was severe housing shortages, which parallel the contemporary housing shortages in the contemporary urban environments of the Southern nations. In 1850, one-third of Liverpool's population lived in unheated crowded cellars (Chambers et al. 1983).

It became impossible to provide for adequate sanitation in these industrial centers. There was simply no capacity to deal with the human, municipal, and industrial waste generated in these cities. Narrow alleys quickly filled with rotting garbage, as the infrastructure to move waste from the cities to the countryside was inadequate. Throughout the city of Paris clean water was available only at a few scattered fountains, while in London, water companies allowed it to flow for only a few hours a day. For the vast majority of urban residents, bathing was out of the question. Wealthy residents paid carriers to bring buckets of fresh water to their homes. Water in most cities came from what were already dangerously polluted rivers and lakes. There were simply no sewage treatment systems in place. In the 1830s Manchester had indoor toilets for only one-third of its buildings. In the 1840s the ratio of indoor toilets to population was 1 for every 212 residents. Today, such ratios for the cities of the South are much worse.

In addition to the stench and filth of raw sewage and rotting garbage, industrial and municipal smog was overwhelming. Homes that were heated were heated primarily by burning coal. Industries, too, burned coal and emitted a wide variety of untreated chemical smoke and smog. This smog literally darkened the sky, preventing sunlight from penetrating. Similar conditions exist today in cities such as Shanghai and Mexico City, as the nations of the South experience their own industrial revolutions. Because cities grow up around industries, the factories are at the heart of the urban centers. Workers cluster around these pollution sources, bearing the full brunt of toxic industrial effluent. The ability of local environments to absorb urban industrial additions was, and is, rapidly exceeded, creating nightmares of disease, smog, filth, stench, and squalor.

Despite the overwhelmingly oppressive nature of the urban environments produced by the industrial revolution, relatively few saw these conditions as an indictment of the benefits accruing from the emergence of new technological facilities. Although many recognized the problems that came with urbanization and industrialization, for the most part, these problems were (and still are) seen as the price that must be paid for the unquestionable advantages of industrial society. As Lewis Mumford has noted, "The smoking factory chimney, which polluted the air and wasted energy, whose pall of smoke increased the number and thickness of natural fogs and shut off still more sunlight—this emblem of a crude, imperfect technics became the boasted symbol of prosperity" (Mumford 1963:168).

In the industrial revolution, environmental destruction and decay were the markers of enormous wealth and power. Whereas environmentally sensitive individuals at the end of the twentieth century may come upon a factory emitting endless streams of choking smoke and decry the foolishness of such ecological imbecility, earlier generations saw jobs, money, consumer goods, and power. Like those earlier generations of industrial Northerners, many of those living in the South today, plagued by landlessness, joblessness, hunger, and disease, see industrialization as a glimmer of hope in an otherwise intolerable situation.

While the cities of Europe and North America in the industrial revolution were slowly able to use some of the wealth generated by industrial mass production to create sewage and sanitation systems, industrial pollution control devices, and housing, the situation in the South is quite different. Industrialization comes much later for the South. In addition to the search for industrial jobs, rural to urban migration is fueled by a massive population boom, creating endemic conditions of landlessness for agrarian societies. Since 1950 this migration has overwhelmed the cities of the South. Whereas the total population of Southern urban centers was 257 million in 1950, by 1980 that population had reached 950 million. These populations continue to soar. Mexico City had a population of 2.87 million in 1950; by the year 2000, that population was expected to exceed 31 million (Population Reference Bureau 1981).

As we will see in Chapter 8, global socioeconomic and technological circumstances are much different now than they were during Europe and North America's industrialization. Labor-saving technological innovation in the past century has drastically altered labor to capital ratios. It costs much more money to employ one industrial worker in the late twentieth century than it did in the nineteenth century (Schnaiberg 1980: ch. V). The increased cost of employing industrial workers, together with the decreasing employment capacity of new industrial technologies, has meant that the nations of the South are not currently, and will not in the future, be able to absorb rural to urban migrants as industrialization expands. In addition, the international flow of capital has resulted in a situation in which capital accumulation in the South, resulting from industrial facilities located in the South, is at a much lower (often negative) rate than was capital accumulation in the North (see Chapter 8). This means that impoverished Southern nations will not be able to provide sewage and sanitation systems, pollution control devices, and housing for their rapidly increasing urban populations. In the South, modern industrial urban development is simply not sustainable (Teitelbaum 1985). However, as Chapter 8 will demonstrate, alternative development trajectories are often difficult, if not impossible, to implement.

EMERGENT "ENVIRONMENTAL SCIENCE" AND THE "RETURN" OF ECOLOGICAL LIMITS

If the industrial revolution of the nineteenth century is typified by the apparent obliteration of the constraints of ecological limits on human activities, the late twentieth century is typified by the startling and catastrophic reimposition of those limits. The optimism of industrial enthusiasts like Karl Marx and Adam Smith, as well as the belief that the problem of production had been solved, has come crashing down in the late twentieth century in the realization that the earth simply cannot provide for unlimited resource extraction. Nor can it absorb unlimited chemical additions. In the late 1960s as the peoples of the earth were treated to their first glimpse of their small blue home from space, the limits of that finite mass were being reached, resulting in unprecedented pollution, depletion, extinction, and famine crises. Just as humanity seemed to be breaking free from that final ecological limit, our restriction to habitation of the planet of our origin, the natural limits of the earth reimposed themselves forcefully, as if to thwart our scientific and technological arrogance with humility before the forces that had created us. The earth is finite, and we are dependent on it for our survival, no matter how sophisticated our powers of innovation or rationalization become. We have only one planet to live on. If our activities make the continuation of the earth's essential life support systems impossible, we will perish along with the other lifeforms with which we share it.

Clearly, there had been earlier warnings of the reimposition of ecological limits. Epidemics in cities resulting from overstressed ecosystems alerted us to the dangers of exceeding the capacity of our ecosystems to absorb our wastes. In Chicago and elsewhere, the entrance of increasing volumes of human waste into our fresh water supplies at the turn of the century cost the lives of thousands. The extinction of the forests of Europe, and later much of North America, foretold of the hazards of extracting more from the planet than the planet could renew. Famines in Ireland and elsewhere indicated our vulnerability to nature despite, or as a result of, our "modern" and scientific agrarian technologies. But, save for a few lonely souls speaking from a nearly universal blind faith in science and technology who saw danger where others saw only profits, these warnings went unheeded. Human society continued unabated in its headlong rush beyond the limits of nature.

By the 1960s and early 1970s a growing number of people in the industrial societies of the North began to see the tip of the ecological iceberg floating in our course. Rapid extinction resulting from toxic chemical additions was bringing us to the brink of a *Silent Spring* (Carson 1962). The proliferation of nuclear weapons threatened to destroy us all. Precipitously declining mortality rates due to our modern sanitation methods and medicines resulted in the emergence of a *Population Bomb* (Ehrlich 1968). Spiraling consumption of nonrenewable fossil fuel resources raised the specter of an *Energy Crisis* (Schnaiberg 1975). And futurists began to rediscover that there might be *Limits to Growth* (Meadows et al. 1972), and that exceeding those limits could lead to a catastrophic *Eco-Spasm* (Toffler 1975) of environmental collapse.

Throughout the 1960s and 1970s scientific evidence of the ecological limits to industrial economic expansion began to surface in political circles. Although most readers have been conditioned to think of scientific research as an objective, free-standing source of information for social policymakers, the roles and relationships that constitute science and our political structure are actually closely intertwined. Environmental science emerged in the public arena in the 1960s as much because of the political concerns expressed by Rachel Carson as because of any new and startling findings. Note that the presence of mechanisms through which environmental and economic interest groups provided alternative sets of often contradictory scientific research findings (e.g., Graham 1970) implies that scientific data are inconclusive; that is, they are imprecise in generating agreement about environmental "impacts" (Schnaiberg 1977, 1980: chs. VI–VII). Moreover, it also suggests that scientific information is often gathered and presented in a subjective manner in order to promote the specific interests of particular sets of social actors.

Although scientists are not unfamiliar with the process of choosing sets of data and theories that best support their scientific arguments, the utilization of these arguments in the decision-making process takes scientific disputes out of the "ivory towers" and into the realm of public politics (Gould 1988). Disputes over appropriate methodology and proper modeling are a fundamental aspect of the unique scientific institution. Environmental policy-making typically places these scientific disputes within a political context, where the objective scientific disagreements are used to promote and/or undermine the arguments of political partisans

(Schnaiberg 1980: chs. VI–VII). In such a context, the relative scientific merits of various models and methods are rarely debated extensively.

At the center of the debate in public hearings, congressional committees, and lobbying efforts is the acceptability of the various sets of scientific data and conclusions that these different methods and models have produced (Brodeur 1989, 1992). In this context, each data set represents implicit policy recommendations supported by particular interest groups providing the scientific research (Wright 1992). As a result, debate tends to focus on the credibility of the various data sets mainly in terms of the political impact of their exclusive acceptance (Schnaiberg 1977). Sets of scientific data presented in the course of environmental policy conflicts are most often critiqued for their ramifications for decision making rather than on the merits of the methods utilized in the analyses themselves (Wright 1992). This entire process serves to reduce the perception of science as a fact-revealing enterprise and relegates scientific research to being a tool of interest-oriented political persuasion (Gould 1988; Schnaiberg 1975, 1983, 1986).

Because decision makers utilize the expertise of the scientists largely to determine appropriate government action, these scientists become de facto policymakers themselves (Mukerji 1989). Scientists find themselves in a position to present policy recommendations based on their own research and then to evaluate those policies from an objective scientific standpoint. In order for an interest group to press and defend its position in the environmental policy-making arena, often they not only have a team of scientists that appears to be qualified and credible, but also scientists who are willing and able to produce scientific data that help the political contender pursue its own interests. An environmental organization, a corporation, or a government agency whose scientific staff is continually producing research that runs contrary to the goals or interests of its employer would rapidly lose political clout (Gould 1988; Schnaiberg 1975, 1986).

That is not to imply that all scientific research produced by political contenders is intentionally biased. It is only to say that even the most stringent scientific research ultimately requires significant leaps of intuition, which are likely to be directed by both the objectives of the scientists and the intellectual environment in which they are immersed. If a scientist is working for a corporation that wants to justify the need to construct a huge particle beam accelerator, then that scientist, when finding that research on the potential environmental impacts of the accelerator is partially inconclusive, will be more likely to err on the side of fewer negative impacts rather than greater impacts. The scientific staffs of economic and political actors have substantial incentives to produce research findings that reflect favorably on the positions taken by those actors in specific disputes. Resource development corporations are unlikely to retain scientists who consistently produce results indicating that significant negative environmental impacts are to be expected from resource development schemes (Dietz & Rycroft 1987). In turn, environmental organizations are unlikely to use their funds to sponsor research indicating that environmental impacts are minimal. It is reasonable to expect that industry scientists will produce research that is favorable to industry in the political arena and that environmental groups will produce research that indicates the need for environmental protection (Gould 1988; Schnaiberg 1977).

The time constraints on research resulting from bureaucratic procedures make it easier for political partisans to utilize the inconclusiveness of scientific research (Schnaiberg 1977). Many of the studies required for optimally informed environmental decision making can ideally require many years of research. Political actors, seeking to appear responsive to environmental concerns, hurry the research processes, thereby making it more likely that the results of such research will be inconclusive and open to a wider range of interpretation. Since interpretation of what specific scientific research implies for political decisions is a central element of environmental policy-making, the time constraints on that research tend to produce findings that are more politically malleable (Gould 1988; Schnaiberg 1986).

Such inconclusiveness resulting from time as well as budgetary constraints is quite common in environmental policy research. Such constraints allow the U.S. Environmental Protection Agency (USEPA), for example, to declare that most drinking water supplies are safe, while conducting research on the health impacts of only a handful of the hundreds of toxic chemicals found in many drinking water supplies. Because conclusive data indicating negative health effects from toxics in water supplies are not yet available, the USEPA finds it expedient to determine that the lack of scientific proof of negative health impacts is sufficient grounds to declare that water supplies are safe (Schnaiberg 1980: ch. VI). Similarly, the Reagan administration failed to act on ameliorating the acid rain problem with the excuse that the scientific data were as yet inconclusive as to the causes of the problem. More recently, the Bush administration's opposition to an international treaty on global warming at the "Earth Summit" in Rio in June 1992 was ostensibly based on the inability of scientists to conclusively demonstrate that the phenomenon was indeed manifest in current climate changes (Newhouse 1992). Therefore, political actors may use inconclusiveness in scientific research to promote a belief that problems do not exist.

Ultimately, the most significant problem resulting from the way science is used in environmental policy-making is the fundamental assumption that scientific data can, in most instances, be used to make some objective judgment as to the type of action that is most appropriate, or whether any action is required at all. Despite the way in which interest groups use scientific data to bolster and undermine political arguments, the decisions reached ultimately rest on a subjective assessment of relative values and relative risks (Brodeur 1989, 1992). Given sufficient time and facilities, science may be able to tell us how much radiation a population will be exposed to as a result of a given project and how many cancer deaths per thousand that amount of exposure is likely to result in. Yet the acceptability of that level of risk and the cost-benefit analyses determining the relative merits of various ameliorative actions remains purely subjective and open to political, economic, and social pressures. In this respect, the environmental policy-making process is much more political than it is scientific. Although the process may be perceived as a scientific effort to determine appropriate action, in actuality science merely provides competing foundations for competing political arguments. Therefore, the time, money, and energy expended by environmental organizations to produce compelling scientific evidence paradoxically demonstrates the power of the powerful economic actors in deflecting political conflict away from primary issues (Gould 1988).

Despite the long interval between initial public awareness and the prior *and* subsequent documentation of ecological problems by environmental scientists, there eventually emerged a growing awareness that our socioeconomic and technological trajectories were unsustainable in the long run (despite debate over precisely how far ahead the "long run" actually was). The final jolt that pushed this debate about ecological limits into the political forefront came in the early and mid-1970s, as "oil shocks" led people in the North to contemplate the possibility of life without heat, electricity, transportation, or jobs (Schnaiberg 1975). Ironically, these oil shocks were not a result of ecological scarcity. Although it was clear that unchecked consumption of nonrenewable natural resources would ultimately result in the extinction of fossil fuel supplies, the energy crisis that caused us to contemplate this eventuality was brought on by the efforts of the oil-producing nations of the South. They sought to renegotiate the terms on which their natural resources would be used to fuel the industrial wealth and power of the North. Gas lines in the North resulted from the South's "muscle flexing" (and corporate manipulations), not from a reduction in ecological supply.

Nonetheless, the restricted international flow of oil caused many in the North to become aware, for the first time, of their dependency on the natural environment to provide the resources on which the wealth and power of their societies depended. Although the United States in the 1980s was typified by an apparent rejection of this reality (as if the entire nation went to a decade-long movie to escape temporarily from a frustrating and anxiety-inducing reality—e.g., Lash 1984), the decade of the 1970s ended with the harsh realization that, in terms of our ecological base, we were rapidly moving *From Surplus to Scarcity* (Schnaiberg 1980).

ENERGY LIMITS:
FOSSIL FUEL DEPLETION AND RENEWABLE ALTERNATIVES

The technological capacity to utilize fossil fuels was responsible for much of the increase in the material standard of living through the succeeding waves of industrial revolutions. However, the industrial world is becoming increasingly aware of the economic and ecological consequences of dependence on finite energy resources. Although U.S. expenditures for renewable energy research declined during the Reagan and Bush years, the war in the Persian Gulf, coupled with reports of global warming, has led to new calls for a transition to clean, domestic, and renewable energy supplies. The current fossil fuel-based energy systems will probably not be able to meet projected demands throughout the twenty-first century. Constant increases in such demand are hastening the day when these resources will be exhausted. Unfortunately, neither conservation nor increased energy efficiency are complete solutions. And new exploration will generate still more pollution and depletion problems, the solutions to which will themselves raise energy needs (see ecostrations for Chapters 5 and 8).

Calls for clean domestic energy sources have renewed interest in nuclear energy. Reliance on nonrenewable uranium will only create new unsolved problems of waste and safety, as well as generate high production costs. In addition, nuclear reactors, with their operational lifetimes of only 25 to 60 years, will require ongoing replacement of decommissioned plants, as well as containment of the radiation hazards posed by the storage of these decommissioned plants for thousands of years. The long-awaited arrival of safer fusion reactors does not seem much closer today than it did 20 years ago.

Solar energy is an abundant and clean renewable resource with great application potential. Decentralized *passive* solar energy installations, which are used to heat homes, water, and greenhouses, will help to decrease demand for other energy sources. However, the cost of constructing solar-*electrical* plants remains prohibitive. Current estimates indicate that land-based solar electrical systems would have a cost ten times that of an equivalent coal-fired electrical generating station. Photovoltaic cells are even more expensive. While proposals for space-based solar collector satellites have been made, their costs also limit their potential role as replacement for cheaper fossil fuel sources.

Similarly, wind power is clean, abundant, and renewable, but its costs are too high to replace fossil fuels in most nations. Even in the wealthiest nations, it could only replace a fraction of fossil fuel applications. Large-scale hydropower and geothermal systems are limited by their low efficiencies and their site-specific geographic limitations. More portable alcohol-based fuels, produced from renewable agricultural products, do have great potential in combustion applications (such as automobile fuels), but even they can only meet a small portion of global energy demand. In addition, reliance on alcohol-based fuels will divert farm land from food to fuel production.

Exhaustion of those fossil fuels that have historically expanded consumption cannot, then, be readily transcended by any of these replacement systems. Renewable resources cannot sustain our current levels of energy consumption, nor can conservation and improved energy-efficiency of machines, appliances, and vehicles. Ecological limitations suggest that, after fossil fuels are exhausted, we must get by with using substantially less global energy.

RIO AND THE STRUGGLE TO DEFINE GLOBAL ENVIRONMENTAL DISORGANIZATION

In the early 1990s, as the United States awoke from the "lost decade" of the 1980s, the earlier awareness of environmental problems began to be conceptualized on a more global scale. Much excitement was generated by the so-called Earth Summit held in Rio de Janeiro, Brazil, in the summer of 1992. The Rio conference was billed as a global conference on environment and development. Although the environmental component of the conference received a tremendous amount of media coverage in the nations of the North, the media largely ignored the development component. The disproportionate attention paid to these two intricately interconnected issues reflects the limited view of many governments, journalists, and environmentalists who saw the primary issue of the conference as protecting the environment. The leaders and citizens of industrialized nations pay much less attention to the socioeconomic implications of such protection, both globally and domestically. For people in the South, development is the primary issue, with the environment assuming importance primarily as a constraint on the pace, direction, and scope of development objectives (Bidwai 1992; South Commission 1990).

Historically, those concerned with protecting the natural world have given strong voice to the need to curtail the destruction of the environment, predicting very real disasters if current patterns of natural resource usage are not abandoned. They have been less successful, however, in their ability to prescribe politically attainable solutions to the problems they have found. Many of the proposed solutions have been utopian in their goals and relatively naive in their conceptualization of the social, economic, and political structures that shape current patterns of environmental utilization. Others have tended to be somewhat elitist, nondemocratic, and regressive in their social implications. The utopian solutions have focused primarily on education and consciousness-raising as mechanisms of social change. Clearly, public education is essential to building the broad base of support needed to promote environmental protection. However, it is equally important to recognize that even environmentally aware citizens must achieve survival within socioeconomic structures that currently offer few ecologically benign occupations (see Chapter 6). Other

proposed solutions have demonstrated a limited awareness of the potentially regressive social consequences of specific environmental protection
measures, both globally and domestically. We can do much better.

A brief analysis of the socioeconomic implications of some of the
solutions to global environmental problems presented by governments of
industrialized nations would have allowed those governments to predict
the resistance of the South to certain environmental proposals. Interestingly, the conference was held in Brazil, a relatively poor nation with a
relative abundance of pristine natural resources. While people in the South
may have seen the decision to hold the meeting in Brazil as a global
recognition of the primacy of their aspirations in a conference on environment and development, those in the North tended to view it as a recognition of the need to preserve the environments of the South, on which we
all depend (Goldman 1992).

Much attention has been focused on the need to preserve the world's
rainforests to prevent global warming and preserve biological diversity.
However, the governments of the industrialized nations must recognize
that they are the primary producers of greenhouse gases and that they
have reaped the majority of the economic benefits from the production
of these gases and from deforesting their own nations (Little 1992). If
the nations of the South are to be asked to forfeit much of the economic
gains experienced by the industrialized world in creating the global climate
problem, in order to provide ecological benefits for all, it is only fair that
they somehow be compensated for their sacrifice and rewarded for their
efforts. Thinking globally in terms of a world environment is essential.
However, a failure to think globally in terms of a world economy and the
global distribution of the costs and benefits of environmental protection
and degradation is to ignore many of the macrostructural processes that
have necessitated concern for a global environment.

A similar need to be attentive to structural processes can be seen in
domestic responses to environmental problems. A common response to
the rapid consumption of nonrenewable fossil fuels has been to suggest
that taxation be used to inflate the price of gasoline. Such a gas tax is
already in place in many industrialized nations. Unfortunately, a tax on
gas would necessarily impose an additional economic burden on the working class and poor, while creating little obstacle to consumption by the
wealthy. Flat taxes require the less wealthy to sacrifice a larger percentage
of their total income for basic necessities or to reduce their consumption
in order to make ends meet. For the wealthy, however, a flat tax on
necessities neither absorbs a high percentage of their income nor discour-
ages them substantially from their patterns of consumption, for making
ends meet is not their primary concern. While regressive taxation of
resource consumption would achieve the goal of reducing overall rates
of resource depletion, it would also increase the ever widening gap between

rich and poor. Environmentalists are well advised to consider the distributional aspects of environmental protection measures, especially since the support of the working class and poor will be essential to ensuring the success of future environmental campaigns (see Chapter 7).

Environmental destruction has been linked to a wide variety of health concerns in the industrialized nations, leading many more people to express concern for increased environmental protection. However, it should be noted that the primary health concerns for most of the world's people are malnutrition and diarrhea, not cancer. For the most part, only people who are lucky enough to live relatively long lives have to worry about dying of cancer from long-term exposure to toxins or ultraviolet radiation. If we want those in the South to act to reduce manmade carcinogens in the environment, we must also take into account their primary health concerns and act in ways that will alleviate those ailments.

The *globalism* of those living in the relative affluence of the industrialized world has, until recently, been somewhat narrow. It recognizes our dependence on global ecosystems to provide for our own and our children's well-being. However, it has often failed to recognize the distributional elements of environmental protection, which are especially important to those in the developing world who have not had an opportunity to benefit economically from the processes that are largely responsible for the environmental crisis. The more inclusive globalism that is now emerging recognizes the relationships between Northern wealth and Southern poverty (South Commission 1990). It recognizes that domestic and global conditions of deepening inequality are a primary threat to ecological sustainability. It recognizes that environmental justice is essential to maintain broad support for environmental protection (Young & Wolf 1992). It recognizes the relationship between levels of resource consumption of individuals and the ability of the planet to provide food for growing populations. This new globalism represents the hope that global problems can be alleviated by truly global and equitable solutions, which will make the world a better place for all of us.

SELECTED REFERENCES

ASHWORTH, WILLIAM
1987   *The Late Great Lakes: An Environmental History.* Detroit: Wayne State University Press.
BIDWAI, PRAFUL
1992   "North vs. South on pollution." *The Nation,* June 22:853–854.
BRODEUR, PAUL
1989   *Currents of Death: Power Lines, Computer Terminals, and the Attempt to Cover Up Their Threats to Your Health.* New York: Simon & Schuster.
1992   "Annals of radiation: The cancer at Slater School." *New Yorker,* December 7:86–119.

BROWN, LESTER R.
1992   "Launching the environmental revolution." In *State of the World: 1992*.
        New York: W.W. Norton.
BURCH, WILLIAM R., JR.
1971   *Daydreams and Nightmares: A Sociological Essay on the American Environment*.
        New York: Harper & Row.
CARSON, RACHEL
1962   *Silent Spring*. Boston: Houghton Mifflin Co.
CHAMBERS, MORTIMER, R. GREW, D. HERLIHY, T. K. RABB & I. WOLOCH
1983   *The Western Experience*. New York: Alfred A. Knopf.
DIETZ, THOMAS AND R. W. RYCROFT
1987   *The Risk Professionals*. New York: Russell Sage Foundation.
EHRLICH, PAUL R.
1968   *The Population Bomb*. New York: Ballantine Books.
GOLDMAN, BENJAMIN A.
1992   "Alternative summit echoes U.N. conference's problems." *In These Times*,
        June 24–July 7:10–11.
GOULD, KENNETH A.
1988   "The politicization of science in the environmental impact statement
        process." *Wisconsin Sociologist* 25 (4):139–143.
GRAHAM, FRANK, JR.
1970   *Since Silent Spring*. Boston: Houghton Mifflin.
LASH, JONATHAN ET AL.
1984   *A Season of Spoils: The Story of the Reagan Administration's Attack on the
        Environment*. New York: Pantheon Books.
LITTLE, PAUL
1992   "The Rio summit falls to earth as U.S. snubs global treaties." *In These
        Times*, June 24–July 7:8–9.
MEADOWS, DONELLA H., D. L. MEADOWS, J. RANDERS, & W. W. BEHRENS III
1972   *The Limits to Growth*. New York: Universe Books.
MUKERJI, CHANDRA
1989   *A Fragile Power: Scientists and the State*. Princeton, NJ: Princeton University
        Press.
MUMFORD, LEWIS
1963   *Technics and Civilization*. New York: Harcourt, Brace, & World.
NEWHOUSE, JOHN
1992   "The diplomatic round: Earth summit." *The New Yorker*, June 1:64–78.
POPULATION REFERENCE BUREAU
1981   *World Population Data Sheet*. Washington, D.C.: Population Reference
        Bureau.
SCHNAIBERG, ALLAN
1975   "Social syntheses of the societal-environmental dialectic: The role of
        distributional impacts." *Social Science Quarterly* 56 (June):5–20.
1977   "Obstacles to environmental research by scientists and technologists: A
        social structural analysis." *Social Problems* 24 (5):500–520.
1980   *The Environment: From Surplus to Scarcity*. New York: Oxford University
        Press.
1983   "Soft energy and hard labor? Structural restraints on the transition to
        appropriate technology." Pp. 217–234 in Gene F. Summers, editor,
        Technology and Social Change in Rural Areas. Boulder, CO: Westview
        Press.
1986   "The role of experts and mediators in the channeling of distributional

conflicts." Pp. 348–362 in A. Schnaiberg, N. Watts, and K. Zimmermann, editors, *Distributional Conflicts in Environmental-Resource Policy*. Aldershot, England: Gower Publishing.

SOUTH COMMISSION
1990   *The Challenge to the South: The Report of the South Commission.* New York: Oxford University Press.

STRETTON, HUGH
1976   *Capitalism, Socialism, and the Environment.* Cambridge, England: Cambridge University Press.

TEITELBAUM, MICHAEL S.
1985   *Latin Migration North: The Problem for U.S. Foreign Policy.* New York: Council on Foreign Relations.

TOFFLER, ALVIN
1975   *The Eco-Spasm Report.* New York: Bantam Books.

TRAINER, F. E.
1985   *Abandon Affluence!* London: Zed Books.

VOLTI, RUDI
1992   *Society and Technological Change in China.* New York: St. Martin's Press.

WORLD RESOURCES INSTITUTE
1992   *Environmental Almanac.* Boston: Houghton Mifflin.

WRIGHT, WILL
1992   *Wild Knowledge: Science, Language and Social Life in a Fragile Environment.* Minneapolis: University of Minnesota Press.

YOUNG, H. PEYTON & A. WOLF
1992   "Global warming negotiations. Does fairness matter?" *The Brookings Review* 10 (2):Spring.

Part II

How Does Environmental Disorganization Get Created?

3. Economic Organizations in the Treadmill of Production: How and Why They Create Environmental Disruptions

THE INDUSTRIAL LOGIC: AN INTRODUCTION

To help explain the social roots of the modern logic of production (Schnaiberg 1980: ch. 5), this chapter lays out a simplified logic of how firms operate. In Chapter 4, we follow up how these firms operate within a broader social and economic system, which we examine the label *treadmill of production*. In this chapter about social pressures on *individual* economic firms, we turn to the *society-wide* social and political institutions of the treadmill, which operates to expand both production of the and ecological extraction. The logic of the modern economic firm and the larger treadmill system represent the very antithesis of the Buddhist economics noted earlier: they require maximal consumption in order to sustain firms, so that the economy can generate modest levels of human satisfaction. While the material presented here is somewhat consistent with how economists describe modern production systems, our emphasis is on how this process typically withdraws ecological resources that deplete ecosystems and adds elements that pollute ecosystems.

In order to understand what improvements may be feasible by changing our production practices, we first describe producers that generate more environmental problems. We cover several different types (sectors of production) tracing their interrelations in a representative way. The first production scenario illustrates economic practices where there is a relatively low level of environmental protection enforcement. We then follow with a somewhat more regulated scenario, which constitutes the most feasible patterns of environmental protection in today's society. These patterns can prevail only under favorable economic, social, and political conditions, which we outline later (Granovetter 1985). Common to both illustrations is the core of industrial logic.

45

The Industrial Logic

1. Organizations exist as long as they make sufficient profit (or at least appear to make sufficient profit).
2. Profit is generated by allocating organizational revenues to technological investment and labor in varying degrees, depending on conditions of supply, competition, and financial markets.
3. Each allocative decision has direct and indirect implications for the levels of withdrawals from and additions to ecosystems for the organization and for each unit produced.
4. Because of constraints in the social world, these ecological implications are usually secondary for managers, constrained by their decisions about costs and profits.
5. Therefore, only social, economic, and political forces external to the organization are capable of attracting these managers' attention to environmental impacts.
6. Managers thus have a prime interest in resisting the rise of these external forces and use their influence (economic, political, and social) to resist such forces.

THE LOW-REGULATION SCENARIO: TYPICAL ENVIRONMENTAL IMPACTS

In this chapter, we examine the social pressures on *individual* economic firms. Then, in Chapter 4, we turn to the *society-wide* social and political institutions of the treadmill, which operates to expand both production and ecological extraction.

Let us start with three organizations and their relationships: *Active* Petroleum Corporation, which drills for oil in Alaska and processes it elsewhere, *Basic* Chemical Company, which uses petroleum feedstocks to manufacture industrial and residential products, and *Consulting* Associates, a business consulting firm that advises both of these corporations on their organizational practices. Each of these organizations has the following direct environmental impacts; the italicized impacts are those most commonly associated with each organization.

Direct Environmental Impacts

ACTIVE   *Withdraws petroleum from land ecosystems*

Withdraws some local species from these systems, to make space for drilling and shipping oil

Withdraws fuel resources from a variety of sources, to operate pumps, ships, other vehicles, field staff offices, and residences

Withdraws water for field staff offices and residences, and perhaps to cool pumps

Adds air pollutants from diesel pumps, ships, and heating/cooling of field offices and residences

Adds water pollutants from human wastes and other activities in the field offices, vehicles, and residences

Adds some water pollution from occasional petroleum spills, as well as bilge wastes from ships

BASIC   *Withdraws petroleum for feedstocks for production lines*

Withdraws fuel resources to run production lines for manufacturing chemicals

Withdraws fuel resources to run administrative offices and shipping and marketing products (to transport people and products)

Withdraws water to cool production lines and supply administrative facilities

Withdraws local species to build and operate plant and facilities

Adds other nontoxic pollutants from production and administration waste products to land/air/water

Adds water pollutants from human wastes of workers

Adds some potentially toxic land/air/water pollutants that emerge from production operations to local or more distant ecosystems (landfills, incinerators)

CONSULTING

Withdraws fuel resources to maintain offices and their functions

Withdraws fuel resources to transport staff to the other companies

Withdraws land (and/or air space) to build and operate offices

Adds air and water pollutants from office functions (computing, copying, cleaning)

Adds air and water pollutants from travel of staff to other companies

Adds water pollutants from human wastes of workers

All three types of organizations have a wide range of environmental impacts, and many of these impacts are not clearly recorded in the "accounting" of these firms. These negative externalities of production are kept separately from the profit-and-loss accounts of these firms, in large part because each organization has an economic interest in doing so (see below). Moreover, singly and collectively, these firms attempt to sustain this nonrecording, because affirming their environmental impacts will lead to regulation that will generally reduce their profits; they do so using political, legal, and economic influences.

THE LOW-REGULATION SCENARIO AND
THE LOGIC OF PROFITABILITY

The Spread of Competition

To understand the last statement above, we need to understand the operating context for these organizations. The logic that follows applies most directly to capitalist societies, though much of it overlaps with socialist societies as well. Since many socialist economies are moving toward the adoption of capitalist market systems, the logic increasingly applies to most of the world's industrial systems.

Central to the understanding of these firms is the context of competition: the involvement of organizations in gathering more scarce resources than other organizations. Competition can take many forms: firms compete for volume and shares of markets of consumers (private or corporate), they compete with other organizations to recruit and retain skilled workers, and they compete with governments to gather financial support from banks, other investors, and individual citizens.

Why do they compete? They compete because of the actual or perceived scarcity of all these resources. Why does this scarcity exist? The continued growth in the number and strength of each firm's competitors partly explains this phenomenon. While some of this increase is due to population growth, ironically, more is due to the expansion of the world's wealth, enabling still more entries into markets of all types. (Paradoxically, we thus see that surplus wealth can create scarcities because of expanded competition!) This explanation begs another question, however. While the growth of population and/or wealth explains why competition *may* increase, it fails to explain why it *must* increase. To put this notion most simply, if someone gathers more wealth from whatever source, why should she or he choose to invest this wealth in some form of productive enterprise? Why not just keep this wealth and use it for pleasure? There are two answers to this question, both of which revolve around the same social value. First, even if one keeps wealth to use for pleasure rather than investment, the spending of this wealth in marketplaces enhances the wealth of other entrepreneurs, investors, and firms. Second, and more important, powerful social values in all industrial societies award high social status to those with greater wealth and this encourages people to expand their financial resources through some form of investment. Sometimes it is less the enhancement of our status than the protection of it: people invest for their old age, retirement, or sickness. But they also invest to "live better" or "do better." While the intensity and form of this social pressure vary a great deal, this pressure is nearly universal in the modern industrial societies, either as a defensive or an offensive strategy (Granovetter 1985). Thus, even professors who criticize firms for their environmental disregard regularly invest part of their earnings in pension funds, which in turn invest such money in these same firms!

Is this part of human nature? We cannot answer this question. What we can assert is that competition has expanded in modern industry, spreading within and across countries, and is now spreading still further into underdeveloped as well as industrial countries. Not every individual or firm has the same urge to compete, but all exist today within *competitive economics systems*. Schumacher (1973) and other economics have argued that this is not a necessary part of human nature. Under their Buddhist economics, which minimizes consumption, they argue that we could organize our lives around our basic material needs and derive pleasure from the *non-material* investment of our minds and bodies (see Chapters 6 and 9). However, even for Schumacher, this is possible only if communities exist in isolation from each other, each community being in effect self-sufficient and immune to external competitive pressures.

We feel this is a fantasy on both counts: the world is increasingly moving to a more globalized economy or modern world-system, and fewer community citizens and organizations are committed to a primarily nonmaterial style of life. Paradoxically, the Buddhist countries of Asia are adding to the number of new entrepreneurs in the modern world, Japan and South Korea being the most active participants. While select small communities throughout the world live in "voluntary simplicity," or with a New Age value structure, these do not seem to be likely paths for the foreseeable future in our world. Moreover, even these retreatists exist within the material values and structures of the modern competitive world, which is increasingly privatized and decreasingly communalized. Competition is a bit like heavy traffic: we see ourselves as "in" it, even though we often fail to understand how we are a part "of" it (Granovetter 1990). As Robert Reich (1991: 8) has forcefully put it, "Neither the profitability of a nation's corporations nor the successes of its investors necessarily improve the standard of living of the nation's citizens. Corporations and investors now scour the world for profitable opportunities. They are becoming disconnected from their home nations."

Competition as a Context for the Low-Regulation Scenario

If competition for scarce resources is a fact of economic and social life, then how does it shape the behavior of firms? The most powerful statement we can make is that *competition makes higher profitability a key survival issue* (Williamson 1975, 1981). For the Active Petroleum, Basic Chemical, and Consulting Associates firms discussed above, each must record sufficient profit to avoid economic demise. This demise can occur in many ways in the modern economic system. As in the older economic models, firms must avoid bankruptcy, where losses exceed profits. But they must also make profits at a rate high enough to satisfy investors: in the language of business theory, the firm must maximize the share values of their shareholders. Finally, in the modern world, the firm must in addition use its profits for investments in a way that will discourage other competing investors from taking over the firm to absorb its profits. This represents a formidable challenge for contemporary managers: they can't do too poorly or too well! Let us try to trace these consequences of contemporary competitive systems.

Under *bankruptcy,* the firm is taken over by its creditors—those who have invested in the firm, through stocks, bonds, or loans. It may continue to produce, or it may be shut down. But even if it continues to produce, its future profits will be used to pay off the creditors first, thus limiting the firm's future investments and expansion and competitive capacity. In the process of bankruptcy, many jobs are lost, and the managers lose their control over the technology and finances of the firm.

Under *low-profit* conditions, the firm does not face bankruptcy and loss of control by its managers in the same way. Rather, reorganization of ownership takes place, with more aggressive investors ousting management and buying out some of the less aggressive investors in order to reorient the firm in a more aggressive manner. The object here is to use existing investment and technological capital in a more competitive fashion, and to increase the rates of return of these more aggressive investors. Managers and some other workers lose their jobs, and new managers are given mandates to increase profits in the near term.

Finally, under some *high-profit* conditions, in the past two decades a new form of threat has emerged, the hostile takeover. There are many variants on this form, but the core action is that outside forces view the firm as a desirable acquisition. The firm has valuable capital assets that the takeover firm or investor feels they can sell off with substantial net profits. Alternatively, the firm may have made substantial profits but has not reinvested them sufficiently to become more competitive and earn still higher profits. Thus, it has a pool of undistributed profits, which makes it an attractive target for these hostile investors. Usually, management is ousted in either situation, and other workers may be dismissed as well, especially when capital assets are sold off.

All these actions suggest that management has to operate under increasingly constricted decision-making rules. One way of appreciating the integrated nature of modern production systems is to understand that managers have to push the competitive aggressiveness of the firm in order to protect their own jobs. Because outsiders form a somewhat hostile social and economic environment for the firm, managers have to become increasingly aggressive in their use of technologies to continuously generate profits. The consequence of inattention is loss of employment, especially for the managers themselves, since ever larger numbers of investors and their managers and consultants are looking for new opportunities to expand their investment capital.

Managerial Decision Making under Competition

What does a modern manager have to do? Unlike the fantasy of *It's a Wonderful Life*, the level of investment in most larger firms is sufficiently high that a handful of local, friendly, community investors no longer constitutes the core of investors. Active Petroleum in Alaska is funded by anonymous, impersonal market actors, each of whom has no loyalty to Active, but simply seeks the "bottom line" of profitability or maximized values of their shares. Family firms may be the exception to this approach, but they are increasingly being bought up by external investors, and thus are being shifted from "local" to "cosmopolitan" organizations. Similar statements can be made about Basic Chemical and Consulting Associates. The firm's relations to ecosystems thus change, because the expansionary impulses for investors under their goal of maximizing share values is perfectly open-ended. No longer do more localized investors have as a primary goal the provision of local services or local employment (including employment for family members), or the improvement of the community's economy. Instead, when investors (or potential investors) believe that their investments/shares can earn more under other managerial conditions, the managers in place have to struggle to run even faster on the treadmill of production.

This means that Active's managers must reduce their costs and be aggressive in marketing their oil production. Basic Chemical's managers must also try to control the costs of their feedstocks, putting pressures on Active to keep its prices down. This is because Basic must compete with other firms to expand its chemical market shares and volume of sales, as well as its profits. Consulting Associates has a strong stake in the expansion and profitability and reinvestment of each of these other two firms, because its contracts will grow in profitability, in part related to the volume of profits and reinvestment options for the two firms. Consulting's managers sometimes have greater freedom. When Active and Basic confront lowered profits or the threat of hostile takeovers, these conditions represent new opportunities for Consulting. It may be hired to advise them about new forms of cost control and/or new means to expand their markets and profits.

All three firms have a stake in reducing their costs of environmental control, because of these expansionary pressures. That is the simple reality for rational managers of each firm. Some exceptions to this rule exist but only under unusual and rare conditions. One of these exceptions is where wastes from existing production can be retained and transformed into more cost-effective production (e.g., recycling toxic chemicals or reducing waste heat in a cost-effective way). Another is where only a modest expense is necessary to reduce environmental damages, and legislating this protection as a universal requirement for firms will actually handicap its competitors much more than it will for Active, Basic, or Consulting.

These environmental protection costs are what we normally think of as costs per unit production. They are typically associated with ecosystem *additions* or pollutants, and they fall under what we often term clean-up costs. But as noted earlier, these are only part of the environmental impacts of production. Equally important in most natural settings is the problem of ecosystem *withdrawals*. As discussed earlier, these withdrawals are often linked to the competitive drive to expand production, increase technological investment, and raise profits. Each of the firms is pushed by the many forms of competition—for market shares, profits, and financing—to expand in order not to be scavenged or destroyed by various external actors in its social and economic milieu. The common denominator in these expansionary thrusts is that investors are seeking to maximize the value of or return on their shares of the productive enterprises, and they continue to compete with other investors to attempt to achieve this maximization. Notice that this maximization goal is relative, not absolute: there are no limits to my own investment expectations, except that I seek to do better than my competitors. That is why we must eventually find ways to protect ecosystems through greater control of market forces, since these forces are, by this definition, absolutely boundless.

Generally, this expansion of technology and production involves more withdrawals from ecosystems, for more natural resources are needed to sustain the firm. Active will drill more wells or will increase its rate of pumping from existing wells to expand its oil production. Basic will increase its consumption of petroleum feedstocks and increase its fuel demands to sustain an increased production of chemical products. And Consulting will either hire more consultants or increase the hours and travel of existing staff in order to help these two client firms expand, thereby increasing its energy needs.

Interestingly, this expansionary drive, a push that arises intrinsically from competitive fields of force, produces some environmental gains as well as losses. With Active Petroleum's opening up of new markets, it may invest in a better technology to drill and pump new oil, incorporating some new technical fixes that may reduce oil spill or air pollution hazards.

It may also be able to afford to use somewhat better ships to transport its oil, reducing the risk of future oil spills. Similarly, Basic Chemical may find that new production lines can be equipped with a technology that recycles water coolants in a more closed cycle, along with air scrubbers and energy-efficient conversion equipment. As their workloads expand, even Consulting may engage in computer networking with their two clients, thereby reducing energy needs. They may also relocate some of their staff more or less permanently in each corporation, reducing energy demands for travel. This would occur when consulting services have expanded with each firm. All three firms may thus lower additions and some withdrawals per unit production in their facilities. This is partly because of economies of scale, whereby environmental protection costs can be spread over more product lines, reducing the cost per product produced.

Unfortunately, although expansion can bring some of these environmental protection gains, they also produce ecosystem losses. For while there may be some reductions of impacts per unit produced, the total volume of production has risen fast enough to offset this effect. For each firm, let us say that it produced 1000 units at time 1, as outlined in Table 3.1. By time 2, it had reduced its environmental withdrawals and additions from 100 impacts to 80 impacts per product. It did so in the process of doubling production to 2000 units. Thus, the environmental impact at time 2 is [80 × 2000] = 16,000, versus the level of [100 × 1000] = 10,000, at time 1. In fact, at any increase of production beyond 1250 in this example, there will be a net environmental loss.

This simple exercise suggests that the greatest threat of the treadmill may not lie in deficient technologies that pollute, but in the competitive logic of maximization of share values without limits. For no matter how much technology may improve in reducing additions (or withdrawals) per unit produced, it is likely to be offset by the pressures to expand production in order to increase returns to investors. And this expansionary pressure is likely to be exacerbated by the increase in the number of investors, because of growth in population and wealth. This population/wealth

TABLE 3.1 The Polluting Impacts of Pollution Control versus Production Expansion

	Time 1: No Pollution Control	Time 2: Pollution Control
Constant production	1000p	800p
Doubling production	2000p	1600p
Limits to production to keep pollution constant	1000p	1250p

growth in turn expands the opportunities for any single investor to find higher rates of return on his or her investment. Expanded opportunities create new entrants in investment markets by stimulating more social actors to become active investors, who then seek new outlets for their investments. In the absence of other external limiting conditions, then, this is a positive-feedback system, one that is self-reinforcing in expanding the number of competing investors and the total degree of competition for investors' funds.

Unless these expansionary conditions are altered, the most that those concerned with environmental damage can do is to mobilize politically. They would then force managers and investors to absorb some of the costs of environmental protection, primarily in the area of pollution or additions to ecosystems. Yet, so long as the political system permits withdrawals to expand, whole ecosystems may be destroyed in order to extract more resources for new production. To some extent, we in the twentieth century have not dealt with this problem and we will need to address it in the twenty-first century. In the meantime, we can consider how well we are likely to do, under the most favorable political and economic conditions of our current competitive treadmill.

THE HIGH-REGULATION SCENARIO AND THE LOGIC OF POLITICAL CONTROL

The Spread of Regulation

The preceding discussion of expansionary economic forces helps us understand the political pressures that have led to the creation of the Environmental Protection Agency and similar agencies in the states, as well as the creation of equivalent government agencies in most other industrial and even underdeveloped countries (Hawkins 1984). The expansion of industrial demands on ecosystems has been exponential in recent decades, vastly exceeding the capacity of natural systems for self-protection or recuperation. Equally important has been the rise of political constituencies who have defined the environmental consequences of this expansion as socially undesirable, in light of a variety of social goals ranging from protecting natural beauty, human health, or the future productivity of land and water systems.

We offer two competing perspectives on this dramatic rise in governments' environmental protection efforts. The first, more conventional perspective is that governments are motivated to protect the environment, because of their own social visions, perhaps enhanced by the thrust of the arguments of these new environmentalist constituents who are often mobilized as environmental movement organizations such as the Sierra Club, the Environmental Defense Fund, and Greenpeace. In effect, in this view the government becomes an *ally* of environmentalists, seeking to impose limits on investment and managerial behavior as detailed earlier in this chapter. It becomes an agent of environmental social movements, seeking to find workable ways to impose such limits on economic markets.

The second, less conventional perspective is that governments are actually reluctant actors in this struggle, since countries and government agents appear to be more closely tied to economic expansion. Good times for the economy mean increased powers and freedoms for a variety of government actors (including environmental protection agencies!), but good environmental protection times have far less impact, per se, on government actors. This view goes back to the fundamental aspects of the treadmill of production: much of the social and political and even cultural aspects of modern industrial societies is dictated by the nature of treadmill organization and expansion. In this model, environmentalism represents more of a challenge or threat to the government, whose interest lies in expansion of the treadmill. Governments must *appear* to be doing something to protect the environment, mainly to appease their environmental interest groups, who can cause political troubles otherwise. Whether they actually are doing something is much more variable and depends on the political strength of environmentalists, the speed of the treadmill, and the political actions of treadmill supporters. The most extreme version of this viewpoint is that government actors are actually allies of investors and share their distaste for serious economic regulation. A less extreme version is that government actors want to have their cake and eat it too: they want economic expansion, but they also genuinely want to protect the environment for themselves and their constituents (see Chapters 4 and 5). In this model the government is either ambivalent or a broker between environmental pressure groups and treadmill defenders.

Whichever model actually fits the government of any country and at any historical point, the common outcome of each model is that modern states have developed a broad array of environmental legislation and a complex arrangement of regulatory administrative agencies to implement this environmental legislation in some fashion. From the standpoint of this chapter, what is crucial for managers and investors is at minimum that this regulatory structure is part of the operating context for economic actors. To conduct any kind of business or to invest in any kind of enterprise, this regulatory structure requires what economists call *transaction costs* for treadmill or market actors. Simply put, these costs include all activities undertaken to produce the minimum level of apparent compliance with environmental regulations that will suffice to let the economic actors carry on their desired business. Let us now turn to what this means in practice to Active, Basic, and Consulting firms, and to their larger economic networks.

The Industrial Challenge Posed by Regulation

What does a more aggressive regulatory context mean for Active Petroleum in its oil exploration? There are at least two forms of aggressive regulation (see Chapters 4 and 5). The first is on-site inspection. After treating this form for each of our firms, we will briefly discuss the second, regulation that relies on self-reporting by these firms. Typically, on-site inspection would include a range of regulatory agencies that monitor firms' activities, from drilling to pumping to shipping. It might include physical monitoring of oil drilling, such as having field inspectors observe drilling protocols, and taking air and soil and water samples to test for petroleum seepage and evaporation. It might also mean having state or federal government inspectors following the path of pipelines, inspecting for leaks, checking seals and welds, and taking earth and water samples along the length of the pipeline at regular or spot-check intervals. A similar set of field inspections might occur in shipping the oil, ranging from having government inspectors sampling the waters of the shipping harbor in Alaska to sampling the waters of the refinery unloading ports in the mainland United States, or even traveling on the ships themselves through the whole journey. The common element in this regulatory apparatus is that the government does all the inspectional work.

Under these conditions, what are the transactional costs for managers of Active? There are two kinds of costs. First, Active has to make provision for these government inspectors: they may need to be fed and housed, but equally important, production work cannot go on without being made accessible to these "independent" inspectors. This inspection reduces some managerial freedoms to deploy labor and capital when and how they wish, and thus usually raises costs of production. If there is a break in a pipeline, for example, the welders may be dispatched immediately and repair the break. But pumping may have to be stopped earlier and for a longer period until a government inspector can certify the level of leakage and the adequacy of the repair weld. Since (oil pumping) time is quite literally corporate money, this too is costly. Moreover, if the inspector is dissatisfied with the operations of the firm, he or she may shut down part of the operation for a longer period or assess fines for operating violations, which again are drains against profits. Typically, Active must keep paying its labor force and its creditors for the equipment that is lying idle in these periods of regulatory shutdown. In the next section, this picture of the power of inspectors (cf. Hawkins 1984) will be modified in the light of actual procedures used by both managers and inspectors. However, for Active Petroleum (and Basic Chemical and Consulting Associates), the regulatory structure does always impose some costs.

In the case of Basic Chemical, the regulatory apparatus of the government has a wide potential to impact on managerial freedoms. Legislation that controls air and water emissions offers regulatory inspectors the right to sample air and water streams around the plant; related worker safety regulations may also permit sampling air, land, and water within the private production facilities of Basic itself. Such inspection, as was the case with Active, may lead to shutdowns or fines for violations of operating standards for the plant. It also requires that managers negotiate with inspectors to view all aspects of production lines, transportation facilities, and storage at the production facility and even at their clients' facilities to inspect their products and containers. Again, this reduces Basic's managerial discretion in allocating labor and capital, and it raises costs. Some production facilities that develop leaks or breaks may need to be shut down until an inspector turns up, again increasing shutdown time and corporate costs. New waste-handling procedures may be more labor and capital intensive (sorting and labeling in a more detailed way, for example, to avoid mixups), raising costs without any concomitant short-term profit increases. Moreover, in addition to the official costs associated with inspection, managers and senior workers may experience heightened anxiety and diminished productivity, as they struggle to maintain profits and deal with inspections on an ongoing basis (e.g., putting in unpaid overtime to compensate for down time).

Finally, the situation regarding Consulting Associates' vulnerabilities to regulatory inspections is somewhat less threatening to its profits. Consulting makes no physical end-product and engages in no direct transformation of ecosystem resources. This is the defining quality of all "tertiary industries": they neither extract nor directly transform natural resources. Therefore, it is less involved in the regulatory-inspection routines of the government. Under worker-protection legislation, it might make some occasional visits to inspect the shielding of its computer monitors, but even this is unlikely unless its workers had filed a complaint with the labor agency. In summary, then, on-site inspections pose the greatest threat of disruption for Active, somewhat less for Basic, and the least for Consulting. Generally, tertiary industries like Consulting are less affected by regulatory inspection, while the relative vulnerability of primary/extractive (Active Petroleum) and secondary/manufacturing (Basic Chemical) varies according to their actual processes, products, and scale of operations.

But this is only part of the regulatory burden on these firms. A large component of modern government regulation involves the development of recordkeeping systems by managers. Inspection here starts with inspection of the records rather than the production sites. It requires the application of technical and often legal expertise by government agencies and parallel expertise by the firms involved. This inspection is not usually carried out on a routine basis. Rather, when some individual or organization files a complaint, this labor is used to scan records in either government or the firm's offices. Moreover, if this preliminary assessment shows some apparent violation that regulators confirm in these written records, further record-checks may be carried out, sometimes followed by on-site inspections to assess the validity of the records. The costs to firms are at minimum the expensive labor needed to design these recordkeeping systems, and the capital equipment and lower paid labor required to fill in the record forms. This effort is required to transmit records to government regulatory agencies or to retain them for the eventuality of a complaint made to the environmental regulatory agency that will initiate an investigation of the firm. Once such a complaint has been filed, these costs to the firm may rise substantially: included may be changes in work patterns and recordkeeping, as well as possible shutdowns and fines for violations against regulations by the firm. Again, Active and Basic are probably more affected by environmental regulatory recordkeeping than is Consulting, because of their types of production. However, Consulting Associates may be a key actor in developing these firms' recordkeeping systems. Ironically, then, it may profit from regulatory expansion through its consulting on this regulatory apparatus, at least until the unprofitability of either Active or Basic makes them dissolve their consultancy.

These potential costs to and controls over the firm by regulatory agencies of the government result when government actors seek either to protect environmental systems or at least to present this image of protector to environmentalist constituents. The actual and threatened costs of regulation are indeed a serious component of corporate costs, though it is difficult to find an objective accounting of them: corporations exaggerate them, while environmental movement organizations minimize them. The costs are twofold: (1) the costs of actually complying with government regulations, including making changes that enhance environmental protection (or appear to do so, at minimum); and (2) the costs of resisting regulatory expansion at the political level. From a treadmill or an economically rational perspective, it is understandable that trade associations, groups of investors and their political agents, and other treadmill agents seek to find ways to reduce environmental regulatory costs. Generally, this is true at both the level of individual firms and of whole sectors of the economy. As we go down the scale, however, individual economic actors may be more concerned about reducing only their own costs, allowing other firms and industries to be competitively disadvantaged. Thus, there are both individualistic and collective dimensions to this resistance. Sometimes firms will even support environmental legislation and enforcement, as long as it is uniformly implemented across all firms. More often, however, investors' and managers' collective resistance is designed to reduce the absolute costs of compliance with any regulation being introduced.

The resistance can occur in many different ways. The most cost-effective path is to make sure that the regulation is never legislatively or administratively proposed. Potential political sponsors may be persuaded that this regulation is "uneconomic" or "unfair" or that the environmental problems they are designed to avoid are simply unavoidable (Schnaiberg 1994). The mass media may be used to create unconsciousness by environmentalist constituents, who might otherwise put political pressure on such sponsors. If these efforts fail, then the fight has to be fought more publicly in the media, through litigation in the courts, and by extensive lobbying by trade associations and individual firms in the legislature. Everything from campaign contributions to mass advertising may be part of the strategy. Again, such political and cultural resistance is rational for these treadmill actors, as long as it does not exceed the anticipated costs of compliance with the potential regulation.

If the regulation is nonetheless legislated, then treadmill actors turn to disempowering governmental implementation of them (Lowi 1979), through all means available, from reducing funding for the agencies to altering the administrative procedures in executive hearings. Finally, if the regulation and implementation do become established, associations and individual firms may decide how to work within the letter of the law but to evade its intent. This alternative can entail a variety of active and passive strategies, from delaying hearings and inspections to distorting records and even destroying them. Throughout the process of resistance, treadmill actors have available an array of legal talent, which can strategically assist investors' resistance by using the legal apparatus to delay or eliminate the impact of the regulation. Alternatively, they may resist implementation, thereby raising the economic and political costs of the government regulators. This is designed to get a kind of administrative-economic "plea-bargaining": *"We [the firm/trade association] will comply with only this part of the regulation, and then only if you drop x and y as violations, and delay our compliance for k years."* Faced with conflicting types of resistance by several economic development constituents, the environmental agency representatives may accept this as their only politically feasible option, rather than seeking immediate and full compliance with environmental protection regulations (Hawkins 1984).

To complete this section, we should note that environmentalists have also increasingly struggled to use a similar strategy to extract compliance concessions from firms. This strategy works when the firm is awaiting some permit, either to restart or to expand a production facility. In these cases, "business as usual" is halted, and delay is costly for the firm. The firm is induced to comply to some degree, in order to reduce its operating costs or to sustain future profit streams. In return, the environmentalist organization gives up some of its goals for environmental protection. As with the reverse negotiations, the government actors become intermediary brokers, who lean towards one protagonist or the other, depending on the economic and political context of the negotiation (Gould 1991b).

Managerial Decision Making under Regulation

How do the Active, Basic, and Consulting managers respond to their contexts of greater regulation? Many factors determine these responses, ranging from the economic health of their firms, even to managers' own environmental values. Here we will concentrate on the most common political-economic strategies used by managers.

To set the stage for this discussion, we must first remember how firms are increasingly owned by "absentee" investors: actors who neither live in nor particularly care about the community in which the firm is located. Similarly, with more diffused and remotely located ownership, managers themselves are also largely recruited from outside the community in which the firm is located. Exceptions are primarily family-owned firms and the small number of firms that have had long-standing operations in a single community (though even these have been closed in recent decades when profitability shrinks). Apart from these exceptions, most larger firms, which account for the bulk of environmental degradation, have little or no identity with local communities and local ecosystems. What little identification they do have may relate to social and political pressures on the firm from its employees and other local residents, as well as their personal activities and family situations. In their primary role as manager, however, there is much less commitment to the locality and its environment than used to be the case when most investors were local residents. Moreover, we must remember that managers' behavior is under the substantial control of investors (to whom top management reports), who themselves have virtually no sensitivity to local environments. Indeed, increasingly, such investors reside in foreign countries and thus have little or no concern about the United States (or any other location of the firm) as a natural environment.

Under absentee investment, then, managers must struggle to maximize investors' share values by reducing the economic impact of regulation. In some fortuitous circumstances, political regulation makes managers actually do what is better in the longer run for investors. For example, recent toxic waste legislation apparently led to about 30 percent reduction in such wastes, because firms were coerced to reexamine waste treatment processes in their companies, and discovered that many solvents and other valuable chemicals were being lost. Equally important, they discovered that the costs of improved waste control were less than the eventual benefits of retaining more of their production chemicals for the production itself rather than spilling it into the environment. It is probably true that many such environmental spills are very costly to firms such as Active and that it would seem to be economically rational, as well as environmentally desirable, to prevent such material losses that represent severe ecological additions to natural environments.

Yet firms such as Active and Basic resist tighter regulation that might make them do the economically and ecologically "right thing." Why? Two kinds of answers can be offered. The first is political: firms resist regulat*ions* in order to protect themselves from ever more powerful regulat*ors* and their political supporters, who will coerce them to make other "uneconomic" revisions of production in future circumstances. This resistance is at its core political, although it is based on the expansionary logic of the treadmill (Williamson 1981). This logic has at its core the opposition between unlimited economic expansion and the ecological limitations of natural systems confronting such expansion.

Second, even though investors in Active and Basic might eventually profit from being more careful as to how production is organized, to avoid the economic losses of leakages and spills, the investors may nonetheless resist such compliance and its expenditures. Why? The simplest answer relates to the modern form of volatile investment behavior. If I own shares in Active and Basic today, I may want to sell them tomorrow and invest in Consulting or any other firm in the modern world economy. Thus, investors are interested in maintaining the highest rate of return from Active/Basic today and ensuring that they will have the highest market value tomorrow. Once they sell these shares (and they are always prepared to sell them), they care nothing for Active, Basic, or their community or natural environments of operation. (This is what critical resource economists decry as "discounting the future" and "externalizing negative externalities of production," while the rest of their economic counterparts loudly applaud these cogwheels of economic growth in the treadmill of production.) To the extent that regulators enforce managerial behavior that may create greater profits in the near term, managers can operate more freely to comply with these regulations and still protect the share values of shareholders (e.g., Schnaiberg and Weinberg 1992). The smaller the costs and the shorter the payoff period, the more managers are free to comply. And managers may also act more freely even when expenses are larger and payback periods longer, if they can obscure these realities from shareholders through "creative accounting."

But remember that the above conditions are, alas, optimistic exceptions to the pessimistic rule of antagonism between managers and regulators. The regulators impose on the firm the "unproductive" costs of complying with environmental regulations. Managers, protective of their jobs and their firms, resist such impositions. The fiercest opposition arises when the firm is more disadvantaged by regulations than are its major competitors. Thus, if Active faces stricter regulations in Alaska than its Mexican competitors face in offshore drilling, Active is at a competitive disadvantage in the North American market, especially if there is a glut of oil on the market. Therefore, its profits may shrink, along with its market share, although the per barrel costs of all environmental regulations may still be a quite small portion of production costs. Similarly, if a state agency imposes tighter emission controls on Basic than its competitors face, it may suffer market and profit shrinkages. And managers face still stiffer competition for investors' dollars from large numbers of other enterprises offering higher rates of return.

In any event, this should suffice to explain why managers are motivated to avoid regulatory costs. How do they do so? The range of responses is quite large, and variable in different locales and under different regulatory conditions. First, there are responses to direct inspection. Inspectors can be bribed or threatened directly. They may be shunned and harassed in the performance of their duties by managers and workers. Alternatively, they may be seduced in many different ways. These include a shared moral responsibility for protecting workers' jobs and local tax bases (Hawkins 1984) and drawing inspectors into collusion to overlook "minor" infractions so as not to overburden the firm and create shutdowns and lockouts. These are variations in managers' use of "job blackmail" (Kazis & Grossman 1982). Managers sometimes enlist their workers and local authorities in this effort (Gould 1991a, b; Gould & Weinberg 1991; Hawkins 1984).

In addition to these grosser co-optive and coercive mechanisms, managers may choose to obstruct inspectors in the routine and episodic performance of their inspections. Inspectors may be kept waiting for entry into worksites for long periods; work supervisors may be made unavailable to guide them to the right work settings; records to guide inspections may be "misplaced" or have false entries; and so forth. Often inspectors are underpaid and overworked, and simply pass over inspections that are too difficult to carry out. Thus, raising the costs of inspections may be an effective managerial strategy. Conversely, inspection teams may be overwhelmed by managerial "working to rule," reporting every minor violation so as to swamp the inspectors, thus making them less sensitive to serious violations that managers fail to report. In the case of Active, inspections take place over large geographic areas, often stretching inspection resources very thinly. In the case of Basic, the challenge is less in geographic spread than in the complexity of production (Perrow 1986). Where treadmill supporters have politically succeeded in lobbying for the underfunding of regulatory agencies, as in recent years, these local managerial strategies are even more effective, since the range of tasks for a limited number of inspectors is daunting enough, even without obstructionism by managers. Because Consulting is subject to far less on-site inspection, these managerial strategies are simply moot. For those facing more intense on-site inspections, we can summarize the managerial resistances as falling into active (e.g., threats and bribes) and passive (e.g., delays, obscuration) forms.

Counterparts of these active and passive resistances are also found in the area of recordkeeping, which is a key component of much modern

THE "BUBBLING UP" OF THE TREADMILL:
TRADING OF AIR POLLUTION RIGHTS

Ever since the Clean Air Act was enacted in 1970, most manufacturers and utilities have regarded their legal obligation to reduce their air pollution as a major drag on their profits. Unlike other types of environmental protection regulation, corporate managers see no "bottom line" corporate gains from either of their two major technological options: adding expensive air scrubbers to smoke stacks, or making the changeover from more available and cheaper high-sulfur to more expensive low-sulfur fuels. While managers resist pollution abatement, citizen-workers continue to suffer the hazards associated with air pollution. Pollution problems range from respiratory disease to acid rainfall and affect both local and international areas, depending on the height of corporate smokestacks and the strength and direction of winds.

The major regional and national economic interests have stalemated the air pollution control efforts of environmental groups. As a result, these groups have mobilized to put strong pressures on the Environmental Protection Agency staff. As early as 1971, officials in the Nixon administration proposed a *bubble* concept in order to introduce a single standard for all types of air pollution from a plant. Under this concept, plant managers, using economic criteria, could decide which types of pollutants they would choose to reduce. Although the theory of such trading had been academically debated for many years, this was the first time that government officials (acting in response to proposals of the smelting industry) actually implemented such a policy.

Although this bubble policy was eventually declared illegal for its major advocate, the smelting industry, the concept was eventually included in the 1977 Clean Air Act Amendments. Politicians and EPA officials saw this move as a "solution" to conflicts between economic growth and environmental protection. EPA has in fact recently instituted a broad program of "pollution allowances," allowing managers with older plants in denser, more polluted urban areas to buy polluting rights from newer, more efficient plants, especially those in cleaner rural areas. In May 1992 the Tennessee Valley Authority bought SO_2 pollution allowances for $4 million from Wisconsin Power and Light, which has the potential to sell up to $16 million more of such rights. Investors and managers alike approve this system as economically rational. In contrast, many environmentalists attack trading pollution rights as legitimizing economic values above all other environmental and social values, and as ignoring the distributional realities that health costs for groups in some localities are raised without compensation, while investors in other localities make profits on these transactions. Conversely, the Environmental Defense Fund has strongly supported trading pollution rights as the most practical solution to air pollution problems, given the previous political-regulatory failures to enforce air pollution at the state level.

regulation. Active forms of resistance include the creation of false records and the destruction of true records when a complaint has been filed or threatened to be filed (e.g., Mintzmyer 1992). Thus, Active could either knowingly approve a faulty weld on its pipeline or remove a report of a small spill from its pipeline when the records are checked or an on-site pipeline inspection is made. Similarly, Basic could report that its air monitoring system was fully operational, even though it was down for 12 hours for mechanical problems, and it might lose the records of a leaking waste storage tank when inspectors pay a call.

More passive forms of resistance involve accessibility of records. Recent studies of the Community Right to Know law (Weinberg 1991) indicate that the records produced by toxic waste generators are overwhelming in scale and detail for citizen-regulators to use, and are inaccessible by virtue of having no one in charge of records at state environmental agencies and operating hours that make it impossible for citizen-activists to use in their nonworking hours. Managers also use parallel strategies to swamp and to frustrate official regulators: truckloads of documents may be delivered to litigating lawyers in hearings on violations, or obstructive delaying techniques may be used to inhibit agencies from following through. As with more active forms of resistance, these managerial strategies are most effective when regulatory agencies are underfunded, which often coincides with periods of lowered public confidence in these agencies. Further delays in inspections and hearings lead to still further constituent frustration with environmental regulations, thereby often exacerbating the political and financial vulnerability of these agencies. Under such conditions, corporate "plea-bargaining" or negotiations are a likely outcome. This in turn reduces regulatory compliance costs for managers, putting them into a more powerful political and economic position with their investors ("I have protected your shares through this fight . . .").

ECOLOGICAL IMPLICATIONS OF ECONOMIC ORGANIZATIONS

This chapter has outlined the workings of the modern industrial system and traced their implications for environmental protection. Generally, the historical expansion of production that led to and was facilitated by the treadmill of production has dramatically changed the locus of control over businesses. Investors in moderate and large-scale firms are increasingly drawn from more distant quarters, which has reduced their interest in local communities and local natural environments. Moreover, the rise of wealth (surplus or accumulated capital) has created a more volatile investment pattern in the world today. Freedom of movement of capital increasingly disconnects production facilities that engender ecological additions and withdrawals from those investors whose capital undergirds these facilities. Moreover, investors are primarily motivated to seek a maximum rate of return on their investment.

This goal and the investor behavior exhibited to achieve it constrict management's discretion in responding to environmental degradation. Managers must protect their jobs and their firms from disinvestment by achieving increased values of investors' shares in their firms, or else risk the withdrawal of these funds. Since most environmental protection costs more than it returns to most firms, it is a drag on share values; thus, managers seek to avoid dealing with these problems whenever possible.

This inattention to environmental problems has set up a substantial environmentalist constituency, which has pushed governments to regulate firms. Wherever possible, however, associations of firms resist such regulation, either at the legislative level or in implementing the legislation (in part by limiting the funding of regulatory agencies). Government is also ambivalent about environmental regulation, since it desires expansion of the treadmill in order to enhance its budgets and scope of power. Sometimes government manipulates environmentalists by engaging in sham regulation, and at other times it seeks genuine regulation of production to protect the environment (Granovetter 1985, 1990). But even in the latter case it faces staunch resistance by collective and individual actions of investors and managers. They seek to reduce environmentalists' perceptions of the severity of environmental problems. When this effort fails, they limit the actions of regulatory agencies by controlling direct on-site inspections and by controlling the recordkeeping used by these agencies.

SELECTED REFERENCES

BARNET, RICHARD & R. MULLER
  1974   Global Reach: The Power of Multinational Corporations. New York: Simon & Schuster.
BLUESTONE, BARRY & B. HARRISON
  1982   The Deindustrialization of America: Plant Closings, Community Abandonment, and the Dismantling of Basic Industry. New York: Basic Books.
FANTLE, WILL
  1992   "The new industrial alchemy: Air pollution credits are turning pollution into gold." Shepherd Express [Milwaukee], September 24–October 1 [vol. 12, no. 39].
GALBRAITH, JOHN K.
  1971   The New Industrial State. 2nd edition. New York: New American Library.
GOULD, KENNETH A.
  1991a   "The sweet smell of money: Economic dependency and local environmental political mobilization." Society and Natural Resources 4: 133–150.

1991b "Money, management, and manipulation: Environmental mobilization in the Great Lakes." Unpublished doctoral dissertation, Department of Sociology, Northwestern University, June.

1992 "Putting the [W]R.A.P.s on public participation: Remedial action planning and working-class power in the Great Lakes." *Sociological Practice Review* 3(3): 133–139.

GOULD, KENNETH A. & A. S. WEINBERG
1991 "Who mobilizes whom? The role of national and regional social movement organizations in local environmental political mobilization." Paper presented at the annual meetings of the American Sociological Association, Cincinnati, August.

GRANOVETTER, MARK
1985 "Economic action and social structure: The problem of embeddedness." *American Journal of Sociology* 91 (3): 481–510.

1990 "The old and the new economic sociology: A history and an agenda." Pp. 89-112 in Roger Friedland and A. F. Robertson, editors, *Beyond the Marketplace: Rethinking Economy and Society.* New York: Aldine de Gruyter.

GRANOVETTER, MARK AND CHARLES TILLY
1988 "Inequality and labor processes." Pp. 175–221 in Neil Smelser, editor, *Handbook of Sociology.* Newbury Park, CA: Sage Publications.

HAWKINS, KEITH
1984 *Environment and Enforcement: Regulation and the Social Definition of Pollution.* Oxford: Clarendon Press.

KAZIS, RICHARD & R. GROSSMAN
1982 *Fear at Work: Job Blackmail, Labor and the Environment.* New York: Pilgrim Press.

LINDBLOM, CHARLES E.
1977 *Politics and Markets: The World's Political-Economic Systems.* New York: Basic Books.

LIPIETZ, ALAIN
1987 *Mirages and Miracles: The Crises of Global Fordism.* Translated by David Macey. London: Verso Books.

LOWI, THEODORE
1979 *The End of Liberalism.* 2nd edition. New York: W. W. Norton.

MEIDINGER, ERROL
1986 "The politics of 'market mechanisms' in US air pollution regulation: Social structure and regulatory culture." Pp. 150–175 in A. Schnaiberg, N. Watts and K. Zimmermann, editors, *Distributional Conflicts in Environmental-Resource Policy.* Aldershot, England: Gower Publishing.

MINTZMYER, L. LORRAINE
1992 "An environmental vision thing." *Harper's Magazine,* October: 20ff.

MISHAN, EZRA J.
1967 *The Costs of Economic Growth.* New York: Frederick A. Praeger.

PERROW, CHARLES
1986 *Complex Organizations: A Critical Essay.* New York: Random House.

REICH, ROBERT B.
1991 *The Work of Nations: Preparing Ourselves for 21st Century Capitalism.* New York: Alfred A. Knopf.

SCHNAIBERG, ALLAN
1980 *The Environment: From Surplus to Scarcity.* New York: Oxford University Press.

SCHNAIBERG, ALLAN & A. S. WEINBERG
  1992   "Lubricating conflict: The example of recycling oil." *Environment, Technology and Society* 69:9.
  1994   "The political economy of environmental problems and policies: Consciousness, conflict, and control capacity." Forthcoming in R. Dunlap & W. Michelson, editors, *Handbook of Environmental Sociology*. Westport, CT: Greenwood Publishing.
SCHUMACHER, E. F.
  1973   *Small Is Beautiful: Economics As If People Mattered.* New York: Harper & Row.
WEINBERG, ADAM
  1991   "Community right to know and the environment: Reconceptualizing the law." Paper presented at the annual meetings of the American Sociological Association, Cincinnati, August.
WILLIAMSON, OLIVER
  1975   *Markets and Hierarchies.* New York: Free Press.
  1981   "The economics of organization: The transaction cost approach." *American Journal of Sociology* 87 (November): 548–577.

4. Treadmill Predispositions and Social Responses: Population, Consumption, and Technological Change

DIRECTIONS OF AND MOTIVES FOR TECHNOLOGICAL CHANGE

To understand why we have organized this book around the notion of the *enduring conflict,* we need to move up from the level of individual economic organizations to the system of economic organization. This chapter begins that process, in building on past research and theories in the social sciences, but framing the issues in ecologically significant ways. The general argument here, which follows on the logic of Chapters 1–3, is that powerful and enduring forces within industrial societies tend to increase withdrawals from and additions to ecosystems. These social forces reflect an industrial "culture," which is the outcome of interconnected social roles and interests (Noble 1979). Such interests have become institutionalized in the structure that has been created in the modern world economic system in this past century (Williamson 1985).

These interests are quite diverse. Some are aggressive, and others are passive; some are proactive and others reactive; and some may be seen as offensive while others are defensive. For reasons we will outline here and in later chapters, while these interests differ on social and economic planes, their orientation is similar in their relation to ecological systems. These social and economic interests coalesce around viewing ecosystems as instruments, to be used to achieve current and near-term future economic goals. Unfortunately, the ecological implications of such economic "use" entail a variety of forms of ecological withdrawals and additions. Such ecological changes have the potential to disorganize ecosystems, from the local to the global level, in ways that may influence the longer term economic goals, as well as some immediate social needs and concerns.

Part III of the book will outline the social and political responses to these latter needs which react to the dominant societal view of ecosystems as embodying "natural resources" to be converted into economic gains. Here and in Chapter 5, however, we will outline the contents of this instrumental view and the economic, political, and social structures that shaped and preserve it. We refer to this dominant view as the cultural component of a modern structure which we call the *treadmill of production*. The central elements of this treadmill are listed in Table 4.1.

In its simplest form, the treadmill of production is built around the interaction of two processes. The first process is an expansion of technological capacity, arising from the reinvestment into the production system of surplus values extracted from previous production forces, acting on ecosystems (see the next section, Expanding Production). Associated with expanded technological capacity, especially in modern industrial societies, is an expanded necessity of using this capacity in order to provide economic support for the population. The population of modern societies is increasingly made up of a small number of very large productive organizations and the concomitant growth of the number of wage employees of these and other productive organizations (Granovetter 1984). Both categories are committed to the treadmill but for somewhat different reasons. Investors and managers of the large production organizations seek to survive in a globally competitive milieu (see Chapter 3) and need to grow in order to cumulate wealth.

For some of these investors, their commitments generate ecological-use activities that are aggressive, proactive, and offensive. Conversely, for a large majority of the wage-earning population, their dependence on the expansion of economic organizations in order to gain employment and

TABLE 4.1 The Logic of the Treadmill of Production

1. Increasing accumulation of wealth, through ownership of economic organizations that successfully use ecological resources to expand production and profits.
2. Increasing movement of workers away from self-employment, into positions of employees who must rely on expanded production to gain jobs and wages.
3. Increasing allocations of the accumulated wealth to newer technologies in order to replace labor with physical capital, thereby generating more profits for wealth-holders, in order to sustain and expand their ownership in the face of growing competition from other wealth-holders.
4. Increasing activities of governments to facilitate expanded accumulation of wealth for "national development," on the one hand, and "social security," on the other.
5. The net result of these processes is an increasing necessity for ever greater ecological withdrawals and additions in order to sustain a given level of social welfare.
6. The ecological obverse of no. 5 is the increasing likelihood of an industrial society creating *ecological* disorganization, as economic pressures push toward greater extraction of market values from ecosystems.
7. Extending no. 6, societies become increasingly *vulnerable* to socioeconomic disorganization, as their ecological "resource base" itself becomes disorganized.

wages is passive, reactive, and defensive (Granovetter & Tilly 1988). Yet, regardless of these differences in motives, economic growth is a common value of both of these social segments.

The second process entails the dominance of economic growth preferences, even when many decision makers know that ecosystem disorganization is a likely outcome. This projected ecosystem *disorganization* is often dismissed as merely a temporary *disruption* (see Chapter 1). In other cases, there is even a denial of the disruption, or of any disruption due to the production that is valued for its economic growth potential.

The role of government is often viewed as that of policing the relationship of economic structure to ecosystem disruption (Williamson 1985). It is also seen as that of mediating many relationships between workers and investors/owners/managers of economic organizations. But neither of these ideal roles can be actualized, since governments are not impartial mediators between dominant treadmill values and alternative values (Reich 1991). For modern governments have as their constituencies both major groups of treadmill interests. For political and administrative agents of government, economic growth offers some gains for both constituencies (investors and workers). Moreover, all government expenditures, which can be allocated to either constituency (e.g., subsidies for investors, or social welfare for employees and dependents), arise as a tax or levy on national income. Thus, growing national income, which is typically generated by speeding up the treadmill, simultaneously makes it easier to collect a given level of tax revenue and allows governments to allocate more revenue to its two constituencies.

Thus, the treadmill tends to be the dominant value of capital owners, workers, and governments alike (Granovetter 1979). Economic growth is generally preferred everywhere (Granovetter 1979), as even the recent Rio Conference on Environment and Development showed (see Chapter 8). This chapter and the next emphasize how deeply institutionalized this value structure is, dictated by the worldwide organization of economies. Achieving environmental protection, therefore, requires an enduring conflict with the treadmill of production. We might paraphrase a political slogan of an earlier period by stating: *eternal conflict is the price we will have to pay for ecologically sustainable development.*

EXPANDING PRODUCTION AS A SOCIAL CHOICE

Woven through the treadmill of production is one particular form of economic growth: the expansion of production (Reich 1991). This is by no means the only form of economic growth that is logically compatible with the treadmill of production. Indeed, that is why Chapters 9–10 explore other possibilities of restructuring our societies' productive systems. However, the historical evolution of the modern economic system has been closely associated with such an expansion. Chapter 8 describes the intense struggle of contemporary underdeveloped societies to continue on a similar path in their foreseeable future. Their value preferences and plans follow this path, despite their awareness of the environmental consequences of such an expansionary path. Theirs was the overt commitment to development at the 1992 Rio Conference on Environment and Development (although most of the industrial societies equally maintained these values, only more covertly).

Despite many logical alternatives, our actual past, present, and planned future scenarios for modern societies all encompass continued or accelerated expansion of production. Understanding why this is so requires us to place the analysis of individual economic organizations presented in Chapter 3 in its framework of a broader socioeconomic system. While Chapter 3 outlined the economic logic of expanding profits, this chapter examines how profits are linked to technological changes and how such technological changes are in turn tied to the expansion of production. The competitive framework outlined in Chapter 3 has been present in skeletal form since early forms of trading existed, with horseback transportation of goods. The pace of competition accelerated somewhat with more advanced means of transportation, since it permitted more firms to send their products to more distant markets. Thus, sailing ships and especially steamships permitted industrial country producers to expand their markets in other industrial and underdeveloped countries. At the same time, railroads permitted intrasocietal competition in the industrial countries. In contrast, in the underdeveloped countries, most of this transportation improvement merely facilitated the expansion of monopoly corporations (see Chapter 8). Improved transportation enabled them to exploit these populations and ecosystems on a grander scale, extracting still more ecological resources from these countries (e.g., through mining and forestry especially and, later, through plantation agriculture, with the growth of refrigerated ships).

Improvements in transportation were part of a growing attentiveness to technologies in all forms of production. While "tinkering" was a widespread form of improving and adapting production technologies for several centuries, the twentieth century began to alter this social and economic process (Schnaiberg 1980: ch. 3). Many different historical processes combined to generate these substantial changes. These processes are listed in Table 4.2 on p. 72, in different forms and degrees across societies and production arenas.

These diverse historical factors helped pave a general path to expanded production, especially from the periods following World War II (though the impacts of some of these factors increased as early as the mid-nineteenth century or before, in some cases). From an ecological

TABLE 4.2   The Roots of Expanded Production

1. The increasing portability of production, as sources of energy became more separable from their applications in production (e.g., stream power versus steam, and then diesel and electrical power).
2. The portability of instruments of finance, increasing the "circulation" speed of production and distribution, by establishing national and international banking networks.
3. Improvements in transportation, allowing for more rapid and easier movement of raw materials, sources of energy, products, workers, and distribution agents.
4. Improvements in communication, leading to a reduction in the transaction costs of producing for distant and less familiar markets, and increasing the pace of economic activity.
5. Increased availability of credit from financial institutions, and insurance from such institutions and government agencies in order to permit taking longer distance risks.
6. The rise of technological specialties (e.g., applied scientists or engineers), which would have skills at redesigning capital equipment in production.
7. The rise of financial-organizational specialties (e.g., systems analysts and industrial engineers), which permit reallocation of financial and human resources.
8. Political control over international and domestic trade, through the use of government instruments, ranging from patent and property rights to the use of "gunboats" and armies, as well as trade consuls and small business administrations.

perspective, we should distinguish two different forms of production expansion. The first is a quantitative form: here factories and mills primarily got larger and more numerous, and withdrew *more withdrawals* and added *more additions*. In the twentieth century, however, much greater qualitative changes in production were created: in these qualitative changes, we often had *new withdrawals* or *new additions,* which were previously never extracted from or dumped into ecosystems (see Chapter 2). When the source of power for mills changed from water to steam, we had primarily quantitative changes: they became larger, and they simply impacted on more ecosystems in the production process, as well as in the mining process (which could be farther away, with steam-powered trains to ship the coal). New types of coal were mined, with steam-powered equipment and new explosives. In addition to the quantitative effects of this transformation, some qualitative changes also occurred. New forms of air pollution arose from burning new types of coal, and perhaps some new forms of land and water pollution also occurred near factories, with fly-ash and other effluents from the use of the new coal. This early transformation of production is strongly associated with *changing energy sources.* Moreover, much of the ecological impact of this path to expanding production was associated with withdrawals of fossil fuels, which we termed depletion or resource exhaustion.

When factories changed from coal to fuel oil, and later to electricity, however, the results were often more pronounced qualitatively as a result of further industrial processing. Some quantitative impacts of energy use and transformation occurred. Indeed, some were even seen as positive in environmental terms, such as burning clean oil versus dirty coal, which had left more visible pollutants in the form of particulates made up of fly-ash. But the availability of large supplies of portable energy (especially electricity), coupled with new scientific resources, led to "better living through chemistry" in many fields. This change led to many problems of *additions* to ecosystems, or what we have come to call "pollution," a situation that accelerated in the post-1945 period.

The modern economic system faces technologically induced problems of both withdrawals and additions (Schnaiberg 1980: chs. 2 and 3). Among industrial countries, there has been a historical withdrawal of and depletion of petroleum (on land) and some mined resources. But in recent decades in such countries, additions such as toxic wastes, threatening human health as well as animal species, have become more prominent through the rise of synthetic chemicals in production. By the late 1980s the United States alone produced 275,000 tons of industrial waste per year (OECD 1991). Included in that waste were more than 48,000 different chemicals registered with the U.S. Environmental Protection Agency (National Wildlife Federation 1991). In contrast, in the underdeveloped countries, deforestation and desertification have proceeded from quantitative shifts, including increased extraction of firewood by individuals, and massive timber cutting and some plantation agriculture by multinational companies. Between 1981 and 1990 about 40 million acres of tropical forest were destroyed (Rudel & Horowitz 1993; World Resources Institute 1992). Within both sets of societies, as well as the Eastern Bloc states, there is a wide range of both depletion and pollution, arising from intensified use of traditional power sources such as soft coal (producing toxic air pollution and acid rainfall).

Global problems of warming arise primarily from the combustion of fossil fuels (carbon dioxide) and the waste products of modern agriculture and industry (methane gas), heavily influenced by the level of national industrialization. Ozone depletion is even more skewed to the production of industrial societies, which use chlorofluorocarbons in both industrial and consumer products (e.g., refrigeration and air-conditioning). But local and regional problems of any type can occur in localized ecosystems in any society. Thus, for example, clearcutting in northwestern U.S. forests can deplete local topsoil, as can agricultural expansion in irrigated parts of the Great Plains and other areas. Conversely, the toxic nuclear radiation from Chernobyl or from dismantled nuclear submarines has occurred in relatively nonindustrialized parts of the former USSR. And it was in Bhopal, India, that the world's highest recorded death toll from toxic waste occurred (from a local subsidiary of a multinational corporation, Union Carbide). Because of the mobility of fiscal capital, and of physical productive capital, "advanced" technology can create qualitative chemical pollution anywhere that production is relocated. The obverse is also true: the recent controversy in the Pacific Northwest of the United States over protecting the northern spotted owl has been intensified because of the forest clearcutting there, a practice that removes the owl's habitat. Clearcutting is expanding, with most of the cut logs being sold to Japan and much of it processed in Japan rather than in the United States, which as a result has lost many timber industry jobs.

Why then does the treadmill system favor expanding production, thereby increasing ecological withdrawals and additions and the threat of ecosystem disorganization? In an earlier period, before worldwide competition was so intense, why did production expand? The usual answer relates to the growth of population: in the next section we treat this as a real but very incomplete explanation for the expansion of production. Our interpretation of the work of historians, economists, and sociologists suggests that a tension exists within industrial systems, especially but not exclusively in capitalistic ones. In the early days of the twentieth-century treadmill, the speed was slower, but the directions of modern production systems were already laid out. The process is a relatively straightforward one. For any given producer who is successful in extracting ecosystem resources and in marketing them, a profit is generated. Some portion of the profit or "surplus" is likely to be allocated to new physical capital. This capital is then used to expand production, often thereby reducing the per unit costs of products and improving the company's competitive position and/or the size and share of the total market it supplies.

A first question can be raised: why can't a corporation's level of production simply remain static rather than expand? One answer is that some family-owned enterprises have indeed remained fairly stable and static over protracted periods. These owners typically were satisfied with their rates of return, since they didn't need or want more profits. Often, even in such firms, the next generation of owners may be larger, or seek new challenges, and thereby seek to modernize and expand their operations. (The son or daughter faces an economic organization that his or her parent had the satisfaction of *building*.) When we move beyond family-owned businesses, we encounter variants of the situation described in Chapter 3.

A company that enters a public market which provides it with operating or expansionary funds must compete with other firms for such funds (Williamson 1981). This produces both the resistance to environmental protection regulations outlined in Chapter 3 and the need to expand profits that underlies Chapter 3 (Williamson 1985). From these arguments, we can state that expansion of profits is more of a goal in this public marketplace, while reshaping production systems may be a more important goal in family-owned businesses. Somewhere in the middle of these two positions is the case of family-owned businesses in which the next generation is larger and thereby needs more profits to support more owners. Such owners then expand the pie, rather than just fighting each other for a fixed profit level. In other cases, inheritors of businesses have no skills or desires to continue the business, and they sell off the firm to a market actor, thereby moving the firm onto the "conveyor belt" of the treadmill of production (Granovetter 1979, 1984).

The second question posed has to be: why do owners invest more in new equipment, rather than in adding more workers (Noble 1979)? A conventional answer is that this path results in greater capital efficiency (defined as lower costs of production per unit produced), permitting more rapid expansion of profits through expansion of market size. This path differs from the model in which a social reorganization of workers permits more profits from a given level of production by increasing labor efficiency. Interestingly, most of the examples of a labor-relations path seem to arise within family businesses, where owners are also managers. They retain social relationships to their employees, rather than seeing employment as a business transaction (Williamson 1985; cf. Granovetter & Tilly 1988). In sharp contrast to both of these models, the theory of rationalization or social control suggests that owners of capital and their managers can predict and control their transactions with machinery and physical technology rather than their transactions with workers. Whether this difference in control is always or usually actualized, the *belief* of investors and managers that these transaction costs will be predictably reduced itself creates pressures to develop new technologies to supplant more human labor. Unlike the first two models, the last model treats the employment relationship as only a transaction, peripheral to the major tasks of the production organization (Williamson 1981). It assumes enduring conflict between owners and workers, which agrees with both neoconservative and neo-Marxist views of the firm and the economy. We must add to these models an increasingly common form of economic transaction, which involves the purchase/takeover (hostile or otherwise) of existing firms and the liquidation of that firm's assets. In this scenario productive enterprises are eliminated to provide capital for other investments. Although it may appear that such transactions represent non-expansive investments, production *is* expanded, but in different enterprises and often at different geographical locations (see Table 7.1, p. 158).

In concluding this section, we stress that the expansion of production has both a historical and a comparative dimension. Throughout most of the modern industrialization period, expansion of production has been the general trend. It is not the only possible way to create social conditions in which both capital investment and labor commitment are rewarded in some "equitable" way in generating production and surplus and in allocating this surplus. One simple way of thinking about these future possibilities is to consider the current and historical variation in modern societies in some crude indicators of these processes. For example, the ratio of upper management wages and benefits to those of line-workers has varied substantially across time periods and industrial societies. In the past decade, ratios have risen from 40 to 1 in 1980 to over 100 to 1 in the United States, considerably higher than in other European societies with whom we compete (Galbraith 1992). Similarly, the net rate of return on capital investment varies substantially across periods and societies: this has included variable gross rates of return on investment in productive capital, as well as quite variable rates of taxation of these earnings, to generate a net rate of return. Similarly, the ways in which these tax revenues have been allocated to workers versus owners and managers also vary widely (Granovetter & Tilly 1988).

POPULATION AND PRODUCTION: THE COMPLEX CONNECTIONS

It is tempting to explain the contemporary growth in production by referring to the growth of the human population in each society. At every level of analysis, however, this inference is misleading. Starting with the world as a whole, those societies with the highest rates of economic growth and the highest rates of ecological withdrawals and additions, are precisely those societies with the lowest rates of population growth in the twentieth century. Indeed, the proportion of the global population represented by these high-economic growth nations is shrinking rather rapidly. As we move from this global perspective down to a nation-state and regional level, this disjuncture between population growth and ecological withdrawals and additions becomes more evident—but also more complex. At one extreme, we cannot assume that population growth is irrelevant to both temporary ecological disruption and enduring ecological disorganization. However, the size of a population appears to be most relevant to ecological disruption where populations are closer to subsistence production rather than industrial production. In recent decades, the world has become more aware of drought, starvation, and their connection to the press of populations on limited ecosystems. Desertification in sub-Saharan Africa has been increasingly linked to the attempts of regional nomadic peoples to support larger herds of animals by grazing them in areas of marginal moisture and productivity. Here and elsewhere, this process is accelerated by the collection of firewood through cutting down younger and younger trees, which in turn makes soil more vulnerable to sandstorms and loss of topsoil, when moisture is low.

In establishing any form of environmental protection, we must attend to two features of this population-induced ecological disorganization. First, many of these local and regional ecological problems are "solved" in ways that ecosystems pass on these pressures to all animal species: members of the population gain less nutrition, become ill and disabled, and die in much larger than usual numbers. Paradoxically, this increase in death rate was what the Reverend Thomas Malthus (Appleman 1976) predicted as a "positive check" in his famous/notorious 1798 *Essay on the Principle of Population*. In this late-eighteenth-century analysis, Malthus was careful to distinguish between the rise of such mortality checks and the healthy condition of a growing population that was able to consume more resources by having enough earnings to create an effective demand for natural resources in order to sustain themselves. Only as population "tended" to outrun its local ecosystem's capacity people sickened and die. In the South, and even in the poverty areas of cities in industrial societies, the same process goes on, only somewhat abated by national and international flows of food and other assistance.

Even in 1798, and especially in the six later editions of the *Essay*, Malthus pointed to a different trajectory for human populations. As people became more educated and more knowledgeable about their futures, preventive checks would begin to occur. People would not have children without being able to care for them. Instead, people would begin to plan the size of their families according to their expected livelihoods. To the extent that employers provided more wages and welfare, including education, for the workers and their children, workers would begin to use both abstinence, and later, contraception, sterilization, and other forms of voluntary limitations of births. This less dismal scenario, which later was referred to as the *embourgeoisement* process, was one of balancing population size and resource extraction to avoid higher mortality. From this perspective, then, population would not exceed ecosystem limits. That is, humankind would begin to plan and adjust population size and growth rates, but at the familial level rather than at the societal level, according to local and regional agricultural and related ecological conditions.

Unfortunately, Malthus's contributions to the study of population terminated with his death, before the vast expansion of production through the widening use of fossil fuels and raw materials from distant ecosystems in industrial societies. The form and scale of later industrialization created productive mechanisms in societies whose expansion vastly exceeded the stimulus of population growth itself. That is, it was the growth of industrial production systems rather than the growth of human reproduction that increased societal impacts on ecosystems. To expand production, industrial investment of capital "overcame" local ecological limitations, largely by moving resource extraction activities farther afield to many more and to more distant ecosystems. As we noted earlier, this shift depended on the revolution in transportation technologies. Improved transportation provided ease of movement both of fuels and raw materials from distant resource areas and of the finished products to distant consumers.

To understand the limited role of population growth, we need merely to turn to the South. In the twentieth century, and especially since World War II, Southern societies have experienced the sharpest rates of population increase in part because of food stabilization and in part because of public health controls that together lowered mortality in this period. As a consequence, they have become the youngest societies and thus capable of even more population growth in the future, as the vast numbers of children become parents. For most of these societies, increased poverty and underdevelopment have been a consequence of population growth, according to demographic scholars. Our assessment (see Chapter 8 especially) is that rapid population growth was only a small factor in their underdevelopment: much more important is their remoteness from and lack of control over industrial production systems. The policy guidance offered by family planning programs and other population control advocates is actually as follows: *reduce your rate of population growth, and only then can you invest in modern production systems.* While rising population has indeed led to many local shortages of arable land, fuel, and water, the major impact has been malnutrition, disease, and death. This problem has limited actual withdrawals from and additions to ecosystems, making them well below the rates of such ecological disruptions in industrial countries, some of which even have negative rates of population growth.

In a socially realistic analysis, production expansion has complicated relationships to population growth. Quite different combinations of the population's savings and consumption patterns can produce highly variable patterns of productive investment and production expansion. Thus, for example, the U.S. population consumes more of its per capita income than does Japan, which invests more of its income in Japanese industries (either directly or through government intervention). Thus, the effect of population on ecological demands will also differ in the two societies: more per capita consumer impacts exist in the United States than in Japan, but potentially more industrial impacts can and will occur in Japan in the absence of governmental and private sector environmental protection. As the U.S. economy continues to decline relative to Japan's, *ceteris paribus,* we would expect to find a faster growth of environmental disruption in Japan. Both societies have low rates of population increase, but the U.S. increase is more often due to immigration, which essentially transfers the population growth demands of other societies to the United States, while the Japanese population growth is more domestic. Whereas in all industrial societies, a population represents a potential market for goods and services produced by the economic sectors, with modern flows of investment and goods, markets are increasingly multinational and international, as are flows of capital (see Chapter 3). This further weakens the connections among a society's population size, level of production, and withdrawals and additions within domestic ecosystems. Indeed, the recent renewal of international calls for increased "basic needs" production at the Rio conference and elsewhere, attests to the prescience of Malthus's early distinction between population size and effective demand. For in a world that has generated unprecedented levels of production expansion in recent decades, a large fraction of the world's population goes without adequate nutrition, housing, medical care, and employment. Interestingly, production for basic needs is most closely tied to population size and growth.

Thus, the failure of growing world production to meet basic human needs is additional powerful evidence that no clear link exists between production expansion and population growth. It indicates that the biomass quality of human actors is less significant for predicting their ecological impacts than is the socioeconomic quality of human actors. One way of demonstrating this idea is by reference to social expectations about the size of children and the linkage of family size to nutritional adequacy. In the North, over the past century individuals have grown substantially taller than their ancestors. Yet this growth of biomass actually represents a significant drain on ecosystems, requiring higher food and raw material inputs (e.g., for clothing, bedding, and housing) and increasing human wastes per capita. Once more, it is our social values that take precedence over our biological necessities. The opposite end of this scenario is the *shrinking* size of individuals under conditions of malnutrition and starvation in the South. Contrasting these two sets of conditions (higher weight and diffused obesity in the North versus lower weight and malnutrition in the South), we find that the per capita ecological impact of individual members of the two types of societies as biological demands on ecosystems is higher in the North. Yet we decry population growth as an *ecological hazard* in the South.

A second example of the logical flaws in a crude population-based explanation of expanded production is found in our recent attention to the disappearing rainforests (Rudel & Horowitz 1993). There is often a confusion in our public rhetoric about South American rainforests, since many South American countries have high rates of population growth. But the major forces influencing the cutting of rainforests are industrial investors, who want the land for mining, cattle grazing, and plantation agriculture. First, such investors act to remove the population by killing or forcibly moving them and then they cut the rainforest trees, which they also sell for large profits (Rudel & Horowitz 1993). Some of the more socially and ecologically progressive movements in industrial societies to find alternative, sustainable uses of rainforests by preserving the tree cover may be unaware of actual efforts along these lines by indigenous leaders of local populations. These include groups of rubber-tappers and others involved in more sustainable forms of production. Some of them, like Chico Mendez, have died in the process of opposing miners, cattle ranchers, and other industrial investors (Gore 1992). As we note in Chapter 8, however, these groups face serious pressures from industrial and other economic elites, who look to industrial societies for models and money to expand high-technology production, with all its attendant ecological risks.

In summary, from a local and global ecological perspective, population growth represents a clear and present danger. Contrary to some analysts, we see little social or ecological advantages to a growing population in most societies. At the same time, however, the historical record is clear: it is not population growth that has created the national and global environmental disruption we confront today. Rather, following Chapter 3, it is the expansion of profits or surplus that has led to an enormous expansion of production in the past century, especially in the last half-century. With the modern potential for global diffusion of money, physical production equipment (technology) and information, goods and services, to both producers and consumers, the role of population growth in expanding production becomes attenuated. Instead, the generation of surplus and the allocation of this capital influence production expansion. Both domestically and internationally, not only are production decisions controlled disproportionately by a small number of decision makers, but also consumption capacity is increasingly being allocated to a smaller share of the world's consumers (Galbraith 1992; Reich 1991).

EMPLOYMENT, WAGES, AND THE TREADMILL: LABOR AND TECHNOLOGY

With historical changes in industrial societies and in most of the modern world-systems, more and more surplus is going into physical technologies, which then accelerates the withdrawals from and additions to global ecosystems. Increases in carbon dioxide reflect increased fuel consumption in industrial countries and the expansion of auto-truck usage. Global warming is, therefore, primarily an ecological warning that our technological systems are pushing against global ecological limits. The impact of carbon dioxide (and, to a lesser extent, of methane from agribusiness operations such as animal feedlots) has been exacerbated by the application of massive mining and forestry operations which have removed tree cover from much of the world's forests. This has slowed the natural process by which carbon dioxide is converted into plant material through photosynthesis (only to be returned to the atmosphere when the trees die or are cut and burned), and has increased global warming risks (Gore 1992).

The treadmill has also created substantial material benefits for workers through this historical process of replacing human labor with physical technologies. This replacement involved the substitution of fossil fuels for human and animal energy, and the later substitution of new chemicals to produce a whole range of new products and production processes (e.g., plastics, electronics, pharmaceuticals, and other hydrocarbon-based products). These products have become more available to workers through expanded markets, both private and state-run. In order to participate as consumers in these markets, however, individuals have needed to earn more money to purchase more goods and services.

One of the perennial problems associated with a growing production stream is simply overproduction: that is, there will not be enough consumers with enough money to buy these products. This situation creates periodic recessions and depressions in industrial societies. In either of these cycles, when goods cannot be sold, inventories build up, as in Basic Chemical in Chapter 3. Then production facilities are slowed and eventually shut down. Ancillary business services (e.g., Consulting Associates in Chapter 3), finding their services in less demand, lay off workers and reduce the hours of other workers. Similarly, when manufacturing decreases, the demand for raw material inputs decreases, forcing slowdowns or shutdowns of facilities such as those of Active Petroleum in Chapter 3. This represents a deceleration, but not generally a dismantling, of the treadmill. It produces some temporary decreases in ecological withdrawals and additions. When conditions change, this process is reversed, and ecological pressures typically rise again, often exceeding the pre-recession levels.

What happens to workers in these processes? The general theory of wages suggests that, as workers become more productive, generally through the application of more technology per worker, management can afford to pay workers more wages. Thus, each of these high-tech workers can consume more of the products produced in an accelerating treadmill, thereby permitting the withdrawals and additions of production to continue, as well as increasing the level of postconsumption wastes. This result can be traced to three simultaneous processes operating on worker-consumers: (1) they buy more, and hence they have more to discard; (2) they tend to find it more profitable to spend hours at work rather than repairing domestic goods, and hence they throw out more products that are potentially reusable; and (3) they are subject to higher levels of advertising, being encouraged to discard old products and buy newer ones, so that firms can avoid recessions.

So blue-collar workers involved directly in applying higher technology to production (i.e., using more energy and/or chemicals) earn more and consume and discard more. They seem to have gained more comforts from consuming the fruits of industrial expansion. Some social critics (e.g., Braverman 1974) claim that such workers may actually be less stimulated than their predecessors by boring production processes, but other critics increasingly point to the occupational stresses of the "bad old days" (e.g., Rodgers 1978). Yet other social critics point to the lack of stimulation in passive activities such as television viewing, but others note new forms of learning and recreation by these workers. Generally, few observers could in good conscience claim that such workers have been materially "impoverished" by this history of production expansion. And many workers, with relatively high levels of literacy and increased leisure time, would claim that their lives are intellectually and emotionally superior to those of their ancestors (Rubin 1976; Schor 1991; Sennett & Cobb 1974).

Moreover, with advanced technologies that have expanded production, many new types of white-collar workers have a variety of new career prospects in a variety of positions that do not involve direct extraction or transformation of environmental inputs. Expansions of sales and clerical jobs whose tasks are to sell and keep track of expanded production, have also occurred, as have professionalized jobs with higher levels of human capital, including financial experts, research and development scientists and engineers, marketing experts, public relations professionals, communications specialists, and even environmental experts. All have been an essential part of the processes by which expansion of production occurred. Higher wages for these "head-work" positions have permitted such professionals to absorb more of the growing production stream and to become more proficient in stimulating even higher levels of production and consumption. And some of them (like the authors) have devoted their professional lives to dealing with the human and environmental problems caused by the rise of production.

These employment and wage consequences are frequently said to be part of the "progress" generated by an expanding production system. Less frequently mentioned are their negative outcomes, the most striking of which is the displacement of many workers at both very low and very high skill levels. As a result, it has been charged that workers have become "de-skilled" (Braverman 1974) and even dehumanized (Schumacher 1973). Historical accounts of the rise of industrialization (Rodgers 1978) indicate that from the start many workers from traditional industries tried to avoid factory work, because of employment and wage conditions.

Generally, we can say that some portion of the workforce has lost discretionary control over their work processes, often in return for higher wages generated by application of new technologies. Conversely, until recently, it was argued that white-collar workers gained such controls, but office technologies such as typewriters, word processors, and computers have made white-collar work increasingly routine. More recently, white-collar and "elite" blue-collar workers from the so-called labor aristocracy (e.g., auto and steel workers) have suffered some loss of employment, wages, and work control, in the United States at least, with the increase in competitive pressures noted in Chapter 3 (e.g., Blumberg 1980; cf. Granovetter & Tilly 1988).

Unemployment, underemployment, poverty, and ill-health have also been side-effects of the expansion of production. High-technology corporations have grown at the expense of thousands of smaller enterprises and more labor-intensive crafts. Except for the elite consumers of modern society, far fewer of the consumer goods are produced by the more direct application of skilled labor to raw materials. Much of the modern basket of consumer goods is machine-produced, with workers operating machines they cannot build, or, in most cases, even repair. This development has led to the charge that workers have become more "alienated" from their production activities. Hand-made goods are much more expensive than machine-made goods: that is the core goal and logic of our history of production expansion. Many hand-workers were initially displaced by early industrialization. The Luddites, for example, were quite rational when they opposed the rise of steam-powered weaving mills, for through this new technology they lost the freedom of producing in their own cottages. In like manner, successive generations of industrial workers have been displaced as a result of changes in technologies and markets. The flight of capital from the United States to the Pacific Rim and other countries is merely the latest in a long series of such social disruptions. The United States' new free trade pacts with Canada and Mexico may produce a net gain for some American workers. But in the foreseeable future, it will mean actual losses for many production and other workers, along with some gains for Mexican and perhaps some Canadian workers (Galbraith 1992; Reich 1991).

Our urban ghettos and other poverty areas are a byproduct of this historical expansion of production. With more energy and chemicals, and fewer unskilled or low-skilled workers in production, the employment market has collapsed for many residents of these areas. Moreover, to avoid dealing with the urban problems of crime, drugs, and poverty, employers using higher technology often prefer to operate away from large urban areas. Their more portable technologies and reduced dependence on low-skilled workers permit this migration (e.g, Bluestone & Harrison 1982).

The same processes that occurred in the larger central cities from 1945 to the 1990s repeated themselves in smaller towns and older suburbs in the 1980s. The problems that were earlier associated with the unemployment of African-American and other minority groups have now become apparent in many communities with nonminority populations, and often have extended from blue-collar to white-collar careers (Reich 1991).

Even with the continued expansion of the national economy, government programs to take some of the surplus thereby generated through taxes and to allocate it to displaced and impoverished workers have been contracting relative to growing needs (Galbraith 1992). Rising government health care costs, as fewer workers are in positions to have adequate health insurance from their jobs, are among the several categories of increased pressure on government from rising production. It has also been suggested that this process will accelerate, lowering the material standard of living for many more working- and middle-class Americans (Ehrenreich 1990, 1992; Gallagher 1992). For all kinds of workers who have lost access to employment, whether temporarily or permanently, this history of production expansion has meant additional costs. The welfare state is based on the theory that the government will allocate a substantial share of the surplus generated by production and profit expansion to cushion the costs of expansion for workers who have been negatively impacted. This *safety net* includes provisions for: workers injured on the job (worker's compensation or disability), workers suffering job loss (unemployment insurance and employment offices), workers unable to find new employment (welfare or the dole), workers unable to afford decent housing (housing allowances or public housing) or adequate food (food stamps and surplus food allocations), or workers too old to work (old age pensions). But in recent years states and localities have faced increased pressures to reduce all types of social welfare costs. At the same time, the number of food stamp recipients in the United States has reached an all-time high.

Ultimately, these pressures devolve from one of several causes: (1) owners and managers seek to retain more surplus for use in reinvestment or to pay greater returns to investors (see Chapter 3), and (2) workers and managers who are employed seek to retain more of their earnings for private consumption rather than public redistribution (Lapham 1989). Both groups support scenarios of lower taxes, with private production, private investment, and/or private consumption preferred over public goods such as a social security net. These two scenarios reinforce each other to some extent and create two classes of laboring people: (1) those who are on the "rising tide" of production expansion, and (2) those who have "fallen overboard" without an adequate life preserver.

WOMEN'S WORDS AND WORLDS:
THE STRUGGLE FOR A VOICE AT RIO

Although many leaders of environmental movements are male, women have played more central roles than men in local campaigns dealing with children's health risks. But the specific concerns of women are often treated peripherally in environmental programs. This is a painful paradox in environmental policy-making, since the role of women has been vital to adjusting family size to ecological and economic restraints, as well as in rearing, educating, and providing the cultural roots for the future workers of the world-system. Moreover, women as workers themselves have played key roles in both education and health care, and are moving into policy positions in both the private and public sector. Finally, women's multiple roles make them both key participants in the treadmill processes *and* as "whistle blowers," alerting communities to the impacts of the treadmill on local economic structure and family life, especially in cases of drought, deforestation, natural disasters, and toxic waste hazards.

In planning for the United Nations Conference on Environment and Development in Rio de Janeiro, Brazil, in June 1992, women around the world sought to avoid being dismissed in the new world economic and ecological agendas. Early planning in Nairobi during 1990 continued this trend, spurring Bella Abzug and Mim Kelber to organize other activists into the Women's Development and Environment Organization. This social movement organized the World Women's Congress for a Healthy Planet in Miami, Florida, in November 1991, which prepared a Women's Action Agenda to introduce correctives to the male biases of both treadmill supporters and opponents at Rio. The Earth Summit incorporated a number of the agenda items, which included greater integration of women as managers and field workers in environmental protection and economic development projects. Equally important, the Summit's Declaration of Principles and Action Agenda 21 stated the importance of both women's and men's freedom in deciding on family size, and women's enhanced access to reproductive and other health care services. Social research has strongly indicated that the greater involvement of women in these roles, especially where women also have broader extrafamilial roles and rights, is likely to reduce family size in both Southern and Northern nations.

This transformation of feminist frustrations into more organized and "moderate" movements parallels the historical transformation of earlier feminist activists, such as Margaret Sanger, a "radical" proponent of birth control. According to activist Ellen Chesler's 1992 biography, *Woman of Valor: Margaret Sanger and the Birth Control Movement in America*, Sanger used the skills of the radical feminist movement to move the broader society towards acceptance of family planning (a pattern common to other feminist crusaders, including Frances Willard). Indeed, Sanger herself was the founder of an organization that eventually became Planned Parenthood. This now international organization has actively promoted women's and children's rights and health concerns, often against socially draconian proposals made by "overpopulation" alarmists.

WHO'S IN CHARGE? PRIVATE CAPITAL, GOVERNMENT, AND/OR LABOR?

Some social analysts have cited runaway technology as a major cause of environmental disruption. For us, this position is a distortion of social reality in several ways. Economic decision makers change technologies rapidly, but the technologies themselves cannot act without human control. Thus, the concept of technology "running away" actually refers to a set of economic decisions, and, as we have tried to stress, these decisions are taken by individual social agents, acting in a variety of social roles. These roles are part of a contemporary institutional system (see Chapter 5), which we refer to as the treadmill of production. To understand this much is to understand the points at which we can alter the technological and treadmill conditions. Therefore, we want to underscore the misleading quality of the concept of runaway technology.

First, to *design* any technological change requires a substantial amount of money/capital for research and development. This funding has to come from a major institution, either in the private or public sector, or through some joint activity of theirs. Second, to *implement* a new technology also requires considerable capital and expertise, for some basic scientific/engineering design has to be transformed into a pilot plant (essentially, a small factory) or a major workshop or clinic or office. The capital and expertise must be allocated to transform ideas into physical equipment and processes of labor control to operate it, along with procedures to ensure access to the raw materials and often to markets to distribute the product. For this reason many new inventions are never patented; or if patented, they are never applied to production; or if applied to production, they fail and become moribund. Third, to *sustain* a new technology, the application must not only work occasionally, but must also operate steadily and predictably, with low enough costs so as to compete in markets (Williamson 1985; Reich 1991).

Take, for example, the contemporary concern about recycling post-consumer wastes. We know that paper wastes make up a high proportion of landfill content. By removing inkstuffs and repulping the paper fibers, newsprint can be recycled to produce new paper products, albeit with shorter fibers than the initial paper contained. While waste inks are responsible for some additions in the remanufacturing process (Gould 1991), biodegradable soy-based inks are also available for short-use printed paper. Moreover, communities have become mobilized to gather newsprint and other "recyclable" wastes for transport and remanufacturing, often through convenient (but expensive) curbside recycling from homes and apartments. One might imagine, then, that recycling paper would become a runaway technology in the late twentieth century. On the contrary, newsprint and other paper wastes have become a glut on the market, because the rate of collection of newsprint has vastly exceeded the rate of remanufacturing at paper recycling mills. Why? The most common answer is that recycling paper has not yet become economic enough for investors to build more paper recycling mills. This is true despite the fact that much of the waste paper is obtained for very low charges (Schnaiberg 1992) from voluntary associations and municipalities. Paper industry investors and managers contend that "the market" for recycled products is not yet profitable enough to generate profits for new recycling mill investments. They have urged government agencies to buy recycled products, as well as to collect waste papers in communities and their offices, in order to increase private sector profits.

This example indicates that capital interests are the driving force in technological change. Far from being runaway, the example shows that paper recycling is a "limp-along" technology. Only when profit expectations change might it become "runaway." (There is no certainty even then, since other investment opportunities may preclude this.) But technological changes under the treadmill of production are the products of many influences, albeit in our society they rest most heavily on capital owners and their allocation of funds. Governments may influence this process of change through any or all of the following:

1. Tax "virgin" paper products, increasing the relative profitability of recycling paper wastes.
2. Offer tax incentives to recycling mill owners in order to reduce their costs of production.
3. Set up new research plants to test new and cheaper technologies of paper reprocessing and new products.
4. Offer incentives to recycling mills that locate in areas of high unemployment, paying a tax rebate or credit for each worker employed in the operations.
5. Offer tax revenues to municipalities in order to further subsidize curbside collection.
6. Offer employment tax rebates to hire more workers to separate different types of waste paper, increasing the ease of reprocessing and quality of recycled products.

These government actions influence owners, managers, and labor and community action groups. They require tax revenues from other sources to pay for most of these changes, and in turn they offer different mixes of incentives and disincentives to segments of the investor and labor organizations in the country. Therefore, they are involved in the politics of taxing and allocating revenues, and the decision to take any of these actions is likely to be made on political and economic grounds. Pressures from investors, labor groups, and municipalities would tend to move federal and state legislators in one direction or the other. Once again, the nature of neither the technology itself nor of the ecological disruption it creates determines the government's actions with regard to changing technologies. Rather, it is the political actions, typically based on economic interests, that permit government changes to add or withdraw support for the private use of technologies.

Conspicuously absent from much of our discussion on technological change is the role of labor. We believe that this absence reflects the actual behaviors of organized labor in the United States, although its role is different in Western and Eastern European societies, which indicates that other roles are possible in the United States as well. In many ways, labor groups are reactive to proposed changes in technology, with the possible exception of problems of occupational safety and health (e.g., Brodeur 1974; Claybrook 1984). That is, most labor groups have little capacity or will to propose changes in technologies, except where direct constituent interests are at stake around issues of health and safety. This doesn't mean that labor groups are powerless in the process of technological change. They may occasionally veto proposed changes, because of employment or safety and health conditions (Granovetter 1985). More commonly, they resist some changes that would be disadvantageous to their labor members. In such cases, the most common outcome of negotiations between labor groups and employers is a phasing-in process for new technologies, and some compensation for older workers (buyouts, pensions, guaranteed employment, severance bonuses) to "smooth" the path for implementing new technologies. Finally, at the government legislative level, they may appear to testify in favor of or in opposition to new regulations for a particular technology (e.g., in the Clean Air Act, or in the Resource Conservation and Recovery Act and Superfund decisions) (Granovetter & Tilly 1988). They may also appear as a litigant, especially when the litigation is about compensation for occupational illnesses, such as in the asbestos industry trials (e.g., Brodeur 1974).

Returning to the question of who's in charge of technological change, the answer seems to lie most centrally in the private sector. Governments can induce or prohibit certain technological changes, such as in prohibiting chlorofluorocarbons in the future or in supporting a supersonic transport fleet that would also have reduced the ozone in the upper atmosphere. But these political controls over economic markets are limited and crude policy tools. More reasonably, governments in the industrial nations can accelerate or decelerate the rates of technological change, but *they don't control many of the directions of change* (Reich 1991). A significant exception to this is the arena of the military, where there is more government specification in the direction of technological innovation trajectories (Mumford 1970). For some technologies, societies, and periods, though, governments have been much more direct technological actors within civilian sectors. That means that, under certain social and political conditions of responsiveness to environmental disorganization, they could shape technological change more directly. Labor groups have a more limited role, both currently and historically, although their compliance has been an important element in many technological changes (Ehrenreich 1990, 1992). Perhaps their major role is a political one, acting through, with, and in opposition to government leaders, programs, and policies by means of lobbying, voting, and political support of candidates for public office. Their other political role is through litigation: even individual workers can sometimes mobilize a labor lawyer through a class action suit based on individual workers in similar working conditions. But it is generally suits by organized labor that typically carry more legal clout in court.

One exception to the reactive and limited role of labor is the role of professional research and development workers. Much of the modern regulation of the civilian nuclear power industry, for example, is a product of the political actions by professional nuclear scientists and engineers. Both individually and in organizations such as the Union of Concerned Scientists (see Chapters 5 and 7), they acted to counter the promotion of nuclear power by the federal government to subsidize its military use of nuclear weaponry. Their insider knowledge of the technologies they helped to develop and operate gave them a capacity to blow the whistle on industrial glossing over of problems with nuclear safety—both operating and proposed systems, such as high-level waste storage. Their role has been unique with regard to the projected impacts of future technological changes. However, some of the importance attached to their whistle-blowing role has carried over into new federal legislation to protect and reward future laborers, who report illegal actions of their employers. (They can receive up to 25 percent of the fines resulting from their reports.) Of course, such economic rewards paradoxically retain the highest values of the treadmill of production: expanding profitability!

Nonetheless, this is neither a fixed nor a dismal picture. Indeed, the fact that technology is not runaway should give us political heart: what institutional decision makers propose can be altered by other political and economic actors. The treadmill is not a mystical system but a construction of human interests. In our next chapter, we point to the institutional underpinning of this system in order to note both the treadmill's resistance to structural changes and its limited points of vulnerability to opposing forces.

SELECTED REFERENCES

APPELMAN, PHILIP, EDITOR
   1976 *An Essay on the Principle of Population—Thomas Robert Malthus—Text, Sources and Background, Criticism.* New York: W. W. Norton.

BARNETT, RICHARD J.
1980   The Lean Years: Politics in the Age of Scarcity. New York: Touchstone, Simon
        & Schuster.
BLUESTONE, BARRY & B. HARRISON
1982   The Deindustrialization of America: Plant Closings, Community Abandonment,
        and the Dismantling of Basic Industry. New York: Basic Books.
BLUMBERG, PAUL
1980   Inequality in an Age of Decline. New York: Oxford University Press.
BRAVERMAN, HARRY
1974   Labor and Monopoly Capital: The Degradation of Work in the Twentieth Century.
        New York: Monthly Review Press.
BRODEUR, PAUL
1974   Expendable Americans. New York: Viking.
CHESLER, ELLEN
1992   Woman of Valor: Margaret Sanger and the Birth Control Movement in America.
        New York: Simon & Schuster.
CLAYBROOK, JOAN
1984   Retreat from Safety: Reagan's Attack on American Health. New York: Pan-
        theon Books.
DIAMOND, DEBORAH B.
1992   "A mother of invention: Activist finds new meaning in Margaret Sanger's
        contraception crusade." Chicago Tribune, August 16th.
EHRENREICH, BARBARA
1990   Fear of Falling: The Inner Life of the Middle Class. New York: Harper
        Perennial.
1992   "Are you middle class? Maybe–but it doesn't mean the same thing it
        used to." Utne Reader September/October: 63–66.
FOWLER, SUSANNE
1992   "Earth Summit: Rio session puts needs of women on the map." Chicago
        Tribune, June 28th.
GALBRAITH, JOHN KENNETH
1992   The Culture of Contentment. New York: Houghton Mifflin.
GALLAGHER, NORA
1992   "Feeling the squeeze: In tough times, the fallout from money fear affects
        us all." Utne Reader September/October: 54–61.
GORE, SENATOR AL
1992   Earth in the Balance: Ecology and the Human Spirit. Boston: Houghton
        Mifflin.
GOULD, KENNETH A.
1991   Money, Management, and Manipulation: Environmental Mobilization in the
        Great Lakes. Unpublished doctoral dissertation, Department of Sociology,
        Northwestern University, June.
GRANOVETTER, MARK
1979   "The idea of 'advancement' in theories of social evolution and develop-
        ment." American Journal of Sociology 85 (3): 489–515.
1984   "Small is bountiful: Labor markets and establishment size." American
        Sociological Review 49 (June): 323–334.
1985   "Economic action and social structure: The problem of embeddedness."
        American Journal of Sociology 91 (3): 481–510.
GRANOVETTER, MARK AND CHARLES TILLY
1988   "Inequality and labor processes." Pp. 175–221 in Neil Smelser, editor,
        Handbook of Sociology. Newbury Park, CA: Sage Publications.

HECHT, SUSANNA & A. COCKBURN
1992 "Rhetoric and reality in Rio." *The Nation,* June 22: 848–853.
LAPHAM, LEWIS H.
1989 *Money and Class in America: Notes and Observations on the Civil Religion.* New York: Ballantine Books.
MUMFORD, LEWIS
1970 *The Myth of the Machine: The Pentagon of Power.* New York: Harcourt, Brace, Jovanovich.
NATIONAL WILDLIFE FEDERATION
1991 *The Earth Care Annual.* Washington, DC: National Wildlife Federation.
NEWHOUSE, JOHN
1992 "The diplomatic round: Earth summit." *The New Yorker,* June 1: 64–78.
NOBLE, DAVID F.
1979 *America by Design: Science, Technology, and the Rise of Corporate Capitalism.* New York: Alfred A. Knopf.
ORGANIZATION OF ECONOMIC COOPERATION & DEVELOPMENT
1991 *Environmental Indicators.* Paris: OECD.
REICH, ROBERT B.
1991 *The Wealth of Nations: Preparing Ourselves for 21st Century Capitalism.* New York: Alfred A. Knopf.
RODGERS, DANIEL
1978 *The Work Ethic in Industrial America, 1850 1920.* Chicago: University of Chicago Press.
RUBIN, LILLIAN B.
1976 *Worlds of Pain.* New York: Basic Books.
RUDEL, THOMAS K. & B. HOROWITZ
1993 *Tropical Deforestation: Small Farmers and Land Clearing in the Ecuadorian Amazon.* New York: Columbia University Press.
SCHNAIBERG, ALLAN
1980 *The Environment: From Surplus to Scarcity.* New York: Oxford University Press.
1992 "The recycling shell game: Multinational economic organization vs. local political ineffectuality." Working paper WP-92-16, Center for Urban Affairs & Policy Research, Northwestern University, Spring.
SCHNAIBERG, ALLAN, N. WATTS, & K. ZIMMERMANN, EDITORS
1986 *Distributional Conflicts in Environmental-Resource Policy.* Aldershot, England: Gower Publishing.
SCHOR, JULIET
1991 *The Overworked American: The Unexpected Decline of Leisure.* New York: Basic Books.
SCHUMACHER, E. F.
1973 *Small Is Beautiful: Economics As If People Mattered.* New York: Harper & Row.
SENNETT, RICHARD & J. COBB
1974 *The Hidden Injuries of Class.* New York: Alfred A. Knopf.
WILLIAMSON, OLIVER
1981 "The economics of organization: The transaction cost approach." *American Journal of Sociology* 87 (November): 548–577.
1985 *The Economic Institutions of Capitalism.* New York: Free Press.
WORLD RESOURCES INSTITUTE
1992 *The Environmental Almanac.* Washington, DC: World Resources Institute.

5. *Lubricating the Treadmill: The Role of Institutions*

THE INFLUENCE OF INSTITUTIONS: INTERDEPENDENCY WITH THE TREADMILL

Chapter 4 presented an overview of the major society-wide trends associated with maintaining and accelerating the treadmill of production. In this chapter, we focus on how the institutional structure operates to sustain these major national and international trends. From a sociological perspective, an institution is a relatively stable clustering of social rules, roles, and relationships which operate as a set of guiding principles for major activities in the society, in spheres such as education, the economy, the cultural media, and the family. This chapter serves in some ways as a bridge between the societal perspective offered in Chapter 4 and the individual perspective provided in the next chapter.

There are two somewhat competing perspectives on institutions: the first is that they tend to be durable or enduring features of social life. Yet, because they are social creations, they are also adaptive to many different types of changes—both those external to a particular institution and those internal to it. In the next section, for example, we talk about the changing nature of environmental sciences: the modern period has witnessed the expansion of roles for scientists studying the impacts of modern industry on ecosystems. Universities, government agencies, and even the firms noted in Chapter 3 are employing more environmental analysts in the 1990s than in the 1960s. Yet the very process by which this has occurred has to some extent transformed the work roles of these environmental scientists, often reducing the scope of their research and the freedoms they have to disseminate their concerns about the environmentally negative features of production. At some point, a tension is thereby created between our view of these new environmental institutional roles: rather than subverting the treadmill, they may be subverted by it. The means of subversion are the familiar positive outputs of the treadmill outlined in previous chapters: higher salaries, consulting contracts, prestige, and positions of power and influence.

Much of our analysis in this chapter follows a simple argument: *the major institutions of modern society are "addicted" to economic growth and treadmill expansion.* There are two versions of this argument: (1) the conspiratorial view, which attempts to explain uncritical institutional support for tread-mill expansion as a result of coercive applications of power by major treadmill interests, to persuade potentially critical institutions to cooperate, "or else!"; or (2) the mutualism view, in which there is a common interest in sharing in the fruits of the treadmill, which induces institutions to actively collaborate in accelerating the treadmill. While both versions have a role in modern society, we emphasize the second here because it is both a more pervasive explanation and one that is less likely discussed in most communications media (which are themselves institutions with similar addictions).

To illustrate how pervasive these institutional supports for expanding the treadmill are, consider the broad context in which we are writing this chapter. Recently, increased attention was paid to global environmental problems, especially at international conferences such as the United Nations Conference on Environment and Development in Rio de Janeiro, Brazil in June 1992. Yet, at the national level, in the 1992 U.S. presidential elections, for example, the dominant emphasis was on expanding jobs, creating larger free trade zones in the North American Free Trade Act in order to expand trade and profits, increasing local tax bases, and increasing exports through greater technological expansion. Interestingly, Al Gore, the new vice-president, is himself an environmentalist and an author of *Earth in the Balance: Ecology and the Human Spirit*. However, very little of the electoral campaign addressed even national ecological problems, let alone those global issues whose dimensions Gore (1992) has so eloquently described.

This chapter seeks to explain why we remain institutionally committed to accelerating the treadmill of production, despite all our knowledge about environmental disorganization and its social consequences. The short answer is that, despite our cumulative knowledge and repeated challenges to the reported social and ecological benefits of the treadmill, our social institutions do not perceive that there is any other way of sustaining themselves. This is similar to the political science aphorism "Democracy is the worst of all political systems . . . except for the alternatives!" Our modern political-economic equivalent is that the treadmill of production has many imperfections, but it's the best we can do. One feature of modern history that underlies this position is that we "consume history" through the treadmill and thereby have limited awareness of historical alternatives to the modern treadmill. A second feature is that the treadmill spins off many benefits for the leaders and professionals in modern institutions, those who are important intermediaries in shaping the opinions and behaviors of many publics.

While we focus on what we consider the most central institutions and social mechanisms that reinforce the modern treadmill in this chapter, we are aware that we are excluding other important ones as well. For example, we choose not to discuss religious or legal institutions or the military. To some extent, we hope to encourage the reader to explore the themes of this chapter in these other institutions. To some extent, too, we note in passing some of the major themes that predominate in these other social institutions. And finally, we believe that the examples in this chapter are sufficiently representative that attentive readers will be primed to scrutinize other institutions and their organizations.

KNOWLEDGE CREATION AND DISSEMINATION: ECONOMIC VERSUS ECOLOGICAL REALITIES

To many casual and even sophisticated observers, it would appear that modern societies are environmentalist. How do we come to this conclusion? Increasingly, two indicators are being used to support this assertion: (1) in many public opinion surveys, larger proportions of respondents than in earlier decades espouse environmental values, and (2) in such surveys, larger proportions of respondents than previously indicate that they have engaged in additional environmental behaviors. However, these apparent social scientific facts are misleading indicators of our institutional supports for environmentalism versus the treadmill (Dunlap & Mertig 1992).

First, the values expressed by survey respondents have no consequences for their daily lives, so they may not be realistic expressions of what these respondents actually do in their everyday roles. One way to understand this freedom to espouse values is to examine the ways in which respondents answer the question: Is there a conflict between economic growth and environmental protection? Typically, a preponderance of responses indicate that there is no conflict, which contradicts the major argument of this book. And, unless we are grossly inaccurate in our analyses, it will also contradict the experiences of these respondents. In short, this response is an accurate description of a grossly inaccurate analysis. It does not affirm the ascendance of environmental education or the diffusion of ecological sciences (Rohrschneider 1991).

In like manner, the environmental behaviors of mass publics expressed in these surveys are misleading. In recent years, these actions often refer to subjects' recycling actions. Once again, the ecological sciences indicate that recycling generates very limited deceleration of the treadmill of production. Indeed, the fact that mass publics have enthusiastically climbed on the recycling bandwagon is itself an indicator of flawed understanding of ecological realities. Actually, recycling is only slightly more ecologically efficient than the simple discarding of wastes. This is because modern industrial societies have chosen to recycle not by reusing consumer and producer wastes, but by remanufacturing them. Remanufacturing creates many ecological withdrawals and produces many polluting additions. Ecologically, it would be best to limit production and use of these recyclable products; second best would be to reuse materials, which might also have the social benefits of providing employment for less skilled workers (Schnaiberg 1992a). Thus, the dominant version of recycling is hardly compatible with sustainable development (see the section Cross-Pressures on the Modern State later in this chapter).

If these naive attitudes and behaviors had been observed in the 1950s, we might have simply chalked up these misperceptions as being due to public ignorance. We would have attributed them to the failures of scientific research to describe ecological systems and their relation to societal production. Yet these misperceptions have continued into the 1990s, after almost three decades of ecological research, environmental education, and mass media development of an environmental beat. Why does this ignorance or false consciousness continue? Two institutional realities explain this perpetuation of ignorance:

1. Severe limitations of social support are placed on ecologically oriented scientific and technological education and research, which has been dwarfed by the competing influence of production-oriented scientific and technological research and education.
2. Strong seductions are exerted by the treadmill's economic structure, which ripple through communications institutions and serve to highlight the benefits of the treadmill rather than its ecological and social costs (Schnaiberg 1994).

We examine the first of these factors in this section and the second in subsequent sections. One way to understand the history of environmental science and technology is to consider a behavioral model suggested by the modern oxymoron of "environmental consumption." By using a credit card issued by environmental movement organizations, individual environmentalists believe they are supporting environmental action. This is because fully 5 cents of every dollar that they spend goes to the environmental movement. It is also true, however, that *only* 5 cents goes for this anti-treadmill organization. In contrast, the remaining *95 cents goes to support the treadmill of production.* Thus, this environmentally responsible behavior has a ratio of pro- to anti-treadmill influence that is actually 19 to 1!

Using similar analytic reasoning, we can be cheered that expenditures on scientific environmental research may have increased by 150 percent from 1970 to 1990. But this is also compatible with the fact that production research-and-development expenditures may have increased even faster in the same period. Thus, it is entirely possible that the proportion of total scientific and technological research expenditures that went to environmental issues may have actually decreased in this period. While we are encouraged to focus on fully how much has been devoted to environmental research, or to recycling of products, we are simultaneously discouraged from looking at expanding support for the treadmill's "business as usual" (Stretton 1976). This view induces us to take a more critical look at how "only" a little environmentalism has crept into everyday institutional roles and social decision making (see Chapter 10).

This background expansion of treadmill commitments is a kind of creeping event (Molotch 1970) that characterizes much modern environmental research and education, as well as modern production systems (as noted in Chapters 3 and 4). Since Rachel Carson published her popular environmental-alarm book, *Silent Spring*, in 1962, a change has certainly taken place in environmental research and education. As we note in Chapter 7, in the United States and some other Western societies, a broad expansion of membership in old-line conservation movements has occurred and many new environmental-action movement organizations have been created. These movements have indeed benefited from the expansion of environmental scientific research. Each new scientific discovery of some ecological disorganization mobilizes more of the citizenry into environmental movements. Similarly, each new technological research discovery induces more political pressures to have the government mandate that industries (or consumers) introduce such "feasible" innovations. Thus, for example, new techniques of solvent recovery have emerged under the pressures of the Resource Conservation and Recovery Act, which was passed as a result of new scientific discoveries of toxic waste hazards. Eventually, this also led to pressures against expanding local landfills and to pressures in favor of governmental and industrial collaboration to increase postconsumer waste recycling. Curbside pickup was a key social and economic innovation that made this economically feasible (Schnaiberg 1992a).

Along with their actions in using scientific ecological discoveries to mobilize citizens and government to change production systems, environmental movements have also lobbied federal and state agencies for more funding of future environmental research. They have also sometimes increased pressures to expand the personnel and tasks of such agencies as the Environmental Protection Agency, which are supposed to use the new scientific discoveries as one basis for regulating industries (Landy et al. 1990). Interestingly, Rachel Carson herself did no original scientific research for her important consciousness-raising book. Rather, she read widely in the existing scientific literature and talked to many scientists who had data and insights on chemical pollutants (additions). Carson's environmental "research" achievement was thus to accumulate and organize scattered scientific findings that pointed to ecological disorganization and to publicize such findings. The prior reality was that scientists kept many of their ecological findings within their private intellectual "inventory." Many of them feared occupational reprisals if they challenged their employers with such data (Graham 1970). For these scientists, not only was there no public "demand" or rewards for such information; in fact there were career penalties for creating and disseminating such information.

In the three decades since Carson's seminal book, it would appear that modern industrial societies have changed substantially. We now assume that environmental research goes on routinely in every sector of the society and that our children and young adults have all become exposed to environmental education. As a consequence, we accept the conclusions from the public opinion surveys that the U.S. population has become a bastion of environmentalism. Yet during all of this period, economic growth, not environmental protection, dominated the research and development agenda of every major industrial society, in every decade. This emphasis is echoed in the curriculum of every level of our educational system, which has increasingly been attacked for failing to prepare young citizens for the demands of work roles. No educational reform campaign has yet attacked educators for perpetuating the values and behaviors of the treadmill—to produce and consume more (Williamson 1985). Indeed, quite the contrary: new workers graduating from high schools and colleges are deemed to be unproductive; that is, they don't help accelerate the treadmill sufficiently. When recent graduates are found to lack reading or mathematics skills, no political or economic concern is expressed that they will misread hazardous waste site warnings or miscalculate the energy efficiency of their appliances. Rather, the concern is that employers cannot use these workers' labors to extract sufficient profits from the firm's direct or indirect processing of natural resources (as noted in Chapter 3).

As in the example of the "environmental credit card," what recent history reveals in industrial societies is a very high ratio of treadmill-to-environmental research and teaching. There are many more environmentalists among our student body, but even these groups show very limited appreciation for the realities of ecological disorganization. Student groups have been in the forefront of recycling efforts: when asked why, the response of one group at a major midwestern university has been, "because we could *do* something there," without entering into sustained social and political conflict. Responses such as these point to the wider reality that most students in most schools and universities never have *any* serious environmental education. In natural science courses, a brief module may be directed toward this subject in some schools. In social science courses, a brief chapter outlining what mass media report as a social problem will be a typical offering. In examining the curricular history in Illinois, for example, we discovered that not until 1990 had the state created any formal educational mandate to introduce any environmental curriculum in high schools. Thus, the bulk of education is far more congruent with, if not directly tied to, the treadmill of production (Scitovsky 1976; Schor 1991). Students go to school and attend classes not to help shape the future of their societies as much as to "get a good job," which enables them to "have a good home" and to reproduce or expand the experiences of their parents in the treadmill of production (see Chapter 6).

Is the story different with regard to scientific research? Are we increasingly devoting ourselves to documenting how the treadmill produces ecological and social harms, and struggling to develop more benign patterns of production and consumption? The answer is somewhat more hopeful than the educational dissemination story above. Nonetheless, most research and development expenditures are still allocated to expand production and enhance competitiveness. Indeed, one of the new spurs to North American competitiveness in world markets is the North American free trade agreement NAFTA, which environmentalists have attacked (Hecht & Cockburn 1992; Burke 1992). The fear is that ecological disorganization will move from the United States and Canada to Mexico, where pollution laws are weaker and enforcement even more sporadic. In one sense, the United States and Canada would become more environmental, and Mexico would become more an ecological victim of the treadmill, reproducing the unhealthy air pollution of Mexico City in other regions and depleting ecosystems of energy and other natural resources throughout the country. Interestingly, the rise of new environmental protection legislation in the United States has increased engineering research and produced new forms of "cleaner" technologies, essentially reducing energy inputs (withdrawals) and pollution outcomes (additions) per unit of production. But it appears that only a small fraction of this knowledge will be transformed into actual North American production systems and that the Japanese will be likelier to export this technology (as with earlier ones created in the United States) to industrial and developing nations alike (Newhouse 1992).

Thus, the reports of an environmental revolution in industrial societies seem to be greatly exaggerated. Part of the reason, despite an increase in environmentally relevant scientific research, is that the creation of the treadmill provides a routinized support system in the main paths of scientific and engineering research. This means that high schools prepare students to enter college training programs that direct students toward treadmill careers in *production*-oriented sciences and applied sciences (Schnaiberg 1975, 1977). Business and trade cycles and changes often reduce the employment prospects of both pure and applied production researchers; the same is also true for the minority of scientists and engineers doing work related to environmental and social impacts. During the 1980s, for example, the Reagan administration attempted to reduce the role of environmental regulators in the Environmental Protection

Agency (Landy et al. 1990). These effects rippled out from this agency, reducing research grants for environmental researchers in universities and independent research institutes, as well as employment for government scientists and engineers. Thus, while treadmill-supporting scientists and engineers confront economic oscillations in demands for their services, environmental-supporting professional researchers confront both economic and political oscillations. In keeping with the orientation of this chapter, then, it seems fair to assert that environmental research and environmental education are far less institutionalized in the United States and other industrial countries than is true of treadmill research and treadmill education (Schnaiberg 1977).

We see the same imbalance in the international arena. Industrial nations committed themselves to far fewer ecological "deeds" at the much-heralded Rio Conference on Environment and Development. In contrast, their words appeared to be oriented more toward the ecosystem than the treadmill. Ironically, one reason President Bush gave for failing to sign a global warming agreement to reduce carbon dioxide was that he feared that a U.S. failure to live up to the agreement would lead to litigation against the government by environmental movement organizations (see Chapter 7). This indicates that the major role of ecological research has been to increase political pressures on the U.S. government through the political and legal mobilization by environmental movement organizations (Hecht and Cockburn 1992; Burke 1992; Little 1992).

To some extent, such mobilization has been greatly enhanced by the somewhat naive environmentalism of mass publics (Dunlap & Mertig 1992) noted at the outset of this chapter. For it is these publics, especially the educated middle-class constituents, that support the lobbying and litigation of national and regional environmental movement organizations. Importantly, some of this concern has diffused to working-class and low-income minority grass-roots communities as well, especially in the case of toxic waste hazards, which have historically been disproportionately located in these communities (Bryant & Mohai 1992; Krauss 1992). Some of these groups have begun to expand into national networks, especially through Lois Gibbs's Citizens' Clearinghouse, which started with the campaign against toxics in Love Canal in New York (Levine 1982). Thus, even though ecological science has not deeply penetrated into the understandings of many citizens, enough of it has broadly diffused through the media to alert citizen groups to their health risks at least (Brown & Mikkelson 1990). (We will return to this distinction between ecological concerns and health concerns in Chapter 7.)

Despite this local and national mobilization, we must stress the socialization to accelerate the treadmill by natural and social scientists in laboratories, pilot plants, and schools and universities. This is a major routinized, sustaining force of the treadmill, which receives the lion's share of funding by the private corporate grants and public governmental support for knowledge creation and dissemination (Schnaiberg 1977).

CULTURAL INFLUENCES ON CONTEMPORARY WORKERS: FROM FAMILIES TO LABOR UNIONS

In Chapter 3, we outlined the constraints that managers and owners of individual business enterprises operate under in trying to maintain their occupational roles in the face of attempts at environmental regulation. Chapter 4 charted the major structural trends that produce such constraints on these economic actors (Williamson 1985). Together, these two chapters outline some of the processes and structures of the treadmill of production, which produces ecological disorganization. In this section, we trace the treadmill's influences on the other major component of economic organization—human labor. Within classical economics, the three factors of production were land, labor, and capital. In the contemporary world, we have broadened the first category to include the environment, but labor and capital remain major factors of production.

Breaking with social science conventions, we attempt to explore how the treadmill operates on human labor by examining two apparently unconnected institutions, the family (Coontz 1992a,b) and organized labor. Workers' orientations to treadmill acceleration versus ecological sustainability actually begin in their family of orientation and are altered in the educational systems described in the previous section. They are further modified as young adults enter into the workforce, encountering labor organizations ranging from labor unions to professional associations, as well as the attitudes and practices of their employers (see Chapter 3).

Let us start with family systems and how they shape the expectations of future (and present) workers who are members of the family. The first reality (Lasch 1977) is that the modern family in industrial society is a highly permeable institution. That is, the family's boundaries are readily penetrated by other institutions. For adults, these particularly include workplace influences; for children, they include the influence of schools. We have dealt with how the treadmill operates through some of these mechanisms earlier. Generally, we view the modern family as less of a separate collective entity and more of an aggregate of individuals, each of whom is subjected to the external socializing forces of the treadmill. Some of the social concern about this process predates modern concerns with environmental problems. In the 1950s sociologists decried the emergence of a mass society, which would be dominated by massive organizations, especially businesses and government agencies. The fact that a variety of critical social movements emerged in the following decade should warn us that overgeneralizations are risky (Coontz 1992a, b). Therefore, we note that this section does not argue that families have no existence separate from dominant treadmill institutions. Basically, here we want to elaborate on how some of these institutional forces impinge on family life. Our view is that these institutions operate in ways that tilt these familial members toward treadmill values and behaviors rather than sustainable-development values and behaviors, including the value of emotional commitments to family roles instead of material achievements (see Chapter 1).

Perhaps the most critical attention to the modern family in the past four decades of social science research has been in its saturation by mass media, as highlighted in recent decades by the role of electronic media, especially television. It also includes print and other media, including other forms of live entertainment. From our perspective, the centrality of the impulse to consume is the most important form and content of modern print and electronic media. One dominant feature of modern electronic media is the core role of advertising, which is in turn tied directly to the defining features of the treadmill (Ewen 1976).

Stripped to its essentials, the crucial linkage for us is that both knowledge dissemination (Molotch 1970; Molotch & Lester 1975) and entertainment (which includes social role modeling for young people) are made possible only through the operations of an accelerating treadmill of production. Advertising revenues, which support electronic media, are tied to the expansion of markets, which in turn permit the expansion of production. Thus, regardless of the content of the media, the form of the media ensures, at least through its advertising displays, reinforcement of the treadmill. When analysts of advertising (Ewen 1976) study the content of these displays, their central message typically is: "you are what you consume." Whether the family viewer wants to be big, powerful, handsome, pretty, smart, sexy, or whatever—the message is that such achievements can be attained only through the consumption of some goods and services. Thus, while the consumption of computer dating services may not lead directly to disorganizing ecological withdrawals and additions, this form of interpersonal relationship reinforces the influence of the treadmill's market orientation.

Beyond the advertising influences, it should be noted that a medium that depends on advertising revenue for its maintenance must program according to its advertisers' preferences. Thus, with the exception of "public" or some government-supported media, programming itself responds to the desires of advertisers (Molotch & Lester 1975). This makes it quite remarkable how much coverage of "environmental problems" has emerged in the past twenty-five years in Western societies (Albrecht 1977). However, this media coverage has also failed to link these problems with the operations of the treadmill itself, leading viewers (children and adults alike) to anticipate that "something" will "fix" the problems. Programming presents treadmill roles in a positive light, emphasizing income, wealth, and consumption as the major achievements of modern work roles. Occupational safety, community preservation, and ecological protection roles are rarely found in entertainment programming, and not all that much more in informational programming (though "scientific research" may be very positively presented). Interestingly, although there are periodic episodes about "suppression" of the media, Molotch and Lester (1975) have stressed that media directors more properly share the treadmill values of their economic sponsors. Hence, the media themselves have institutionalized treadmill values and need little external control. Perhaps the following recent commentary on a panel discussion of the failures of the major media to do an adequate job of reporting on the 1992 (and earlier) U.S. presidential campaign platforms (including both environmental and economic policies) most graphically addresses these realities:

"Just get in the middle and move with the mass; don't cause any trouble; don't ask any tough questions; don't take the risk." Rather added, "to change the atmosphere is the challenge," but said he did not know how to do that. Nor were there any answers forthcoming during the panel discussion with Rather and his fellow-anchors.

"Here were five of the most powerful men in America, and they were acting as if they had no power to change what was going on in their own newsrooms," marvelled Howard Kurtz, who covered the event for the *Washington Post*. Yet the anchors may not have been ducking responsibility so much as being realistic about the system they are part of. They, of all people, recognize that *money is at the root of virtually all decisions in television news these days;* it goes without saying that *newscasts must enhance a company's competitiveness and profitability or they will not stay on the air.* (Some of the *same pressures* confront nominally non-commercial *public broadcasting,* which is becoming increasingly reliant on big corporate sponsors.)

Rather hinted at these constraints when he explained during the panel discussion that the reason the networks had not devoted more time to investigating campaign issues was a fear that "these *serious but dull" discussions would damage ratings"* (*New Yorker,* 1992; emphasis ours).

Two features of this modern penetration of family life should be noted. The first is that most parents have exercised very limited influence in the amount and form of media penetration of their households (Coontz 1992b). Thus, electronic media socialize through advertising and through programming directly to young people, with very limited intervention by parents. Indeed, with the increased participation of women in the labor force, there are even fewer adult members around to supervise electronic media consumption by young people. This represents a powerful socializing force in modern society, especially since the basic electronic media (television, radio, and recording devices) are almost universally diffused in some form throughout the class structure of the society. Color television sets, for example, are found in 92.7 percent of U.S. households (U.S. Energy Information Agency 1987).

Some political and social critics have argued that mass media undermine "family values" by promoting deviant behavior such as premarital sexuality, homosexuality, and out-of-wedlock births. Paradoxically, few have noted that the consumption pressures of modern media may equally well undermine other family values such as thrift, hard work, savings, reuse of materials, pride of workmanship, craftsmanship, safety and health, or emotional investment rather than increased consumption (Coontz 1992a). Not surprisingly, perhaps, these latter values promote sustainable development, for they emphasize a lower level of the "comforts" that Scitovsky (1976) has noted come from marketized, material transactions, and more attention to the "stimulations" that arise from intrapsychic and interpersonal, non-market relationships. The actual family values that these modern cultural media do seem to emphasize are values of increased consumption and decreased leisure and family relationships (Schor 1991).

Young people then move from this early milieu of consumption orientation into schools, which tend to reinforce it by encouraging learning for the sake of "getting a good job" and being able to eventually consume. At the point of school-leaving, at whatever level, they enter the workforce and confront a third level of socialization—labor organizations. For about forty years, the dominant form of such organizations in the United States and other Western industrial societies was labor unions. In recent decades, however, the percentage of the workforce that is unionized has been shrinking. This decrease has been due to a decline in stable, blue-collar jobs in large-scale manufacturing since the 1960s, as capital has fled to less regulated and less costly wage centers in less developed nations. This decline has been evident even in the social welfare states of Scandinavia. The collapse of the USSR and the Eastern European bloc has signaled the demise of state-centered worker organizations as well. To this historical shift in capital (see Chapters 3 and 4) should be added the political influence of conservative regimes such as those of Ronald Reagan and George Bush in the United States and Margaret Thatcher and John Major in the United Kingdom, all of whom chose "union-busting" as a mechanism to accelerate their respective treadmills (with only mixed success).

Some of the numerical attrition of formal labor unions has been offset by the rise of professional associations (Larson 1977) of skilled white-collar workers. While these differ from traditional labor unions in some important ways, they also share some central features. Key among these is the centrality of their concern with economic protection for their members. Whether expressed in wages, fees, bonuses, or contracts, the shared concern is with expanded consumption power of the members of unions and professional associations. Both types of organizations have sought to control entry into and promotion through their respective occupational systems, in order to preserve something approximating a monopoly over labor supply. Just as labor unions often overlooked health and safety conditions for their workers (Brown & Mikkelson 1990), so too do modern professional associations overlook the "speedup" of modern white-collar work (Braverman 1974). In the United States, Schor (1991) has noted that fully employed workers have had increasingly long work-hours since 1960, and a concomitant decrease in "family time" and "leisure" (Rybcznski 1991). This is consistent with the findings of time-researchers, who note that workers express "values" for "family time" but in fact choose to work longer hours if they can earn more. Schor (1991) notes that treadmill employers have more control over their workforce if they can get a given cohort of workers to expand or contract their work-hours rather than having the employers risk the more costly route of recruiting and laying off new employees in their workforce. Thus, workers who choose or are pressured into working longer hours per week help accelerate the treadmill of production by increasing profits through their working and through their consumption. This exemplifies John Kenneth Galbraith's (1971) model of the squirrel-cage model of workers, in which workers run faster to consume more. Not surprisingly, this squirrel-cage model is one corollary of the treadmill of production.

Thus, from family hearth to workplace organizations, strong institutionalized forces are at work inducing workers to consume more. Not all families or workers succumb (Coontz 1992a). Some families avoid having electronic media in their homes or limit their children's passive listening or viewing. Such families assert some of their nontreadmill family values by increasing the strength of their family's boundaries. They often substitute collective activities and relationships for individual consumption. Similarly, some workers drop out of the professional or union culture and opt for handcrafts production, countercultural production, voluntary simplicity, or simply more leisure for hobbies and families. But, as we note in Chapter 6, strong institutional forces are at play that would get activated, if these "deviant" patterns were to be adopted by a majority of families and workers. Thus, new age participants who eschew the treadmill are permitted to grow, because their numbers are small and there is already a surplus of willing workers at all levels to fill the treadmill's slots. In addition, there are growing numbers of "new age entrepreneurs" who are merely applying treadmill logic to a new "green" market segment.

"GREEN" ADVERTISING:
THE GOOD EARTHKEEPING SEAL OF APPROVAL

Responding to marketing polls indicating increased public support for environmental causes, many corporations have attempted to gain advantage in the marketplace by using "green" advertising to create a positive corporate image. One example of this manipulation of environmental concern is Du Pont's "Applause" TV ad. The commercial features seals, dolphins, whales, sea otters, and penguins ostensibly responding jubilantly to news of Du Pont's ecologically enlightened corporate actions. Scenes of coastal splendor are accompanied by Beethoven's Ode to Joy as the words "Du Pont: Better things for better living" appear on the TV screen. Why are the animals so happy? Because Conoco, Du Pont's oil-refining subsidiary, announced that it would build two double-hulled tankers. Double-hulled tankers are more resistant to collisions such as that which caused the *Exxon Valdez* to run aground, devastating the fragile ecology of Prince William Sound.

The move to build two double-hulled tankers was only a minor business decision for Du Pont. Anticipating congressional action on double-hulled tanker legislation and finding that the double-hull adds only 15 percent to total cost, Conoco quickly concluded that the double-hulled tankers were a good investment. At the time the TV ad was produced, Conoco had no double-hulled tankers in its fleet, which is one of the smallest in the oil industry. Conoco operates primarily in the Gulf of Mexico, where its tankers are unlikely to encounter the sea otters, penguins, and seals who are portrayed as their beneficiaries. Conoco's new tankers are not supertankers; rather, they are medium-sized vessels that may be used to unload supertankers at sea, thereby increasing the risk of oil spills.

Du Pont's enthusiasm for inflating a minor business decision into a major ad campaign stems from its concern for its own environmental image. Behind the jumping dolphins and applauding seals lies the largest single corporate polluter in the United States. In 1989 Du Pont and its subsidiaries reported emitting more than 348 million pounds of industrial pollution, 10 million more pounds than the year before. Du Pont discharged more pollution in 1989 than Ford Motor Company, Union Carbide, and Allied Signal combined, an amount equivalent to 14 times that produced by Dow Chemical. Du Pont is betting that such dramatic anti-environmental deeds can be concealed with a few pro-environmental words intended to distract the public.

Du Pont's "green" advertising is an attempt to create an image of Conoco as an environmentally sensitive corporation, one that can be trusted to proceed prudently in ecologically fragile environments. The environments they have in mind are the Arctic National Wildlife Refuge in Alaska and a national park in the Ecuadorian Amazon (see ecostration for Chapter 8). Both "protected" environments sit atop valuable fossil fuel reserves, and oil development in both areas is vehemently opposed by environmentalists. America's number one industrial polluter is hoping to be entrusted with some of the earth's most unique and fragile ecosystems on the basis of its environmental sensitivity, as reflected in its ad campaign. Don't believe everything you see on TV.

CROSS-PRESSURES ON THE MODERN STATE: CAPITALIST VERSUS SOCIALIST EXPERIENCES

One of the most common responses reported in public opinion surveys is that "government isn't doing enough to protect the environment." A minority of respondents even claim that they would be willing to pay more taxes to protect the environment, albeit usually a small sum, under $100. An even smaller minority (well under 10 percent) claim that they would be willing to forgo some wages if that would help protect the environment. In the 1960s and early 1970s a variety of radical environmental analysts (e.g., Anderson 1976) argued that a socialist form of government would solve environmental problems by eliminating the drive for corporate profits in the modern treadmill system. These arguments persisted (e.g., O'Connor 1988) despite the early warnings (e.g., Goldman 1972) that the USSR and other socialist states were confronting environmental problems that were almost as severe as those of Western capitalist societies.

In some Eastern European socialist states, one of the latest dissenting movements that preceded the collapse of the communist government was an emergent environmental movement. Whether this interest emerged from genuine concerns about environmental hazards or merely deflected other political and social dissent into a relatively "safe" channel is not clear. But after the political and economic collapse of the USSR and its satellite states, the environmental damage wrought by communist administrations was revealed, and it is a tale of ravaged ecosystems and dangerous habitats. The account recently documented in *Ecocide in the USSR: Health and Nature Under Siege* (Feshbach & Friendly, Jr. 1991) is sobering, and data that subsequently came to light underscore the problem. Perhaps the most chilling account is the dumping of high-level nuclear wastes from the Soviet nuclear submarine fleet in a Ukrainian harbor, with attendant birth defects and illness and mortality that has previously only been associated with the U.S. atomic bombing of Japan in 1945. This recent account seems to place the USSR in the unenviable position of having been the world's worst environmental state, although there are other major contenders, including China and India.

While there are substantial comparative differences between industrial nations and equally substantial historical variations within any given modern industrial society, it seems fair to assert that all industrial states have had a history of increasing ecological disorganization in the twentieth century. Two related explanations can be offered for this parallel trend. The first is that every government has been induced to play a similar role in supporting its own domestic version of the treadmill of production. The second is that the structure of the modern world-system has globalized the treadmill, from its roots in Western industrial societies (Wallerstein 1984). In this world system, all states are compelled to compete in an international capitalist economy in which winning and losing often hinges on the breadth and depth of national commitment to the capitalist path of expansion of the treadmill. Put another way, the first explanation suggests simultaneous discovery or diffusion processes, while the second is a form of cultural imperialism. There is considerable evidence to support either perspective, and we have opted here not to choose between them.

These two explanations share the reality that the modern history of industrial development is a history of the treadmill of production. In particular, it is a history in which the role of governments has been at least important in every industrial society, if not central in the economic trajectory of each. This model prevails in capitalist and socialist nations that have a high degree of coordination between governments and economic sectors—the corporatist and neo-corporatist nations such as the former USSR, Germany, and Scandinavia. But it also applies to those with a lower degree of such coordination—the noncorporatist nations such as the United States and the United Kingdom in some periods (Lehmbruch 1986).

How does this model pervade the history of governments in modern industrial society? Generally, regardless of the conceptual approach we use—whether it is Gabriel Kolko's political capitalism (1966) or James O'Connor's model of the dual functions of the government (1988)—the pattern is similar. At some point in the creation or acceleration of the treadmill of production, governments get involved in the process of stimulating economic growth. The particular form this involvement takes varies quite widely, ranging from political support for dominant economic elites (major owners of productive wealth), to direct accumulation of fiscal capital and its allocation to production elites. All of these means bind governments into the process of accumulating capital, as governments observe that their political survival depends on promoting sufficient economic growth to generate the tax and other revenues needed to placate their constituencies.

To do this, governments engage in the process of taking surplus (e.g., taxation) and allocating it (e.g., subsidies, credits, military protection) to the economic sector. Ironically, the modern rhetoric of free trade obscures much of this process, for it seems to suggest that trade exists in a social and political vacuum. This has never been true, and it remains untrue even today when, following the collapse of most socialist systems of production, we have witnessed an *apparent* "triumph of the market over politics" (Lindblom 1977; Williamson 1985). Government enters as both a vocal and especially as a silent partner in all free trade. The range of government supports of treadmill expansion is very large. For example, protecting national and international banking and stock exchanges is a major social and political role of governments. In the United States, for example, the collapse of savings-and-loan associations in the late 1980s led to government repayment of as much as $500 billion, using tax dollars to repay investors for the losses (Barlett & Steele 1992).

These losses were incurred under the deregulatory pressures of Reaganomics, which was supposed to take the U.S. government out of the economy! This government bailout was partly statutory (under the political support for the banking system of the United States): this guaranteed repayment of up to $100,000 per savings account. Interestingly, the Federal Deposit Insurance Corporation actually repaid *all* investors who had savings well beyond this level of formal insurance in order to maintain public confidence in the banking system. It is worth noting that those with $100,000 or more in savings represent a very small elite stratum of American society. By what political process were such losses actually incurred? The story that has thus far emerged is that financial and real estate entrepreneurs essentially inflated the values of property and supported a round-robin of S&L loans to support this action. They then took the money and allowed the Reconstruction Finance Corporation to take over the bankrupt properties and sell them for a small fraction of their initial "free market" (more realistically, politically "negotiated") values. In effect, the federal government wound up underwriting the private gains of the Reagan administration's political supporters, using tax revenue collected from the citizenry as a whole (Barlett & Steele 1992).

How was this process politically rationalized? The original rationale for deregulation was that this policy would liberate "the market" to accelerate the U.S. treadmill of production, thereby providing new economic opportunities. Instead, what evolved was in effect a highly unproductive allocation of federal revenues. This in turn increased the national debt by increasing annual budget deficits. The growth of this national debt then raised the subsequent annual costs of servicing the substantially expanded national debt and actually decelerated the treadmill, leading to subsequent economic recessions.

Was this good news for environmentalists, since the treadmill was slowed down? (I.e., there were reduced rates of increase of gross national product in the 1985–1992 period.) Generally, we would argue that this was bad news, since the goal of accelerating the treadmill remained both a national and an international priority. That meant that environmental protection expenditures were viewed as a drag on capital accumulation. Thus, pressures were increased on the Environmental Protection Agency budget (Landy et al. 1990), especially through the efforts of the Council on Competitiveness, which labeled environmental protection of all types as an impediment to U.S. competitiveness and economic development. (But note that our Japanese competitors, according to Newhouse [1992], instead seem to view exporting more environmentally benign technology as a treadmill accelerator!) Instead of focusing on the burdens of deregulation, then, the dominant political response of the Reagan-Bush administration was to ignore them and push for still greater deregulation as a treadmill accelerator, despite the failures of this policy in the previous decade. Strong parallels to this policy existed in the Eastern European socialist bloc, where failures of collectivization in production, especially agricultural production, led to ever greater government pressures to control agriculture, including massive use of fertilizers and pesticides to stimulate production (Feshbach & Friendly, Jr. 1991).

Thus far, we have described a one-dimensional view of the role of government. In both capitalist and socialist societies, governments have a second major role. Governments must allocate what O'Connor (1973) terms *social expenses* in order to maintain the administration's social legitimacy. Some of these expenses can be coercive, such as police and army expenditures to control political and social dissidence within their populations. Typically, in many societies we refer to these expenses as social welfare, for example, food, health care, pensions, shelter, education, and protective services. Most analysts believe that environmental protection expenditures are among the newer forms of such expenses.

This is an interesting political and analytic dilemma, since investment in new ecologically benign technologies and services should more properly be viewed as a form of capital investment. Part of the puzzle is solved when we understand that such forms of investment generally differ from the historical criterion of allocating investment capital, where the return is in terms of money and not ecological sustainability (Redclift 1987). Social expenses in general refer to all government activities apart from supporting capital accumulation or treadmill expansion. Governments use these expenditures to relieve the most pressing citizen complaints about the society's and government's functioning and serve to maintain the acquiescence of worker/consumers. This pressing need for social expenses has a contradictory impact on governments, however. On the one hand, revenues allocated to social expenses are not directly available to reinforce the capital accumulation portion of the treadmill. Thus, there is an apparent tradeoff between supporting treadmill growth and responding to social needs. One typical government response to this tension is to accelerate the treadmill in order to "increase the size of the pie." The total taxes that a given tax rate thereby produces rise because of the growth in taxable income and/or property that treadmill expansion yields. Thus, economic growth is advertised as a panacea, as a way to enable us to live better. Even environmental protection, many conservatives have argued, needs treadmill acceleration, since it generates more revenues for ecological clean-ups. Unfortunately, this can become an endless regression, as the accelerated treadmill tends to generate still more ecological withdrawals and additions.

Two contemporary responses to this policy dilemma have been offered: (1) we can only afford serious ecological protection by growing more; and (2) environmental protection creates new jobs. The first response argues that treadmill expansion is the solution to ecological disorganization; the second holds that environmental protection is not as great a problem for economic growth supporters. Our evaluation of this position is as follows. We concur that the economic system has to meet social needs as its first priority. (This position is in disagreement with that of the deep ecologists; see Chapter 7.) We also agree that the state must produce sufficient tax revenues to help deliver needed goods and services to citizens who cannot obtain sufficient income through the labor force. However, we sharply depart from the assumption that the treadmill organization is the only way to deliver these socially desirable outcomes. Treadmills are very inefficient, on both ecological and human grounds, because they require enormous ecological throughput to deliver a given level of income, taxes, and social services.

One way of contrasting the dominant models of government responsibility to support the treadmill forms of economic expansion is to consider two types of government mechanisms to allocate tax revenues, thereby supporting their constituencies. Governments can generate public goods, or they can generate public services, as a way of delivering needed social welfare to underemployed, unemployed, and poor citizens. Studies indicate that creating public services, such as health, education, or environmental protection, can generate seven times more employment than building public works, such as bridges, highways, or airports. Moreover, services that employ more labor tend, on the average, to require fewer ecological withdrawals and additions. Finally, governments can tax the wages of the workers they employ in public services, or some of the services they provide, and thereby recycle some of the tax monies for use on other projects.

What does this offer as a set of options for government economic policies, taking into account the realities of long-term environmental and social needs? First, we should note that all governments need to construct some public goods: health care workers need clinics and hospitals, public transit workers need buses and trains, teachers' aides need classrooms, and so on. Second, however, if the primary task of government is to help expand the employment and earnings capacities of disadvantaged or displaced workers, then the balance of government tax allocations should be tilted toward labor costs rather than capital costs. To do this, governments need to alter the current imbalance favoring capital interests in their societies through political mobilization of a broader constituency favoring our model here of a more sustained development program.

We can illustrate these alternative paths by considering a recent set of government policies that favor recycling as an environmental policy. Recent analyses (Schnaiberg 1992a,b) indicate that current recycling programs are exemplars of treadmill logic, and thereby suffer from a defective ecological and an inequitable social welfare logic. United States recycling

policy is actually a public goods policy, involving heavy reliance on remanufacturing. Private sector remanufacturing is congruent with the treadmill
principles of expanded capital investment. Governments at all levels have
begun to support curbside recycling of postconsumer wastes in as many
as four thousand communities as a means of stimulating investment in
remanufacturing plants. Such plants include most notably aluminum can
remanufacturing facilities, plastic goods remanufacturing plants, and a
much more limited proportion of paper. Essentially, each level of government uses citizens' tax money to gather this dispersed waste (as well as
citizens' labor to sort and clean some of it).

Large-scale multinational corporations then use this public subsidy to
build new plants, which are the de facto public goods of our recycling
programs, and then to privately remanufacture the publicly gathered
waste materials in order to make profits. They have increasingly lowered
the amount they pay for collected materials, raising the cost of waste
collection by governments. When there is insufficient profit to be made,
then capital owners and managers follow the logic of Chapter 3. Specifically, they

- reduce the costs of remanufacturing, in part by weakening environmental controls on the process;
- abandon the remanufacturing process;
- reduce the prices they pay to collectors of wastes; and/or
- urge governments and citizens to increase their purchases of remanu-
  factured products, even if it generates higher prices for these products.

The net effect of this policy is (1) a larger cost for governments
than they had anticipated, (2) some heavy pollution and energy use in
remanufacturing facilities, and (3) limited employment prospects and the
displacement of marginal scavengers who used to gather urban wastes
(Schnaiberg 1992a,b). What public service alternatives do government
agencies have for waste processing? One major alternative is to have
consumers sort wastes at least as carefully as they do, and to try to use
community labor forces either (1) to reuse as much of these wastes
as possible, by collecting and transporting and selling them at outlets
(such as thrift stores and flea markets), and repairing goods for resale
(this works better for larger household furnishings and appliances); or
(2) to perform minimum processing of locally gathered goods, turning them into socially usable products for government agencies and
citizens.

What could governments accomplish by this policy? There would be
more allocation of local and regional tax money to support local workers
and to reduce the energy and other ecological costs of long-distance transportation and remanufacturing of our current system. But this would

entail resistance from current remanufacturers, whose profits and markets would be more restricted under this alternative policy. One of the more subtle antitreadmill implications of the alternative policy is the discouragement of waste generation. Under tax-supported public service funding, governments will always be under pressure to reduce their operating budgets by reducing waste services, although they may face resistance from local workers' organizations. In contrast, successful private sector remanufacturers of wastes seek to widen the production of wastes, since they become valued inputs to production and profit, and thereby accelerate the treadmill. The current system is actually the worst of public services and public goods policies, since it reflects costly local collections and ecologically malign remanufacturing operations. Moreover, recent analyses have reported that much of the recyclables collected actually wind up in landfills or incinerators, which is a further waste of taxes and generates more ecological withdrawals and additions.

We close this chapter with our recycling example, for it illustrates the direct and indirect ways in which our social and political institutions reinforce treadmill patterns. Recycling has elicited considerable enthusiasm from environmental movement organizations, mass media, and citizens alike. This activity, reinforced by the adoption of recycling by polling analysts as strong indicators of environmental behavior, has blunted the serious consideration of waste policies by these and other social actors. Neither the ecological nor the social distributional aspects of current versus alternative policies has been examined. And in the zeal to recycle more, far less attention has been paid to the generation of wastes. This is true despite the tripartite exhortation by some more radical environmental movements to reduce, reuse or recycle. Only the last of these, recycling, has received massive social and political attention, in part because, among the three alternatives, it requires the least transformation of the treadmill's economic organization.

SELECTED REFERENCES

ALBRECHT, STAN
   1977   "The environment as a social problem." Ch. 15 in Armand L. Mauss, editor, *Social Problems as Social Movements.* Philadelphia: J. B. Lippincott Co.
ANDERSON, CHARLES H.
   1976   *The Sociology of Survival: Social Problems of Growth.* Homewood, IL: Dorsey Press.
BARLETT, DONALD L. & J. B. STEELE
   1992   *America: What Went Wrong?* Kansas City: Andrews & McMeel.

BRAVERMAN, HARRY
  1974   *Labor and Monopoly Capital: The Degradation of Work in the Twentieth Century.* New York: Monthly Review Press.
BROWN, PHIL & E. J. MIKKELSON
  1990   *Toxic Waste, Leukemia, and Community Action.* Berkeley: University of California Press.
BRYANT, BUNYAN & P. MOHAI, EDITORS
  1992   *Race and the Incidence of Environmental Hazards: A Time for Discourse.* Boulder, CO: Westview Press.
BURKE, WILLIAM K.
  1992   "More hot air: U.S. chokes up Earth Summit emissions talks." *In These Times,* April 22–28: 12–13.
CARSON, RACHEL
  1962   *Silent Spring.* Boston: Houghton Mifflin.
COONTZ, STEPHANIE
  1992a   *The Way We Never Were: American Families and the Nostalgia Trap.* New York: Basic Books.
  1992b   "On the edge." *Chicago Tribune Magazine,* October 11:13–21.
DOYLE, JACK
  1991   *Hold the Applause: A Case Study of Corporate Environmentalism.* Washington, DC: Friends of the Earth.
DUNLAP, RILEY E. AND ANGELA G. MERTIG, EDS.
  1992   *American Environmentalism: The U.S. Environmental Movement, 1970–1990.* Crane Russak.
EWEN, STUART
  1976   *Captains of Consciousness: Advertising and the Social Roots of Consumption.* New York: McGraw-Hill.
FESHBACH, MURRAY & ALFRED FRIENDLY, JR.
  1991   *Ecocide in the USSR: Health and Nature Under Siege.* New York: Basic Books.
GALBRAITH, JOHN K.
  1971   *The New Industrial State.* Second ed. New York: New American Library.
GOLDMAN, MARSHALL I.
  1972   *The Spoils of Progress: Environmental Pollution in the Soviet Union.* Cambridge, MA: MIT Press.
GORE, SENATOR AL
  1992   *Earth in the Balance: Ecology and the Human Spirit.* Boston: Houghton Mifflin.
GRAHAM, FRANK, JR.
  1970   *Since Silent Spring.* Boston: Houghton Mifflin.
HECHT, SUSANNA & A. COCKBURN
  1992   "Rhetoric and reality in Rio." *The Nation,* June 22: 848–853.
KOLKO, GABRIEL
  1963   *The Triumph of Conservatism: A Reinterpretation of American History, 1900–1916.* New York: Free Press.
KRAUSS, CELENE
  1992   "Women and toxic waste protests: race, class and gender as resources of resistance." Paper presented at the annual meetings of the American Sociological Association, Pittsburgh, August.
LANDY, MARC K., M. J. ROBERTS, & S. R. THOMAS
  1990   *The Environmental Protection Agency: Asking the Wrong Questions.* New York: Oxford University Press.

LARSON, MAGALI SARFETTI
1977   *The Rise of Professionalism: A Sociological Analysis.* Berkeley: University of California Press.
LASCH, CHRISTOPHER
1977   *Haven in a Heartless World: The Family Besieged.* New York: Basic Books.
LEHMBRUCH, GERHARD
1986   "State roles in the articulation and mediation of distributional conflicts." Pp. 337–347 in A. Schnaiberg, N. Watts, & K. Zimmermann, editors, *Distributional Conflicts in Environmental-Resource Policy.* Aldershot, England: Gower Publishing.
LEVINE, ADELINE G.
1982   *Love Canal: Science, Politics and People.* Lexington, MA: Lexington Books.
LINDBLOM, CHARLES E.
1977   *Politics and Markets: The World's Political-Economic Systems.* New York: Basic Books.
LITTLE, PAUL
1992   "The Rio summit falls to earth as U.S. snubs global treaties." *In These Times,* June 24-July 7: 8–9.
MOLOTCH, HARVEY
1970   "Oil in Santa Barbara and power in America." *Sociological Inquiry* 40 (1): 131–145.
MOLOTCH, HARVEY & M. LESTER
1975   "Accidental news: The great oil spill as local occurrence and national event." *American Journal of Sociology* 81 (2): 235–260.
NEWHOUSE, JOHN
1992   "The diplomatic round: Earth summit." *The New Yorker,* June 1: 64–78.
New Yorker
1992   "Talk of the town: News and notes." August 24:20.
O'CONNOR, JAMES
1973   *The Fiscal Crisis of the State.* New York: St. Martin's Press.
1988   "Capitalism, nature, socialism: A theoretical introduction." *Capitalism, Nature, Socialism* 1 (Fall): 11–38.
REDCLIFT, MICHAEL
1987   *Sustainable Development: Exploring the Contradictions.* New York: Methuen.
ROHRSCHNEIDER, ROBERT
1991   "Public opinion toward environmental groups in western Europe: One movement or two?" *Social Science Quarterly* 72: 251–266.
RYBCZNSKI, WITTHOLD
1991   *Waiting for the Weekend.* New York: Viking Books.
SCHNAIBERG, ALLAN
1975   "Social syntheses of the societal-environmental dialectic: The role of distributional impacts." *Social Science Quarterly* 56 (June): 5–20.
1977   "Obstacles to environmental research by scientists and technologists: A social structural analysis." *Social Problems* 24 (5): 500–520.
1992a   "Recycling vs. remanufacturing: Redistributive realities." Working paper WP-92–15, Center for Urban Affairs & Policy Research, Northwestern University, Spring.
1992b   "The recycling shell game: Multinational economic organization vs. local political ineffectuality." Working paper WP-92–16, Center for Urban Affairs & Policy Research, Northwestern University, Spring.
1994   "The political economy of environmental problems: Consciousness, conflict, and control capacity." In Riley Dunlap and William Michelson,

editors, *Handbook of Environmental Sociology*. Westport, CT: Greenwood Publishing.

SCHOR, JULIET B.
1991 *The Overworked American: The Unexpected Decline of Leisure*. New York: Basic Books.

SCITOVSKY, TIBOR
1976 *The Joyless Economy: An Inquiry into Human Satisfaction and Consumer Dissatisfaction*. New York: Oxford University Press.

STRETTON, HUGH
1976 *Capitalism, Socialism, and the Environment*. Cambridge: Cambridge University Press.

U.S. ENERGY INFORMATION AGENCY
1987 *Residential Energy Consumption Survey*. Washington, DC: Government Printing Office.

WALLERSTEIN, IMMANUEL
1984 *The Politics of the World-Economy: The States, the Movements, and the Civilizations*. New York: Cambridge University Press.

WILLIAMSON, OLIVER
1985 *The Economic Institutions of Capitalism*. New York: Free Press.

Part III

What Has Been Done?
What Can Be Done?

6. What Can I Do about Environmental Problems?

SOCIOECONOMIC STRATEGIES

This chapter offers a perspective that encompasses the realities of (1) environmental protection struggles and (2) the reader's multiple roles in everyday life, together with the social embeddedness of those roles. Accordingly, we have crudely divided these routine roles into two categories. The first relates to your roles as citizen-worker and citizen-consumer, which together constitute the dominant socioeconomic roles in most of your lives. In the first three sections, we discuss careers, the use of credit, and patterns of consumption and family formation, which together focus on your socioeconomic options or choices.

The second category relates more to your role as political citizen. We start with your role as a politically conscious consumer, by talking about choices (and their absence) in the area of recycling and recirculation of consumer wastes. Again, our emphasis is on routine, daily actions rather than on more dramatic but sporadic decisions, such as the purchase of solar energy roofs or energy-efficient cars. We then move on to your more uniquely political role in the formal electoral politics and related behaviors around legislative support for environmental proposals. As we acknowledge, timing is important in any push for an environmental protection agenda, and there are offsetting concerns about social justice that need to temper environmental protection legislation. Finally, we close with a brief treatment of your role as a social and political volunteer in environmental movement organizations. Our view of voluntarism is often more critical than the usual call for volunteer actions: not all volunteers are equally helpful to movements, and not all actions of a given volunteer may be equally appropriate for that volunteer to offer.

Decreasing Expectations in Careers

Students, as well as other citizens, are often told that they are part of the environmental problem, and that only they can solve it. This is at once both an appealing and an appalling perspective, since the individual is faced with the potential to do something, and yet is confronted with overwhelming uncertainty about how to deal with the wide array of environmental problems. In this chapter, we explore how individuals may play different roles in environmental degradation. But we do so in the context of a social order that offers scripts for the roles we play. What we offer is a model of individual freedoms and social constraints on how we live, and the connections these have with patterns of resource utilization that create and modify ecological functioning.

We offer two complementary perspectives here. The first is a structural approach that outlines the cultural, political, economic, and social factors that influence each of us in society. Conversely, we offer a vision of individual behaviors, which in small and cumulative ways can alter how society places pressures on ecological systems. One view of these two perspectives is how social structure influences the individual's degree of freedom. An alternative view is how the aggregation of individual behaviors can alter the structure of society. This is the modern sociological approach to the classical philosophical debate between free will and determinism (Granovetter 1985).

As sociologists with a strong sense of the regularized structures of society, we lean toward the first perspective. Most of this book follows this social-structural vision. In this chapter, however, we offer you a sense of how changes in your behavior, both in itself and, more importantly, in conjunction with similar changes in others' activities, could stimulate societal changes. This chapter is designed to be consistent with our arguments in the other chapters. Thus, our view of individual choices and freedoms focuses more heavily on the reader's economic roles ("careers"). We also focus on the reader's specific actions as an individual and a familial consumer of products. Finally, we focus on the individual's political role in his or her political backing for candidates supporting environmental policies and social movements to protect the environment.

We contend that changes in the routine economic operations of our society will have the dominant impact on environmental problems. Thus, in this chapter we emphasize the routine economic activities of individuals, as the major components of the socioeconomic structure that currently produces many environmental problems. Among the possible range of such routine economic activities, we start with two major dimensions of our work roles—careers and credits. They are connected through issues of wages or earnings of workers in their careers. Workers' *careers* refer to broader roles than just professional-technical ones. In the sociological sense, a career refers to a trajectory of past, present, and future work roles, coupled with the argots, cultures, and collective sense of identities of the workers. Essentially, this is one of the individual's key roles in the treadmill of production. Within this role, we emphasize the wage structure, which influences the economics of production, on the one hand, and the profitability of consumer markets, on the other. Credit is allocated to individuals, in part based on creditors' expectations of what these worker-consumer-borrowers will be able to pay off in future years. In turn, credit is largely predicated on the basis of job stability and average earnings projected for the credit card holder. Whereas itinerant dishwashers cannot gain $5,000 or $10,000 credit in the form of bank cards, credit union loans, or credit accounts in large stores, professional industrial managers can readily obtain such levels of credit, because they are believed to be more "credit-worthy," or *credit*able. Credit-worthiness can be viewed as an extension of the earning power of workers. Thus, a choice of a less remunerative career will generally also involve a lower use of credit.

Unlike most standard economic treatises, in this work we emphasize two options that every worker-citizen has available. Choosing to follow a less remunerative career (Saltzman 1991) is actually a choice that most workers can readily opt for, regardless of many institutional pressures. Similarly, every worker can choose to apply for and use less credit. Both actions can decelerate the treadmill of production and hence reduce the demands that society makes on ecosystems. Even students attending colleges, who are building up debt to pay for their education (see the next section), have some options. If they choose to work for a public service rather than in a higher paying private sector, for example, their monthly payments may be much smaller since payments are partly based on income levels. Some professional schools are introducing some form of debt forgiveness for public service work, and President Clinton has proposed that a similar option be made widely available through the federal government as well. Conversely, if more students choose less remunerative careers, college loans may become less available, because the rates of return on them may be too low for both the government and private lenders.

To the extent that broad groups in the population move in this direction, changes in the economic structure may emerge, which again could be more environmentally supportive (Kelly 1992; Needleman 1991). Although the origins of this chapter derive from other works, the argument here is compatible with Juliet Schor's recent (1991) book, *The Overworked American*. She argues that Americans have chosen, or been induced or coerced into, working longer hours in order to have more "things." In this process, we have abandoned genuine leisure, and at the same time have helped to accelerate the treadmill of production and its environmental impacts. An earlier view by the economist Tibor Scitovsky (1976) framed the issue as one of seeking more consumer comforts at the cost of more stimulation in our work and domestic lives (Mogil et al. 1992; Robinson 1977; Robinson et al. 1989).

A distinction needs to be made here between the content of work and its remuneration. It is possible, for example, for worker-citizens to do similar types of work as they had originally planned, but simply do it for less pay per hour or work for fewer hours. With some realistic assumptions, this situation could lead to more environmental problems, for corporate profits could rise initially and this surplus could be invested in more environmentally destructive technologies (e.g., getting more efficient clearcutting equipment to strip forests faster). At some point, if average wages were decreasing, as more and more worker-citizens chose leisure and lower stress over more work, higher stress, and higher income, there would be a glut of goods on the market. Profits would then fall, and presumably many of these producers would reduce production, for inventories would rise too fast. This is, of course, a classic scenario in any business recession. Most worker-citizens have been trained to fear and avoid such recessions and with good reason.

If only a handful of worker-citizens engage in these less remunerative careers, this scenario is unlikely to occur, of course. But their deceleration of the treadmill and protection of the environment is also going to be minuscule (although they may feel better, knowing they are not personally such a drain on the ecosystems). Conversely, if more workers begin to decide to avoid making more money for more goods and services, are there alternative paths other than the painful business recession model, which typically leads to substantial immiseration of displaced workers, even with our so-called safety nets of unemployment insurance? Historically, the major alternative model that has been used is some form of public service or public works, both of which could include environmental protection, as in the U.S. model of the Civilian Conservation Corps of the 1930s. To the extent that workers are willing to accept lower wages, more public employment can be created with a given level of taxes or other government revenues. On the other hand, business recessions typically reduce corporate profits (which is in part how environmental demands get lowered) and thus also reduce tax revenues. Moreover, in this political situation corporate taxes cannot be raised to offset these losses.

What can be done, then? One threat in such a situation is that investment capital will flow to other countries, if business opportunities are higher there (see Chapter 3). In a narrow technical sense, this outcome would itself slow the U.S. treadmill of production, although it might accelerate the global treadmill by using natural resources and labor abroad. Another possibility is that more capital will be reallocated from industries where goods are no longer finding strong markets, to those industries closer to meeting more basic worker-citizen needs. If more efficient methods of producing such goods can be generated, using new technologies and less costly workers, then prices for such goods will drop and more workers can have more of their basic needs met from private production. Conversely, as such shifts occur, government programs can employ more workers displaced from the earlier private production in less appealing industries. Government might also contract with private corporations to offer more goods and services necessary for social needs, such as health, education, recreation, and environmental protection.

To create such a transition would require a prolonged process that in some ironic ways is a mirror image of Eastern Europe's efforts to stimulate more private production of goods and services (i.e., to accelerate or restructure their own treadmills of production). This is because the government would need to have considerable flexibility to cushion the shocks of industrial disinvestment and to help masses of individuals scale down their salaries and still have a decent life. But unlike Eastern Europe we would be coming from a history of privatization: private hospitals and doctors already provide health services, there is a vast spectrum of private schooling, and many manufacturers are already engaged in supplying pollution abatement and energy-efficient equipment and contracting. Thus, many of the transition problems of Eastern Europe would not be substantial problems for the U.S. public services. In this model public employment, especially in tasks such as environmental protection, would become "shock absorbers" for the losses of private consumption and private employment (e.g., substituting public transit services and employment for automobile use and manufacturing/service jobs).

To make this work, however, the government would probably need to create a substantial transition fund, which would be easier to generate under budget surpluses rather than the current deficits. Hence, one of the preliminary tasks for the United States is to substantially reduce the current budget deficits. Ideally, the government should also draw down more of the accumulated national debt, which was tripled by Reaganomics in the 1980s. Without this mechanism, future governments have less freedom. Therefore, it is important to consider the nature of credit and debt, and how the more judicious use of credit may be another option for individuals and institutions, including government.

Credit: Less Is More Environmentally Protective

The simplest definition of credit is a borrowing from the future to achieve present satisfactions. Any form of credit essentially implies that we would rather have some benefits now and pay the costs in the future. It has a first-order consequence, however, of constraining our future options. The debt we incur today has to be repaid in some future period. Thus, we have one of only two options for our indebted future: (1) we will have to earn more, so that we can "afford" to repay our debt more readily than we can do with today's earnings, or (2) we will have to be more prepared to consume fewer additional goods and services in the future, assuming that our earnings continue at their present level into that future. Each option represents ways in which we can "service" the debts we incur today at our future career points.

To the extent that each of us incurs more debt, through various forms of credit, then, we are committing ourselves to one of two scenarios. The first is the treadmill's growth scenario in which treadmill acceleration will somehow allow us to earn more and repay our current debts more easily. This is probably the nearly universal expectation, when we incur all forms of debt, including educational loans, home mortgages, and auto loans. Increasingly, due either to increased job instability or growing limits on earning potentials, this scenario is becoming less realistic for many workers, though somewhat less so for college graduates. Both outcomes are a function of worldwide economic shifts that have been shrinking economic returns to American labor.

Among other reasons for these shifts is that other nations have been saving and investing more of their current "surplus" (returns on labor or capital beyond that needed for individual or organizational maintenance or subsistence). This in turn has permitted them to produce goods and services more efficiently, thereby competing more aggressively than U.S. firms in world markets. As Chapter 3 has noted, this process is exacerbated when some capital owners in the United States or, increasingly, in Japan or other countries derive greater profits and apply this liquidity to buying up and consolidating or making leaner U.S. firms. In this downsizing process, both blue- and white-collar jobs are eliminated. As a result, even traditional professional-technical careers become more unstable, influencing job stability and earnings potential for these as well as those of less skilled workers. American economists increasingly point to the widespread increase in the availability of credit in the United States in the 1970s and 1980s which encouraged consumers to spend more and save or invest less. In the 1980s, United States capital owners leveraged their limited profits, taking over productive firms by greatly expanding corporate debt under "supply-side" Reaganomics (Phillips 1989). As with individual debtors, corporate debt carries the same limited options for future behaviors in servicing this debt: expand profits or consume/invest less in the future to pay off the debt incurred today.

Thus, credit at the individual worker-consumer as well as the corporate-producer level has a paradoxical impact on our economic and therefore our ecological futures. By consuming more now, we help make ourselves more vulnerable in the uncertain future. We either have to depend on an acceleration of the treadmill of production to make more, or we have to confront our limitations and buy less in the future. Because both consumers and producers try to avoid the latter consequence, which is understandable in the context of the materialistic structure of modern industrial society, economic decision makers are pressured to expand production, and thereby to expand employment and raise wages (Needleman 1991). In addition, in the presence of a slowdown or deep economic recession, as in recent years, government operations of governments have even wider consequences.

Governments operate much like individuals and firms with regard to credit. When government revenues are too low to sustain state activities, either taxes must be raised or expenditures lowered, or government debt increased. In the United States, the debt grew at an unprecedented rate in the 1980s as a result of supply-side economics. The national debt multiplied threefold as taxes were reduced to stimulate corporate expansion. However, such expansion was often shortcircuited by quick profit-taking and wasteful expenditures by corporate executives. Nowhere was this more clearly exemplified than in the savings-and-loans debacle (see Chapter 5). In lieu of investing in new forms of innovative and competitive physical capital, much of the income transferred from the government to the private sector and some classes of individual taxpayers wound up supporting current consumption rather than savings and investments. Thus, the government had to borrow increasing amounts of money from financial institutions to support a rapidly growing national debt. Similarly, individuals overspent their current incomes, even with their new tax savings, and wound up deeper in debt at the end of the 1980s than at their onset.

Therefore, government, corporations, and individuals all started the decade of the 1990s with the burdens of debt servicing from their behaviors in the 1980s. All of these components of our sociopolitical system sought to pass blame and responsibility for such debt servicing onto the other sectors of the political economy. Governments sought to reduce transfer payments and services in order to balance the budget. In highly tentative and often devious moves, elected officials also sought to increase taxes in order to achieve the same goal. This meant that, alongside other restrictions of other government activities, in the interest of saving money even environmental protection was often cut back (Goodwin 1992).

But at the same time, individuals and corporations resisted both of these government efforts. Individuals, faced with mounting personal debt, resisted any increase in their taxes, protecting their current consumption and debt repayment. Yet, many individuals also resisted cutbacks of those government services that benefited them. The rallying cry of many such individual political actors was to "reduce wastefulness and inefficiency" in government agencies. These same responses were simultaneously found in the corporate sector, which sought to reduce the burden of its debt repayment by (1) reducing government taxation of corporations, on the one hand, and (2) reducing government enforcement of costly regulations, on the other. Therefore, environmental protection was under special attack, because it was both costly for the government to fund its agencies, such as the Environmental Protection Agency and the Bureau of Land Management, and it was costly for corporations (see Chapter 3) to fund their compliance with the government's environmental regulations. In the face of such interests a variety of antitax movements flourished in the 1980s and 1990s.

Thus, whether at the individual or the corporate level, the recent period has seen enormous pressures opposing growth of government expenditures on environmental protection. Even where taxpayers do not directly pay for enforcement, such as in Superfund clean-ups of toxic waste sites, corporate actors have continued to try to reduce their charges for such programs. Thus, the "road to Rio" in the 1992 U.N. Conference on Environment and Development was paved with many good words for environmental protection, but they were far outweighed by more American bad deeds, which grew out of pressures to expand economically, despite environmental costs. Rather than focusing on reducing the clearcutting of U.S. forests, for example, the U.S. organizations (both movement and governmental) focused on rainforest protection in the South. Generally, while many commentators and even social scientists found solace in social surveys reporting a growing diffusion of environmental values in the 1980s, indebted citizens were more often engaged in economic behaviors that contradicted these values (Bidwai 1992).

Once more, as with diminished career expectations, a reduction of credit has different impacts at the individual and collective levels. If you as an individual restrict your uses of credit for nonessential goods and services, then you effectively pay now and can choose to fly later or opt for other strategies for your satisfaction. You can feel comfortable in knowing you have less need to earn more money in the future to pay for consumption that you have engaged in, using credit as a leveraging device.

As substantial numbers of individual worker-consumers use less credit, however, profits will decline in both the finance industries and in those industries whose products are purchased using credit (e.g., automobiles, household appliances, and air travel). As in the previous section, declining use of credit enhances the prospects for wider and deeper business recessions. The solution here is the same as that noted earlier in this chapter: a gradual transition of investment into more basic individual and social needs. Overall, this could lead to a net loss of U.S. capital to other countries, and thus a displacement of environmental problems, rather than a decrease of global problems. But insofar as other countries face similar shifts, this threat may not be so pressing. Because some of this capital would flow to underdeveloped countries, it would help to upgrade their standards of living, thereby reducing the ecological threats associated with Third World poverty. Some increased industrial environmental demands in the South would partly offset the decreased environmental demands from the North.

Consumption and Reproduction: Higher Quality and Lower Quantity

In keeping with some recent theorizing about children as consumer goods, we are including a discussion of family formation strategies in this section as well. The general principle we share here is one of lowered throughput from the environment into socioeconomic systems. In the following section, we deal with the reverse question: How can we limit the output from social systems back into the environment, so that we can reduce pollution and other environmental problems?

Our principle here is very simple: to reduce individual environmental impacts, consumers ought to obtain their individual utilities from goods and services that are more durable and efficient. This is a somewhat circular argument, since increased durability and efficiency really mean that these items entail lower withdrawals from and additions to ecosystems, per unit of consumer satisfaction or utility. Another way of making the same statement is that we urge individuals to use less disposable goods and services, and generally to share goods whenever possible (e.g., using public rather than private goods and services). Households living on the same suburban street, for instance, could conceivably share a lawn mower rather than purchasing separate mowers for each home, all of which would remain idle most of the time.

But to do most of this is not as simple as it may appear. Recent experiences in the late 1980s and early 1990s with green marketing (Office of Technology Assessment 1992) indicate that many producers have more "green-ness" in their advertising than in their production of the goods being marketed. First, much distortion occurs, for example, in labeling goods as being of recycled content; the ratio of recycled to virgin materials may be quite low, and the recycled component may be of producer wastes rather than postconsumer wastes. Moreover, even if goods consist of more recycled content, the process of remanufacturing, using recyclable materials, may be highly polluting (e.g., using recycled newspapers and washing inks into nearby bodies of water) or energy-inefficient (e.g., recycled crushed glass for new containers).

Second, much of the environmental impact information purveyed by manufacturers may be partial: a product touted as energy-efficient may nonetheless have components that may lead to ozone depletion (e.g., room air conditioners). Similarly, most appliances contribute to global warming through their consumption of electricity or gas, whose combustion generates carbon dioxide. In addition, wood products might tout their biodegradability, while ignoring the effects of cutting these trees in terms of reduced absorption of carbon dioxide. Thus, they, too, may contribute to global warming, or local soil erosion, or local water pollution as fertilizer and pesticide runoff leaches from the forests into waterways.

The reasons for this piecemeal or partial information are threefold. First, producers involved in green marketing are attempting to gain the greatest market penetration for the least production expenditures on environmental protection (Schnaiberg 1992). Since most producers operate in highly competitive consumer and financial markets, their economic interests constrain them to behave in these ways (see Chapter 3). Second, those who manage and design production systems are more trained to evaluate and develop economically efficient modes of technology than they are to create environmentally benign technologies. The criteria and applied science for the first task are more elaborated in educational systems, which have only recently even begun to diffuse the rudiments of ecological analysis. Thus, technological sciences lag in modifying the scientific criteria for reducing withdrawals and additions, although countries such as Japan have moved forward rapidly in the last decade and a half, especially in energy efficiency (cf. Office of Technology Assessment 1992). Third, most consumers themselves have a very limited sense of eco-logic, because of the limitations of educational systems on this plane. For example, only in 1990 did the state of Illinois mandate environmental education in the secondary curriculum. Even most college and university students are not routinely exposed to environmental education.

Despite what seems to be an information overload, therefore, consumers have to rely on very limited cues to become more ecologically benign consumers. Many more products today are being marketed by smaller firms, which at least claim to be chemically benign, not leading to toxic pollution when they are used or their containers are discarded. But even nontoxic chemicals can disorganize ecosystems (see Chapter 1) in sufficient quantities. For these daily consumer items of food, cosmetics, cleansers, and the like, an initial investment of time and money in reading and buying items whose labels indicate more natural components may be ecologically helpful.

There are much broader arenas of consumption beyond the grocery or drugstore items. Automobiles, homes, and electrical appliances are among the heaviest consumer items impacting on ecosystems. Some of these items have widely varying ecological impacts, and more producers, sometimes under the pressure of government regulation, are providing consumer information. So, for example, a careful consumer has available information demanded by the Environmental Protection Agency (EPA) on automobile gasoline consumption and, from this and other agencies, on the energy-efficiency ratio of major appliances such as refrigerators, stoves, air conditioners, and humidifiers-dehumidifiers. But this consumer can still be in the dark about whether the refrigerant liquids in some of the older appliances may contain chlorofluorocarbons, which deplete the ozone in the upper atmosphere. And they may not know which parts of the equipment may be repaired or recycled through remanufacturing processes. Nor do they know what the production processes underlying these products are. This is why governments must act in the production and recycling arenas, often under political and/or legal pressures from environmental movements (e.g., see the remaining sections of this chapter).

This consumption discussion has neglected to mention that many products or services are not available in the market because of a variety of corporate and government actions. Private firms may lack financial incentives to produce more durable goods, for example, because durability of goods will reduce the market for replacement goods. Many illustrations exist in the area of automobiles. For example, in the 1930s a major steel company produced stainless steel auto bodies, and these bodies were far more durable than standard steel ones. This would have reduced land use for auto scrap yards, the energy and mining demands required to produce new steel bodies, and so on. Interestingly, it might also have generated some "offset" jobs (since some would be lost in the steel and manufacturing process) in replacing mechanical parts and engines on these durable auto bodies. The popular mechanics literature has discussed a variety of fuel-saving and metal-saving propulsion systems for automobiles, ranging from the rotary Wankel engine to electric vehicles, which have been largely unavailable because private companies have been unable or unwilling to devote more capital to perfect such products, and governments have been unwilling to subsidize this research and development. Even more modest recent technical innovations such as systems to clean used automobile oil have been hampered by a lack of government regulation (which would provide market pressures for companies to recycle oil rather than produce new oil products) and funding of market research and other research and development.

These details notwithstanding, the other element absent in many communities is an efficient and affordable public transportation system, which would reduce the need for automobiles or at least for auto use for daily journeys to work and shopping. Substantial political disagreement exists over why public transit in the United States is so limited compared to that of our European counterparts. The explanations for the differences range from consumer cultures, to diffused suburban living patterns, to auto-truck corporate conspiracies in buying and dismantling private transit systems in the 1940s, and finally to government limitations and shortsightedness. Thus, in the absence of public goods such as public transit, more energetic pro-environmental consumers have a truncated range of choices. They can walk or bicycle to work/shop, or they can move their households so as to be closer to their work and shopping areas. If they are less energetic, they can car-pool or use more efficient "trips" to combine work, shopping, and recreation in a single automobile circuit. But it is only through *political mobilization*, at a collective level, that consumers, acting as citizen-worker-consumers, can coerce or induce governments to set up or extend public transit systems. Similarly, as our next section indicates, only by such collective political mobilization can citizen-consumers get governments to establish more ecologically efficient re-use and recycling programs for postconsumer discarded items (Goodwin 1992).

While our emphasis has been on the individual consumer, we now extend this analysis to the familial level. One important act that you as a consumer and a reproducer can make decisions about is your choices about family size, or the number of children you seek to bring into this ecologically pressed world. Microeconomic theories of middle-class families suggest that children are less investments than they are durable consumer goods, which bring parents satisfactions. Hence, the choices here can be viewed as paralleling the other consumer choices above. As our discussion in Chapter 4 indicates, issues of population size and global/national ecological impact are complicated and sometimes counterintuitive. But as a citizen of an industrial world, with a career anticipation that will permit (and require) you to raise "high-quality" middle-class children, you have the possibility of controlling your future familial impact on the environment.

We live in a world in which countries such as China have been legislating a one-child limit for couples. Social movements such as Zero Population Growth advocate two or fewer children per couple. In our own society, with high rates of divorce and remarriage, even the calculation of the per couple denominator in the children:parents ratio is confusing. However, one thing is clear. Generally, having fewer children will be more environmentally (and socially) benign than having more children. Because you will have fewer economies of scale in childrearing, each additional child you have will eventually demand more production and withdrawals and additions (though whether this is a linear or nonlinear function of demands per multiple children is unclear). Moreover, if you have fewer children, slots will open up in the opportunity structure for more lower income children to receive more education and better employment, under the *ceteris paribus* assumption (i.e., assuming a fixed level of educational funds and employment openings). One great benefit of familial strategies is that the joys of childrearing can be achieved with only one child. Conversely, even those who savor such joys cannot usually extend their childrearing much farther during their life cycles by having multiple children. This is partly due to the biological limitations of women, who tend to stop childbearing before age 40, unlike men, who can father children at far more advanced ages.

As with other decisions about consumer durables, you should choose wisely and share whenever possible. Instead of having more children, you can become a "big brother" or "big sister" to other people's children. Or you can become a grandparent and be more involved in the lives of your children's children. If you do choose to have a child, you should also be checked out physically for your capacity to produce a healthy child. If there are doubts about your capacities, you should have an amniocentesis. Although induced abortion is a morally and judicially loaded topic in the United States and some other countries, a carefully regulated program of induced abortion is probably ecologically benign. It reduces the ecological demands and social problems that often arise when the children being born are unwanted and thereby neglected by parents or institutional surrogates. When children are born with severe handicaps, some of the same childcare problems may emerge. The problems are often compounded by the needs for energy-demanding equipment for life support and costly care. These financial drains necessitate either the use of taxes or of family income, both of which are likely to accelerate the treadmill of production.

Choices you make about how to raise your child also have environmental implications. You can attempt to create a private world for your child, in which case he or she will have higher environmental impacts during childhood and higher consumption expectations during adulthood (Mogil et al. 1992). Alternatively, you can practice more collective forms of childrearing, ranging from group care, to shared toys and books, to use of libraries and parks rather than just their own bookshelves and backyard playgrounds (Needleman 1991). Of course, if you reduce the remuneration expected from your career, some of these decisions will follow more automatically, since you will have fewer privatized options.

This alternative model of childrearing involves more attentive love for your children, utilizing more of your time for childrearing and less for working, and consuming fewer private goods and services. It will induce them to internalize a more ecologically benign set of values as

PHYSICAL FITNESS AND ECOLOGICAL HEALTH:
BICYCLES AND ECOCYCLES

In the United States, the period of rising environmental concern has also been one of increasing concern about the physical fitness of its citizens. Diet and exercise are the two major components of response to rising obesity, cardiovascular disease, and lack of physical fitness of young and old alike. However, the ecological impacts of the expanded exercise facilities in both the private and public sector have been largely ignored.

Two ecological aspects can be noted: (1) the loss of potential use-value of the human energy involved in such exercise, and (2) the effects of such facilities on ecological withdrawals and additions. Consider the cardiovascular machines, such as stationary bicycles, treadmills, and StairMasters. Fitness advocates expend substantial calories in using these machines, but there is no public benefit from this activity. One simple way of harnessing this human energy would be to transform all these machines into electrical generators by connecting them to small electrical generating turbines (much as water power provides electricity). Another way of capturing this energy would be to have more people use bicycles for the journey to work and shopping, thereby cutting down on energy use for autos (ecosystem withdrawals) and on air pollution from auto exhaust (ecosystem additions).

The second impact of expanded exercise facilities is their substantial energy and water demands. Good gymnasiums require high levels of air conditioning to cool down their users, as well as large-scale water usage for showering. In addition, still more energy and water are required for laundering sweat suits and other exercise clothing (and the ecosystem demands involved in manufacturing them). Open air activities, even for only part of the year, could reduce the air conditioning requirements. Laundering clothing poses more problems, perhaps suggesting that standardized public exercise clothing may have some benefits, especially considering the economies of energy and water that could accrue from public laundering of the clothing. More dispersed public centers could also reduce the additional energy and pollution that are the concomitant of driving to health clubs and gymnasiums. The additional ecological impacts of manufacturing more exercise equipment at home might also be thereby reduced, especially for users who also use other private or public fitness facilities.

adults. To be fair, however, there is some evidence that children reared in a less privatized setting may feel deprived and seek more privatization as adults. This reaction is suggested by the analyses of children of the 1960s communes in the United States (Rothchild & Wolf 1976). But we do not fully understand the emotional development of these young children, and it may be emotional rather than material deprivation to which they responded. Thus, in the production process of your childrearing, you can be more environmentally benign by having fewer children and being more attentive to the few you do rear, without encouraging hyperconsumption on your part or theirs. In this way, you may reproduce more environmentally benign values and behaviors in your children, which they will carry with them into the future of the global ecosphere, and act as more ecologically responsible citizen-workers (Kelly 1992). Conversely, you won't need to justify hyperconsumption because of your children's needs (Needleman 1991).

POLITICAL-ECONOMIC STRATEGIES

Recycling and Reuse: Options for Buying and Recirculating

The late 1980s brought about some interesting changes in consumer and government behavior in the area of waste disposal of consumer wastes. Rather than dumping all such wastes in landfills or incinerating a large proportion of them, innovative programs for recycling were introduced. It was theorized that such recycling would (1) lead to lowered withdrawals of land for landfills and lowered polluting additions to air and water through this reduction, as well as reduced incineration of wastes; and (2) also reduce future withdrawals of ecosystem elements, as wastes would be recirculated into the economy in the form of usable products, substituting for virgin materials extracted from ecosystems.

While the initiative of citizen-consumers was initially substantial, with many of them sorting, packing, and hauling domestic wastes to recycling centers, recent trends toward curbside recycling have lowered these initiatives. Municipalities have sought to reduce waste treatment costs by picking up household wastes on a regular schedule, requiring only that each citizen-consumer separate out their trash into recyclable categories (e.g., aluminum, glass, and paper being the prime categories). Several environmental and socioeconomic problems have emerged in many such programs. In terms of collecting wastes, not all citizen-consumers cooperate in either putting out their recyclables or in properly cleaning and separating them. Clearly, you as an individual can be responsive in both arenas.

A second major problem in the ecological and economic models of recycling is that too few remanufacturers are using these collected materials. This in turn limits how many recyclables are actually recycled through some form of remanufacturing process. Many collected wastes thus end up in landfills or incinerators, thereby incurring greater cost than in earlier "dumping" schemes and raising rather than lowering municipal expenditures for waste treatment. In addition, city revenues from selling such collected recyclables are far lower than expected, since there is now a glut of recyclables available to remanufacturers, who follow supply-and-demand principles of pricing (Schnaiberg 1992).

This problem has led to a variety of consequences for individual citizen-consumers. As noted above, advertising through green marketing is one corporate response. In the context of this section, we focus on producers who advertise that (1) their products are recyclable and (2) their products are made from recycled materials. Although some of these changes are laudatory and represent useful guides for you, there is often much distortion in such advertising, which has led to new regulatory efforts. For example, while a product may in theory be recyclable, if there are no actual programs to recycle then there is no application of the theory in practice. Thus, some manufacturers of disposable diapers advertised the recyclability of their products but were later forced to introduce in small print a demurrer that most communities do not yet have such a program. A problem with such products is that plastic liners must be separated from absorbent materials, and each must be recycled separately. But dealing with soiled diapers is not an appealing task for manual laborers, and machine soaking and separation are rather costly. This is especially the case because currently the profits on plastic or paper recycling are very low.

In response to this problem of nonrecycling of potentially recyclable consumer products, green marketing may encourage consumers to buy product X because its manufacturers have been ecologically responsible in utilizing recycled materials in their production processes. A number of states' attorneys have discovered these claims to be inflated, because it is often cheaper to advertise that a product is made from recycled materials than to modify the manufacturing process to actually incorporate such materials. Thus, you as citizen-consumers should be aware of the epidemic of reports about recycling successes in the products you buy (Office of Technology Assessment 1992). Conversely, many remanufacturers and some environmental movement organizations have encouraged citizen-consumers to pressure their employers and local and state governments to buy more recycled products and to increase markets for remanufactured-recycled goods (especially paper products). Indeed, at the extreme, many "recyclers" have contracts with cities that mandate a minimum of annual volumes of recyclables, and thus encourage the production of wastes to supply them. Thus, as a citizen of a local community, you will be under pressure to increase both the supply of and demand for postconsumer wastes, to help balance the local budgets, and to be ecologically responsible. Some citizen rethinking of this process may be in order, as noted below (Schnaiberg 1992).

A third problem confronting the ecologically supportive citizen-consumer is that, even when recyclables are actually recycled in the remanufacturing process, a variety of withdrawals and additions may be unattended to in this process. For example, the use of remanufacturing of recyclables often increases pollution at these factories, as unwanted parts of the recyclables are disposed of while the valued parts are kept. Newsprint recycling separates inks from paper fibers and disposes of the inks, often creating local and regional water pollution. Even the most successful and profitable recycling, that of aluminum cans, entails energy costs in washing out containers before collection and many problems with contaminants and water vapor accidents in aluminum remanufacturing facilities. Minor commingling or contamination of waste product streams may make such recyclables less recyclable in terms of physical and chemical properties already incorporated into these wastes (i.e., based on past withdrawals from and additions to ecosystems). Thus, some forms of contaminated glass containers may be simply ground up and used as a filler in road asphalt to increase its reflective properties. The net ecological "savings" from such uses may thereby be smaller than anticipated, for many properties of the glass are not used in this application.

Finally, as a citizen-consumer facing the pressures to be a recycler, you need to do your own ecological and socioeconomic thinking. Recycling is generally better than the simple disposal or burning of wastes. However, it is less ecologically benign than a social reuse of these wastes without additional remanufacturing. And it is substantially less ecologically efficient than social nonuse of such products that become wastes in the consumption cycle. Several simple examples should suffice: it is generally better to use refillable containers and bulk purchasing than individual, disposable, or recyclable containers. Retail marketers dislike bulk merchandizing, because it requires higher health standards and more reliable (and hence more expensive) labor to use their discretion in dispensing goods. Manufacturers and wholesalers may dislike these processes because their profit margins are usually lower on bulk sales than on individually packaged goods. Some labor organizations will also have problems, because manufacturing and wholesaling labor will likely be attenuated by bulk marketing, although retail opportunities may rise somewhat (and salaries may also rise there).

This refillability of containers is only one type of recirculation of materials. To reduce ecological withdrawals and additions, a variety of citizen-consumer actions to enhance nonuse and reuse of consumer goods would be helpful. You can avoid buying products with excessive packaging wherever possible. You can give away your used domestic goods to social service organizations that run thrift shops (thereby achieving some social equity, as well as reducing some ecological withdrawals and additions).

Moreover, you can yourselves buy more recirculated goods through thrift shops, resale organizations, garage sales, antique dealers, or used equipment dealers. Some of these actions work at cross-purposes in terms of social equity. For example, if you buy more used equipment, the prices are likely to rise and thereby make such equipment less affordable for low-income groups. The difference between church rummage sales aimed at low-income groups and dealers conducted house sales that attract middle-class consumers and dealers is that the dealers use market values for pricing guides, while the low-income groups use consumer needs to guide more of their pricing.

What guidelines, then, can we offer you as a citizen-consumer? You can be more ecologically responsible by buying fewer goods, purchasing goods that involve more recycled materials and are themselves recyclable, using more durable or reusable goods, purchasing used items wherever possible, and passing on items that you no longer need to social service organizations for recirculation of them. Moreover, as a citizen-consumer, you can organize to help your community to reuse and recycle more effectively, perhaps by concentrating some remanufacturing activities at the community level to create employment. You can also use your vote to support candidates and organizations that promote more social control of reusability, recyclability, incorporation of recycled goods in products, and pollution control of remanufacturing facilities. These economic policies, as we note below, may require a variety of economic incentives (subsidies) and disincentives (taxes or fines) from governments to redirect production organizations to act in more ecologically responsible ways (Goodwin 1992).

Political Support for Environmental Taxation and Job Creation

We now turn to a discussion of more expressly political behaviors, emphasizing your role as citizen more than your role as consumer (Goodwin 1992; Phillips 1989). As Chapter 3 makes clear, governments need to enter into the economic marketplace in a variety of ways in order to restrict access to some ecosystem elements. Without such intervention, there is simply not enough of a long-term ecological calculus that routinely enters into the decision making of economic elites (and as we have seen in the Eastern European bloc, in the decisions of political elites as well). The role of the government is, at the very least, to support ecological monitoring research, since few private institutions or individuals can afford to do so. A closely related activity of government must be the sociopolitical dissemination of these ecological findings to a variety of citizen movements, political organizations, and economic decision makers.

These are the *minimum* tasks of governments in most societies. Beyond this, most governments will have to respond to political initiatives proposing environmental protection through some form of managed scarcity, that is, controlling various aspects of economic market activities. These responses can be widely divergent types of controlling: (1) direct control of access to ecosystems, and (2) economic influences over markets through (a) taxes imposed, (b) fines imposed, (c) subsidies for only some specified forms of ecosystem usage, and (d) various price controls over market producers. We can think about these as either quantity controls or price controls.

Furthermore, every government can take a variety of different stances towards environmental activists. Some will reinforce the narrow and short-term calculus of many economic elites and discourage the protests of most environmentalists to modify market systems of the economy. Others will be formally neutral, neither discouraging nor encouraging such political programs. Finally, some governments will be encouraging of many environmental protests, siding with such groups over the resistances of many economic elites. Apparently, many different factors have influenced governments in any and all industrialized and industrializing societies to respond in these ways. Among other factors are (1) the state of the economy, especially its level of surplus, (2) the strength of the environmental activism movement, (3) the degree to which other citizen protests are in congruence with or in opposition to environmental protests—for example, social welfare movements, and (4) the nature of scientific and popular understanding of environmental hazards.

How should you as an environmentally concerned citizen respond to these conditions? First, you need to understand that there is no "warm fuzzy environmentalism" that ultimately does much about protecting ecosystems and the global ecosphere. We only came to our current environmental problems because many institutions and powerful actors (and indeed, to some limited and variable extent, all of us) have many interests in extracting social system gains from ecosystems. Thus, it is not sufficient merely to point to an ideal end-point of how we eventually want to relate to the environment. We must understand that there are inherent conflicts about how "we" want this relationship to be structured. These conflicts are economic at root and are reflected in political, economic, social, and cultural disputes. These disputes are over two kinds of issues: (1) who will be denied access to ecosystems in order to protect the environment, and (2) who will effectively pay for this scarcity of access, through fines, jobs, wages, social welfare reductions, or health risks (Landy et al. 1990)?

It is sometimes possible to participate in environmental activities that appear to be nonconflictual. These could include new parks, new plantings, and purchases of tracts of undeveloped land. Essentially all of them fit within the normal treadmill procedures, because they do not seriously decelerate the treadmill's use of ecosystems. Correspondingly, they do not achieve much environmental protection, since they do *not* restrict access to major threatened parts of ecosystems, and the costs of such restrictions are disguised from those on whom they are imposed. Virtually every other citizen-based environmental movement will confront serious, enduring resistance from a variety of economic and political institutions and actors. This resistance may be in the form of threats or seductions by economic elites (e.g., job blackmail or green marketing by producers). All forms of communications media can be used, for both types of responses, as can all forms of economic and political exchanges. In recent years, citizen forums have been as prevalent a form of resistance as smoke-filled back rooms are of political arm-twisting. Or they may be in the form of protests by negatively impacted groups of less powerful workers or the poor (whose positions may be supported by economic elites).

What is a concerned citizen to do, then? First, you must understand the social functions of conflict that surround environmental issues. We believe that the slogan "no pain, no gain" applies as much in ecological fitness as in physical fitness. Even if you yourself cannot function well in this conflict, be accepting of other environmentalists who can and do function within a conflictual social system, to reduce ecological "conflict." Second, even when you cannot yourself engage in such social conflicts, you can still offer your political support for political candidates and movements that have serious proposals for economic reforms leading to ecological protection (e.g., through voting behavior or economic contributions to such movement organizations). Third, you should be alert and responsive to innovative ways to distribute the burdens of environmental protection in more humane and sometimes less politically conflictual ways. You should be alert to ways to do this in your school, workplace, family setting, community, and country of residence (Goodwin 1992; Kelly 1992).

Social Movements: Support for and Participation in Them

As Chapter 3 and portions of this chapter show, the market will not routinely solve environmental problems. Nor will the government do so. This is because all citizens and economic actors require the extraction from environments of *some* resources for their subsistence and growth. Thus, every society has some form of ongoing tension (the societal-environmental dialectic) between resource extraction and resource protection. Environmental protection must, therefore, have its own set of social protectors in order to redress the economic pressures that, left unbalanced, will tend to overwhelm most ecological systems. This is especially true in the modern industrial (and postindustrial) era, when successful extraction leads to increased technological and economic power to accelerate the treadmill of production (Landy et al. 1990; Lash 1984). Governments tend to be highly concerned about producing enough social surplus to meet the demands of economically powerful constituents, as well as to offer at least minimal social support to the less powerful, dependent constituents. Social systems need some surplus to accomplish these objectives and sustain their political systems. They do vary considerably, however, in how much surplus is generated, and how it is distributed to social groups.

Social scientists have long noted that power begets power. That is, in the absence of other political activities, those actors who gain economic power will tend to dominate both markets and the political agenda. Only when social and political resistance becomes more organized, in some collective forms of resistance, will the environmental and social equity agendas come into some serious conflict with the dominant group's agenda (Goodwin 1992; Phillips 1989).

What does this imply for you as an individual? It implies that many of your individual efforts may be more useful for "feeling good" about environmental solutions than for "doing good" to actually protect ecosystems. Even as an individual, if your actions run counter to dominant economic agendas, you will find more pressures to conform to the dominant mode when more than a few people join you in your resistance. Conversely, when "everyone is doing it," the resistance itself becomes a new dominant mode. But this level of environmentalist behavior has never happened in any society.

How and where you might participate in some form of collective efforts to enhance environmental protection is a much more open-ended situation. It depends on your personality, your resources, your values, and the social, political, and economic contexts in which you are embedded at any given moment (Gould 1991). Our sense is that, if you can follow the general arguments in this book, you have sufficient intellectual tools to participate in any type of environmental movement organization (see Chapter 7). But many other factors will influence what forms of participation would most suit you at a given stage of your life cycle.

Young students often have much energy and enthusiasm as well as flexible time budgets. Thus, students may join existing environmental movements and serve in street protests and organizational picketing, for example, to raise public and official consciousness about some environmental problem. Young parents may simply not have the time but may still participate by doing home telephoning to mobilize or inform other social movement members, or by doing mailings by stuffing envelopes at home. People starting careers may have less time but more money than when they were students: they may choose to send money to organizations upholding their environmental and social values. More senior members may have some important expertise and be more valuable in doing analyses and writing reports than in participating in public protests. Retired members may be able to do a variety of inside and outside tasks for movement organizations, and they may contribute time, money, and expertise in varying ways (Needleman 1991). For environmental movement members with more work experience, the contacts, lessons, and problems that emerge in their work roles may be valuable assets to the movements. Sometimes these volunteers can be valuable whistleblowers, reporting to movement organizations some insider knowledge about problems in their workplace or in related organizations. Sometimes they can point to fiscal resources (e.g., grant sources) from their employers or to cooperative innovative managers willing to respond to movement initiatives. At other times, they can direct the movement organization in directions of talent or expertise that it may need, from among the networks of their work systems.

Members' activities are among the most valuable resources that environmental movement organizations possess. Thus, the general rule that seems operable is: offer your time, money, or expertise only under conditions in which you are reasonably certain that you are very likely to be able to deliver. And deliver on your promises to the organization. Where members become unreliable—whether by absence, lateness, or inadequacy of their efforts—they often wind up being a greater drag than a boon to the organization. Since environmental movement organizations are voluntary associations, they quickly wind up using scarce resources if their volunteers are unreliable. If you enter as a volunteer but are basically seeking to have the organization do more for you than you plan to do for them, your net effect on environmental protection is likely to be negative. In short, find another social support group elsewhere, because you will absorb more energy than you will be contributing.

SELECTED REFERENCES

BELL, DANIEL
    1976 *The Cultural Contradictions of Capitalism.* New York: Basic Books.
BIDWAI, PRAFUL
    1992 "North vs. South on pollution." *The Nation,* June 22: 853–854.
EWEN, STUART
    1976 *Captains of Consciousness: Advertising and the Social Roots of Consumption.*
    New York: McGraw-Hill.

GOODWIN, RICHARD N.
1992   *Promises to Keep: A Call for a New American Revolution.* New York: Times Books.
GOULD, KENNETH A.
1991   "The sweet smell of money: Economic dependency and local environmental political mobilization." *Society and Natural Resources* 4: 133–150.
GRANOVETTER, MARK
1985   "Economic action and social structure: The problem of embeddedness." *American Journal of Sociology* 91 (3): 481–510.
INGLEHART, RONALD
1990   *Culture Shift in Advanced Industrial Society.* Princeton, NJ: Princeton University Press.
KELLY, MARJORIE
1992   "Are you too rich if others are poor? On ethically gained prosperity and its obligations." *Utne Reader* September/October: 67–70.
LANDY, MARC K., M. J. ROBERTS, & S. R. THOMAS
1990   *The Environmental Protection Agency: Asking the Wrong Questions.* New York: Oxford University Press.
LASH, JONATHAN ET AL.
1984   *A Season of Spoils: The Story of the Reagan Administration's Attack on the Environment.* New York: Pantheon Books.
MOGIL, CHRISTOPHER, A. SLEPIAN, WITH P. WOODROW
1992   *We Gave Away a Fortune.* Philadelphia: New Society Publishers.
NEEDLEMAN, JACOB
1991   *Money and the Meaning of Life.* Garden City, NY: Doubleday.
OFFICE OF TECHNOLOGY ASSESSMENT, U.S. CONGRESS
1992   *Green Products by Design: Choices for a Cleaner Environment.* OTA-E-541. Washington, DC: U.S. Government Printing Office.
OPHULS, WILLIAM
1977   *Ecology and the Politics of Scarcity: Prologue to a Political Theory of the Steady State.* San Francisco: W. H. Freeman.
PHILLIPS, KEVIN
1989   *The Politics of Rich and Poor: Wealth and the American Electorate in the Reagan Aftermath.* New York: Random House.
ROBINSON, JOHN P.
1977   *How Americans Use Time.* New York: Praeger.
ROBINSON, JOHN P., V. G. ANDREYENKOV, & V. D. PATRUSHOV
1989   *The Rhythm of Life: How Soviet and American Citizens Use Time.* Boulder, CO: Westview Press.
ROTHCHILD, JOHN & S. B. WOLF
1976   *The Children of the Counter-Culture.* Garden City, NY: Doubleday.
SALTZMAN, AMY
1991   *Downshifting: Reinventing Success on a Slower Track.* New York: Harper Perennial.
SCHNAIBERG, ALLAN
1980   "Population: Paradoxes of the hydra monster." Ch. II in *The Environment: From Surplus to Scarcity.* New York: Oxford University Press.
1992   "Recycling vs. remanufacturing: Redistributive realities." Working paper WP-92–15, Center for Urban Affairs & Policy Research, Northwestern University, Spring.
SCHOR, JULIET
1991   *The Overworked American: The Unexpected Decline of Leisure.* New York: Basic Books.

SCHUMACHER, E. F.
  1973   *Small Is Beautiful: Economics As If People Mattered.* New York: Harper & Row.
SCITOVSKY, TIBOR
  1976   *The Joyless Economy: An Inquiry into Human Satisfaction and Consumer Dissatisfaction.* New York: Oxford University Press.
STRETTON, HUGH
  1976   *Capitalism, Socialism, and the Environment.* Cambridge: Cambridge University Press.

7. Resisting the Treadmill of Production: Environmental Movements

CONSERVATION AND PRESERVATION MOVEMENTS

Contrary to what many naive observers maintain, the modern world did not discover the environment and its problems. A variety of historical precursors antedate the modern environmental movements, including movements that expressed much more accurate scientific views of ecological reality than are found among many contemporary environmental movement organizations. The sustained yield movement around the turn of the century in the United States (Hays 1969) was built around a scientific awareness of the limitations of ecosystems to simultaneously support competing social uses. Richard H. Groves (1992) notes that similar concerns of both a local and a global nature were elucidated in the colonies of Western industrial countries much earlier. In the nineteenth century, rapid deforestation led to soil erosion and the silting of navigable rivers, especially in Mauritius and India. Because of rising regional famines, social unrest, and decreased agricultural production, colonial trading officials eventually did respond to the scientists' arguments for forest conservation. Groves notes (1992:47) that

> If a single lesson can be drawn from the early history of conservation, it is that states will act to prevent environmental degradation only when their economic interests are shown to be directly affected. Philosophical ideas, science, indigenous knowledge and people and species are, unfortunately, not enough to precipitate such decisions. . . . Our contemporary understanding of the threat to the global environment is thus a reassertion of ideas that reached maturity over a century ago. It is to be regretted that it has taken so long for the warnings of early scientists to be taken seriously.

Interestingly, the cases that Groves refers to include deforestation, desertification, and global as well as local weather changes resulting from overcutting tropical forests in the colonies. A half-century intervened between this global concern and the progressive conservation movement initiated by the scientist Gifford Pinchot and supported by U.S. President Theodore Roosevelt (Hays 1969). In that intervening period, interest in the environment waned. During the Pinchot era that generated another scientifically based conservation movement (leading to the development of modern tree farming), the science addressed primarily local ecosystem problems and issues of producing a single extractive commodity.

What do these older and contemporary preservation and conservation movements have in common, then? Generally, these movements are of two types:

1. Those that seek to isolate parts of ecosystems and protect them from any exchange-value use in social production systems.
2. Those that seek to limit the types of exchange-value uses.

The first are typically labeled *preservation movements,* for they tend to preserve ecosystems from ecological withdrawals and additions. In contrast, the second are more typically seen as *conservation movements,* for they attempt to sustain some market activity, such as soil conservation in agriculture, water conservation in industrial or residential water systems, or timber harvesting. To some extent, each reflects a different superficial relationship to the societal-environmental dialectic. Preservation movements appear to negate the very logic of the treadmill of production, making specific ecosystems unavailable for economic exploitation. Conservation movements appear to accommodate the logic of the treadmill by insuring a steady supply of a particular natural resource, albeit placing limits on the speed of the treadmill.

As the analyses of Chapters 4 and 5 make clear, these distinctions are only superficially meaningful. The system-ness of the treadmill of production offers us a quite different perspective from both of these movement types. It suggests that both types create changes within the treadmill rather than promoting a dismantling of the treadmill. Our reason for this assessment is straightforward: neither preservation nor conservation movements seek to alter the nature of socioeconomic organizations in general and the distribution of power and control over production in particular. They merely limit some types of economic activity in a particular geographic area or limit the use of a particular resource from a local ecosystem.

Ironically, either preservation or conservation can increase the rate of withdrawals from and additions to other ecosystems or other components of ecosystems. For example, when the Redwoods National Parks were created, logging activity in adjacent geographic areas seemed to increase, accelerating the impacts of the treadmill there (Burton 1986). Similarly, in recent years substantial attention has been paid to recycling postconsumer wastes (Schnaiberg 1992), but this effort has often aggravated local pollution problems revolving around remanufacturing facilities

(Gould 1991a). In addition, the energy costs of recycling have been given little attention: it was the so-called landfill crisis that increased political attention to recycling, not a broader concern with environmental degradation. That is, both preservation and conservation movements violate an ecologic of systemic relationships between production systems and ecological systems.

A related way to think about these two types of movements is to consider the social, economic, or political interests that underlie them. Conservation movements often represent a coalescence of economic producers and other social agents in the society. This coalition can include government agencies that support economic development and capital accumulation. This coalition essentially reaffirms the predominance of treadmill values and roles (see Chapter 4). In apparent contrast, many preservation movements reflect passive-aesthetic or active-recreational users, who want to preserve "a piece of the earth" for themselves (Albrecht 1977). But once granted this preserve, they show little interest in the broader ecological disorganization that affects large numbers of people.

It is tempting to argue that, while nineteenth- and early twentieth-century preservationists or conservationists had only limited understanding and goals for protecting environments, more modern movements have improved on both counts (Dunlap & Mertig 1992; Milbrath 1984). The next section qualifies this claim somewhat, although it stresses the uniqueness of modern movements.

MODERN ENVIRONMENTAL MOVEMENT ORGANIZATIONS: SCIENCE VERSUS POLITICS

There is an interesting puzzle in the history of environmental movements. Groves (1992) notes an early period of regional and national concerns in the mid-1800s, and Hays (1969) picks up the history of the progressive conservation movements of the 1905–1915 period. Albrecht (1977) traces the rise of a modern environmental movement some half-century or so after this early twentieth-century movement. Yet all observers of industrial history and ecological change are in loose agreement that for all this nearly 150-year period, there was an acceleration of the treadmill. This upsurge in ecological withdrawals and additions reduced ecological stability throughout industrial nations, as well as in many of their colonies and economic client or dependent states.

Two aspects of this puzzle are of special importance: (1) the role of scientific knowledge in creating, shaping, or supporting environmental policies, and (2) the role of this knowledge in altering the structure of environmental movement organizations. Given the primacy afforded scientific knowledge in modern industrial societies, it is not surprising that environmental problems have often been approached as primarily scientific problems rather than as socioeconomic or political problems. If our current technological complexes produce environmental disruptions, it seems only logical that those disruptions should be examined by natural scientists and solved by engineers. Such a conceptualization, however, ignores the social structural, economic, political, and cultural foundations that result in the development, dissemination, and utilization of environmentally hazardous and destructive technologies.

The difficulties that emerge from a conceptualization of environmental problems as purely scientific in nature are made most apparent when science is utilized on the policy-making level as a basis to justify or delegitimize environmental concerns. For example, the rise of modern recycling was partly supported by the scientific argument that the flow of garbage to landfills would reduce withdrawals and additions. Then scientists turned their attention to finding remanufacturing technologies that would be cost-effective (i.e., profitable). They were not encouraged by the U.S. government or industrial leaders to place their highest priorities on either reduction of wastes or the reuse of wastes, although both paths have had some development under other legal pressures. The most common usages of science in environmental policy-making are in the definition of environmental threats and the assessment of the environmental impacts of various policy decisions. In both roles, however, the scientists' own research priorities are influenced by political and economic mandates and missions, which carry with them scientific funding (Schnaiberg 1977).

One of the most fundamental assumptions of scientific research is that science is objective and politically neutral. It is perceived to be a search for basic truths, and therefore, if done correctly, it will produce facts that are beyond the scope of opinion or ideology. However, because the environmental policy-making process involves competition among various goal-oriented interest groups, often a proliferation of widely divergent scientific analyses are made available to policymakers, as these interest groups provide scientific data to support their political positions (Schnaiberg 1975, 1977, 1980: chs. VI–VII, 1983, 1986; Gould 1988). Environmental organizations, economic actors, public interest groups, and others who have an interest in the ultimate decision regarding a specific environmental policy or project must penetrate substantial political and economic barriers to challenge the scientific rationales used by policymakers (Schnaiberg 1980: ch. VII, 1986). To some extent, they do so by finding other scientists and engineers who take different views. The larger organizations have come to employ their own scientific experts, most of whom are interlocutors between these dissident scientists and the politically mainstream views (Schnaiberg 1977). Some of these movement scientists are themselves dissidents, whose employment terms changed after they challenged the dominant view of their employing organization (Dietz & Rycroft 1987).

From this and similar evidence, we must stress that the rise and fall of environmental protection movements owe far more to socioeconomic and political conditions than to the emergence of scientific evidence of ecological disruptions. Put bluntly, perhaps, the environment does not vote, pay taxes, or raise consciousness by itself. Social action is required to monitor, analyze, and disseminate information about ecological changes. Perhaps even more to the point, ecosystems cannot act on their own behalf: they require social actors to organize themselves in defense of some attributes of ecosystems, based primarily on a set of subjective values that place the environment ahead of the more common economic values promoted by the treadmill. For these reasons we have substantial discontinuities in the historical path of the environmental movement "industry" (Zald & McCarthy 1980) in any single country such as the United States. For these same reasons our comparison of such movements across countries shows such wide variability. Chapters 2 and 5 fleshed out the institutional patterns that have differentiated time periods and places that have been congenial to environmental protection, on the one hand, and treadmill acceleration, on the other.

Thus, although many casual observers have considered it natural that environmental movements emerged in the late 1960s, they misread social and political history. First, the form of mass movements we tend to associate with modern environmentalism did not occur uniformly or linearly across the modern industrial world. As Frances FitzGerald (1979) has noted in her critique of the teaching of U.S. history, such events do not just happen, and their timing and intensity are the result of complex social histories. From World War I until the Vietnam War of the mid-1960s, environmentalism was both present and absent from the U.S. political agenda.

Some observers believe that the question of why environmentalism arose in the 1960s can be answered with the question of why environmentalism declined between 1914 and 1965. Unfortunately, however, the answer to the second question is no clearer than that of the first. A number of factors may have played a part in causing the relative disinterest in the 1914–1965 period. This period, after all, encompassed two world wars and a global economic depression. But then we would also have to argue that the 1960s and 1970s were periods in which other social problems were not primary, which is obviously false. The implementation of certain types of pollution abatement such as mechanisms to separate sewage from drinking water, disposal of waste at sea, tall smokestacks, and other dilution solutions may have mitigated many of the short-term impacts of the treadmill. In addition, the success of the conservation and preservation movements in both insuring a steady stream of natural resources and providing protected areas of natural beauty gave the appearance that ecological problems were being adequately addressed. Nevertheless, such explanations are partial and inconclusive.

We are still left, then, with the question of why the 1960s and 1970s produced an upsurge of environmental concern. One important factor is the rapid expansion of production and consumption in the post–World War II period. The rapid suburban development in this period led to paving over large areas of green spaces around urban centers, displacing farms and recreational areas. This change made "nature" harder to find and more difficult and costly to reach. Rampant consumerism produced an acceleration of waste disposal problems, resulting in litter, landfill, and other unsightly environmental costs. More and more electric appliances sold to more and more households accelerated energy resource depletion problems. And the new materials used in the production of these consumer items resulted in new, often more pernicious ecological additions. Perhaps the turmoil of the Vietnam War, civil rights conflicts, and political assassinations left people longing for what were perceived to be simpler times (Coontz 1992a). An earmark of those quasi-mythical simpler times was a closer connection to the natural world. In addition, as production and consumption accelerated in the postwar era, the ability of ecosystems to absorb negative impacts was overwhelmed as early dilution solutions were similarly strained beyond their capacities. Also, the threat of global thermonuclear war made the concepts of global interdependence and global destruction somewhat more tangible, as did the photos of the earth produced by the Gemini and Apollo space missions. Finally, the lessons in political expression learned through the civil rights and antiwar protests provided citizens new opportunities for the expression of other concerns such as environmental integrity (Morrison 1986).

Whatever the reasons behind it, clearly the 1960s and 1970s witnessed an unprecedented public involvement with some forms of ecological consciousness-raising. Membership in old and new voluntary social movement organizations rose dramatically. The lobbying of national and state legislatures to increase environmental protection followed this increase, heightening public attention to the ecological costs of the cumulative acceleration of the treadmill of production in the post–World War II period.

In the 1960s and early 1970s modern environmentalism incorporated the expansion of older national movement organizations, such as the Sierra Club (founded in 1892), the National Audubon Society (founded in 1905), and the National Parks Association (founded in 1919). It also included new and more confrontational national organizations such as the Environmental Defense Fund (founded in 1968), the Natural Resources Defense Council (founded in 1969), Zero Population Growth (founded in 1969), and Greenpeace (founded in 1972). To make the mixture even headier, new local and regional movement organizations were established in the 1960s and 1970s as well, including the Save-the-Redwoods League (California) and Citizens for a Better Environment (Illinois), and the Adirondack Council (New York). Frustration with the lack of progress in relation to the acceleration of the treadmill led more politicized environmentalists to establish more radical organizations such as Earth First! (founded in 1980). Its founder, David Brower, has more recently moved to create the Earth Island Institute, which has a strong commitment to social justice *and* environmental protection.

The return of relative lack of attention to environmental issues from the start of the first Reagan administration in 1981 to the hot summer of 1988 caused a number of environmental organizations to contract or fragment, as public support for them waned. However, while generalized concern for ecosystems declined, local concern for local hazards grew, and with it emerged a proliferation of small, local grass-roots organizations. From the Home Owners Association of Love Canal, New York, to the rise of minority-led anti-incinerator campaigns in impoverished rural areas and urban centers nationwide, local mobilization against local environmental health hazards grew while national and global concerns shrunk. After the reemergence of environmentalism in 1988, regional, national, and international environmental organizations expanded dramatically. These organizations were challenged to incorporate local concerns and grass-roots groups into a larger network of multilevel organizations, addressing both local problems and their cumulative impact on regional, national, and global ecosystems.

DIVERSITY AMONG VOLUNTARY MOVEMENTS VERSUS THE IMAGE OF ENVIRONMENTALISM

The modern environmental social movement industry (McCarthy & Zald 1977), as it now exists, comprises a variety of international, national, regional, and locally based grass-roots environmental organizations. Many of the regional and national environmental organizations work on both the grass-roots and legislative levels, providing support for locally based environmental groups as well as lobbying, testifying, and providing scientific data in support of increased government attention and action on a wide variety of environmental issues (Gould 1991a).

As mentioned above, locally based environmental groups are usually organized in response to a perceived public health threat resulting from exposure to a local pollution problem rather than from a more general notion of preserving the planet. Local attention to local and immediate environmental contamination episodes is more likely to be based on the local health hazard that each episode may represent rather than the ecosystemic threat that they pose as a group. These more recent local movements focus less on broader issues of ecosystemic integrity or global capacity than do many national and regional environmental organizations. In some instances, locally based groups have even tried to block plans to clean up lakes and rivers, sometimes successfully. This intramovement conflict is often focused on the siting of toxics dredged from other communities' affected bodies of water. The lake or river is often viewed as a better location for toxics than the backyards of local landowners, despite consequences for aquatic remediation. Conflicts along New York's Hudson River are prime examples of this attitude. Clean-up in this area has been blocked by a variety of local interest groups. None of these groups wants to bear the burden of increased environmental hazards locally, in order to improve the environment regionally. Conversely, some community movements often take local action when national or regional organizations are inactive (Dowie 1992; Webster 1992).

The narrower environmental consciousness of the local coalitions often represents a meliorist consciousness in trying to remove a local problem, without challenging the structure of production and consumption that generates these local hazards (Albrecht 1977). National and regional environmental organizations often try to demonstrate the connections between local and broader issues in efforts to raise local environmental consciousness and expand their own constituency. Although the number of local problems and local organizations often precludes an aggressive consciousness-raising campaign in all affected communities, some of these local organizations have broadened their agendas to include more regional, national, and global environmental issues. However, local groups are more often associated with newly discovered toxic wastes that were products of a local industry's history (such as at Love Canal, New York; Times Beach, Missouri; and Port Hope, Ontario) or proposed waste dumps and incinerators, rather than with the reduction of continuing emissions from existing industries. These industries provide jobs for local citizens, tying people into the treadmill and making opposition to them more politically and economically complex (Gould 1991a, 1991b).

The environmental movement encompasses a wide variety of social groups and organizations. As a result, the movement (if it can properly be called that) represents a very loose network of diverse interest groups whose goals occasionally coincide or complement each other (Gould 1991a). The environmental movement may include animal rights advocates, hunting and fishing clubs, Native Americans, labor unions, professional political activists, homemakers, eco-saboteurs, farmers, antinuclear groups, naturalist clubs, and many others. In addition, any specific conflict within the complex network of issues called the environmental problem often draws in other groups that are not usually associated with the environmentalist cause, but have a stake in the outcome (Schnaiberg 1980: ch. IX).

In the antinuclear movement of the late 1970s, for instance, coal miners participated in environmental coalitions to promote indigenous U.S. coal production as a substitute for Middle Eastern oil imports rather than nuclear power (Gould 1991a). The simultaneous public outcry over the hazards of nuclear energy and the increasing price of oil coincided to revive coal development. (Earlier, environmental concerns, focused primarily on acid rain, had put a damper on coal development, especially on high-sulfur coal.) Although the environmental movement did not intend to promote strip mining as an energy alternative to nuclear power, those in the coal industry saw the antinuclear movement as an opportunity to promote their own nonenvironmental economic interests. The emergent alignment with blue-collar coal miners was not overtly opposed by antinuclear activists, but the alignment was of necessity temporary and issue-specific.

Currently, increasing concern among environmentalists about the long-term impacts of fossil fuel consumption on global climate has revived the U.S. nuclear industry. Having been quite successful in preventing the expansion of nuclear power in the United States in the last ten to fifteen years, the environmental movement now finds itself unintentionally aligned with nuclear power developers who are promoting nuclear energy as a clean alternative to carbon-emitting coal and oil-based electricity generation. Although environmental social movement organizations can't control other interests that may try to jump on the environmental bandwagon, they can make efforts to publicly distance themselves from these interests. Such rapidly changing, issue-oriented, temporary, and opportunistic coalitions or political alignments tend to be self-defeating in the long run in terms of promoting environmentally sustainable development. The acid rain issue limited coal development and unintentionally promoted the development of nuclear energy. The nuclear hazards issue then revived coal development, while limiting nuclear power development. The global warming issue is now threatening to limit coal development once again, while unintentionally promoting nuclear power development. In the meantime, oil continues to be the primary energy resource of choice in the United States, with widely fluctuating prices alternatively promoting and undermining the impetus to develop renewable alternatives.

Both the diversity of interests and the resulting instability of large coalitions over time make the environmental movement somewhat less cohesive (though more global in scope) than the American social movements of the 1960s (Gould 1991a). Although the eclectic nature of the antiwar movement presented similar obstacles, the war itself was a unifying issue for a variety of groups. The end of American involvement in the war in Vietnam resulted in the dismantling of this eclectic social movement coalition, as a variety of groups went on to pursue their own specific concerns and interests. Hence, the new left, the flower children, the free speech movement, the women's movement, the environmental movement, the civil rights movement, the back-to-the-land movement, and others were no longer able to maintain a coalition for broad social change. Success in achieving the primary goal of the major unifying issue allowed entropy to split up what might have become a broad-based movement for sweeping social change on a national scale. The environmental movement has produced no similar single leading issue for diverse groups to rally around. Similarly, the civil rights movement of the 1950s and 1960s also produced a diversity of groups and tactics, yet was united behind clearly defined, immediate political goals (Morris 1984). The achievement of those immediate goals—primarily political equality as opposed to economic justice—also fractured the movement, as various groups sought a wider diversity of goals.

The environmental movement's lack of clearly defined unifying goals is partly due to the complex nature of the global environmental condition. The intricate network of environmental problems makes it difficult to define the primary issues. These complex environmental problems are also immutably interwoven with even more complex social and economic problems surrounding issues of social equity. Such overwhelming complexity in problem formation makes finding solutions even more difficult. When solutions are so difficult to identify and goals are so numerous, unity of action among a startling variety of interested parties makes coalition formation and maintenance extremely problematic. Given the powerful forces that promote the treadmill, coalition formation is nonetheless essential if goals are to be achieved in opposition to those forces. The fact that each potential environmental coalition partner has very real stakes in some aspect of the treadmill makes this task even more challenging.

As we have seen, however, the resulting lack of cohesion of the environmental movement has sometimes been used to the movement's advantage, for such flexibility permits "marriages of convenience" in specific resource conflicts (Gould 1991a). These temporary coalitions mobilize the combined power of groups that are usually adversarial but have a common interest in a specific outcome to a specific natural resource conflict. Unfortunately, the power of the treadmill manifests itself in the long-term political outcomes of these issue-specific battles; limiting one area of treadmill expansion often then promotes environmentally destructive expansion in another area. Issue-specific opposition to the treadmill is therefore sometimes analogous to trying to squeeze a balloon: pressure exerted at one end of the balloon tends to produce equal and opposite displacement of air at the other end. The problem then is to find some means to open the inlet to the balloon, to reduce the total volume of air. This is analogous to reducing the volume of influence of the treadmill.

RACE, CLASS, AND ENVIRONMENTAL REMEDIATION:
A TALE OF TWO RIVERS

Washington, D.C., hosts two major rivers. The Potomac River is well known throughout the United States as the U.S. capital's primary river, with the Lincoln Memorial situated prominently on its banks. More than 25 years ago, President Lyndon B. Johnson called for a "fishable and swimmable" Potomac, launching an effort to remediate the polluted waterway. Since then, approximately $1 billion has been spent to clean up the Potomac, with tangible results. However, the nation's capital is also home to another river, the Anacostia. Unlike the Potomac, the Anacostia River is little known outside of the District of Columbia. Also unlike the Potomac, the Anacostia has received neither the attention nor the funding to support extensive environmental remediation. By some accounts, the Anacostia is as polluted today as the Potomac was in the 1960s.

Why is the Anacostia River virtually unknown? Why has it remained extensively degraded while the Potomac has been substantially revitalized? Some experts blame the slow flow of the Anacostia for its inability to cleanse itself. Others blame the draining of wetlands and channelization initiated in the nineteenth century. Yet others offer a third explanation. While the Potomac runs through and past wealthy white neighborhoods, the neighborhoods through which the Anacostia runs are overwhelmingly black and poor. Thus, while the Potomac was attended to, the Anacostia, like the people on its banks, was neglected.

The fate of the Anacostia, in a city in which about two-thirds of the population is black, is generating more environmentalism, a concern generally associated with affluent whites, among blacks as well. In response to the neglect of the Anacostia and to environmental hazards in the black community generally, the African American Environmentalist Association was formed. Its director, Norris McDonald, worked for Friends of the Earth before leaving to form this newer environmental justice organization. He observed that "The powers that be that have worked on pollution have worked on the Potomac but not on the Anacostia." The Anacostia's watershed is home to some 600,000 people, and includes neighborhoods with some of the highest crime and drug-use rates in Washington, D.C.

In a sense, the river's neglect and decay is a marker for the more general neglect and decay of the urban poor and minorities in the United States. Like the socioeconomic problems affecting the communities adjoining the river, the ecological problems affecting the river are complex. And although some remediation efforts have been initiated in recent years, both the river and the communities through which it winds have a long way to go before they can be considered safe and clean environments. In the future, ecological issues are likely to become more and more inextricably linked to social equity issues. This tale of two rivers highlights the need for, and the emergence of, an environmental justice movement, which could become a powerful political force in the years to come.

The web of fluctuating socioenvironmental relationships that comprises the environmental movement is held together primarily by a relatively small network of longer term environmental activists, located in key international, national, and regional organizations throughout the world. Despite the rapidly increasing proportion of the world's population which professes deep concern for the environment, a relatively small network of core activists tends to coordinate most of the coalition formation, agenda setting, and political action of the environmental movement on all but the grass-roots level (Gould 1991a).

As we have seen, the environmental movement is qualitatively different from earlier social movements, both in the scope of the issues it seeks to address and the extreme diversity of interests that flow in and out of it from time to time and from issue to issue. The potential coalition that falls under the environmental umbrella cleaves or coalesces along a number of dimensions simultaneously.

- First, the movement represents a wide variety of issues, from game hunting to environmental racism.
- Second, it represents a wide range of proposed solutions, from recycling to deindustrialization.
- Third, it includes a daunting variety of interest groups, activists, and constituents.
- Lastly, it operates on all levels of action and policy-making, from individual initiatives to global international treaties.

Such a broad and diverse set of problems, goals, participants, and levels of action is unlikely to reproduce the patterns of success or failure of other social movements. Such movement diversity will not even allow us to state any unified criteria for the evaluation of success or failure. Perhaps the best way to assess the impact of the movement will be to look at the condition of the global ecosystem, if and how much it improves, and the ways in which the costs and benefits of improvements are distributed.

DISTRIBUTING ENVIRONMENTAL PROTECTION COSTS: A SOCIAL CHALLENGE TO ENVIRONMENTALISTS

About twenty-five years have now elapsed since the rise of a modern environmental movement in the late 1960s (Dunlap & Mertig 1992; Milbrath 1984). The twentieth anniversary of Earth Day, the United Nations Conference on the Human Environment, and the United Nations Conference on Environment and Development (UNCED) have come and gone. At this point in history, we may conclude that the modern environmental movement has been a startling success. Conversely, we may also conclude that it has been an abysmal failure. Both conclusions are valid, depending on which criterion we use to measure and evaluate success or failure.

From a global overview, it would unquestionably seem that those favoring environmental protection have advanced this struggle over the past two and a half decades. In the bluntest terms, it would appear that future historians will view the last third of the twentieth century as the environmentalist epoch (Hays 1985). However, there are two stories one can tell about the past twenty-five years. The optimistic story begins with the spate of U.S. environmental legislation in the 1968–1972 period. It continues with the rise of an international movement for appropriate technology (see Chapter 8) and the limits to growth movement, and the presence of student, grass-roots, and large multinational interest groups of the late 1980s. It reaches a crescendo with the 1987 Bruntland Commission report on sustainable development and the 1992 Rio conference. This scenario almost always includes new controls on air and water pollution, heightened regulation and clean-up of toxic wastes, protection of endangered species, and the process of environmental impact assessment as an enduring component of public and much private sector decision making (Schnaiberg et al. 1992).

In sharp contrast is the less optimistic overview. During this same period, we have seen increases in the extinction of species worldwide, acid rainfall and forest destruction in industrial nations, deforestation in large parts of the South, and desertification in a variety of regions globally. Growing inequalities between industrial and developing countries have intensified pressures on primary producers, leading to an acceleration of ecosystem extraction for subsistence and exports. In addition, we have observed new patterns of international nuclear contamination through atmospheric flows following the Chernobyl accident in the Ukraine and high casualties from the Bhopal toxic chemical release in India. Moreover, the global warming assertions and ozone depletion scenarios that some natural scientists tentatively accepted a decade ago appear to have garnered more scientific consensus. Thus, global animal and human populations are now seen at increased risk for skin cancers due to ozone "holes" and the subsequent global rise of ultraviolet radiation. Indeed, recent decades have seen such a rise in environmental problems that a kind of global epidemic is now perceived to be occurring. The pace of the increase in environmental problems has outstripped the pace of the increase in global responses to these problems (Schnaiberg et al. 1992).

Environmental protection efforts occur in a national and global system characterized by tensions between economic development and environmental protection. The modern environmental movement, by choosing to deal with these tensions by ignoring them, alienated a large segment of its possible constituency. It forced itself into a situation in which it was proposing policy options that had limited positive environmental impacts and regressive social impacts. Even so, the strategies employed by the movement have allowed it to become a player in the political arena. As such, the movement has created some limited, though significant, gains that are important not for what they have done to safeguard the environment, but for what they could allow the movement to achieve in the future (Schnaiberg et al. 1992).

As we view the past twenty-five years of U.S. environmentalism, two features emerge as most significant: (1) the volatility of membership in individual movement organizations, especially in movement coalitions in any specific environmental policy arena, and (2) the continuing underrepresentation of working- and lower-class groups and minorities in general in environmental movement organizations and in their fleeting coalitions. (Possible exceptions are local groups organized for a short time around local health concerns about hazardous wastes.) Thus, for example, environmentalists have been talking about a coalition with labor groups on and off for these past twenty-five years, but there is no continuity of any such coalition (Schnaiberg et al. 1992).

The problem is that the agenda, rhetoric, and assumptions of most mainstream environmental movement organizations often fail to represent the concerns of the less empowered groups in modern societies. One advantage that minority group members and organizations can bring to environmental movement organizations is the well-grounded expectation that government agencies do not normally take citizens' concerns into account in their regular policy-making (Krauss 1992). This suggests that the bulk of the membership in the environmental movement consists of those middle-, upper-middle, and upper-class individuals who expect government agencies to take such views seriously in policy-making. This may be due, in part, to their experiences in other arenas (primarily economic), where they find that government often does act in their interests.

An equally important problem for the environmental movement is that it deals with ecological changes rather than with the distribution of costs and benefits of the economic changes necessary to produce environmental protection. By doing so, environmental protection places the movement at odds with the notion of environmental justice. This alternative notion entails some positive redistribution of economic resources in order to gain the support needed to achieve ecological goals (Bryant & Mohai 1992).

The difficulty in promoting policy proposals that benefit the poor is that those groups benefiting more from the status quo strongly resist giving up their wealth and income to protect the environment, while at the same time often donating tax-deductible "mail-order membership" money to environmental organizations. Furthermore, the privileged few have the political, social, and economic power to effectively thwart domestic environmental policy proposals. They do so either by opposing such environmentalist proposals or by ensuring that, if the proposals are enacted, they are either not implemented or, if implemented, that the costs of these are redistributed to less powerful groups.

Environmental movement organizations have responded to this problem in a number of ways. In terms of pushing for environmental protection, (1) some organizations have retreated from all attempts at influencing policy and have instead engaged only in voluntary alternative behaviors, such as reducing their own energy and product consumption; or (2) other organizations have attempted to persuade elite groups that it is in the long-term interests of the treadmill to plan for environmental protection, in order to protect their investments. With regard to the dilemma of placing the bulk of the burden of environmental protection on the working class and poor, many movement organizations have (3) retreated from this issue by ignoring such concerns and keeping their distance from less powerful social groups and organizations, or (4) in rare instances, a handful of organizations have tried to build stronger coalitions to oppose treadmill elites by coupling environmental goals with economically and politically redistributive means in an effort to integrate environmental and distributive issues in a single major strategy. These alternative strategies are outlined in Table 7.1 on p. 158.

Many environmental movement organizations profess to be saving the earth for the good of all. When attacked by powerful economic interest groups, which cite the environmentalists' threats to employment, wages, and taxes, the standard response of most environmental groups is to claim that they are acting in the name of broader environmentally-impacted social constituencies, or to deny that any negative economic impacts are associated with environmental protection measures. Frequently overlooked in these claims is that these same environmental protection movements have two kinds of environmentally impacted constituencies: social groups who are victims of environmental degradation, who suffer from diminished use-values of their ecosystems; and social groups who are distributive victims of environmental protection, who may suffer from diminished exchange-value (market) returns from their labor or their local investments, such as jobs, wages, and home values. Recent controversies over the protection of the northern spotted owl by limiting Pacific Northwestern lumbering reflect these socioeconomic realities (Schnaiberg et al. 1992).

Note that we do not argue here that these environmental protection efforts are reprehensible. We simply point out the social impacts of such ecological protection in a context where the environmental movements involved have not proposed any environmental justice program. Such a program might recommend using the federal revenues currently dedi-

TABLE 7.1 Environmental Movement Types: Goals, Assumptions, and Strategies

Structuralist or radical	mobilize to defeat economic elites and the treadmill of production. · key assumption: "most citizens" benefit. · Collective action in *opposition* to the treadmill.
Retreatist or deep ecologist	transform society through appropriate technology and voluntary simplicity. · key assumption: "everyone" benefits. · Individual and small group actions in *opposition* to the treadmill.
Reformist	modify production to substantially reduce environmental problems. · key assumption: "citizens" and investors have equal stakes in production and environmental protection. · Cooperative action *with* treadmill elites.
Meliorist	"buy green," and other consumer actions. · key assumption: consumption leads production. · Individual actions *within* the treadmill.
Cosmetologist	recycle "litter." · key assumption: the government will take care of problems. · Individual action *only* as directed by treadmill elites.
Social equity	the problem is economic survival, not environmental protection. · key assumption: poorer people need to have their basic needs met. · Support of the treadmill *only* insofar as more jobs and income flow to the unempowered.
Anti-environmentalist	the problem is environmental alarmists, not the environment. · key assumption: the market will automatically internalize any short-term problems. · No environmental protection action, and/or individual and collective action in *support* of treadmill.

cated to subsidizing logging by large lumber corporations to retrain, relocate, or subsidize potentially dislocated workers or to create local employment alternatives to logging.

One interpretation of this environmental protection history is that environmental movements have been more successful in getting issues on the broad political agenda than in getting policies institutionalized within this agenda. The good news for environmental reformers is that there is some form of cultural and/or political legitimacy to a consideration of environmental protection policies. Environmental concerns can no longer be casually devalued and ignored. However, this also represents some bad news, since the price of this legitimacy is that most environmental movement organizations have obtained it by failing to engage in the politics of environmental justice. That is, environmental movements are necessarily distributive movements, influencing the allocation of increasingly scarce natural resources among and between users. By not raising new social standards for such access, environmental movements have often become negatively redistributive movements, aligning themselves with large-scale capital interests and government bureaucracies against the interests of organized and unorganized labor, the poor, and minority groups. Ironically, this practice recapitulates the "progressive conservation" strategy during Teddy Roosevelt's administration (Hays 1969), which presaged the long decline of U.S. environmentalism from 1914 to 1965.

This present alignment disempowers the environmental movement in two ways. First, opponents of environmental protection can point to the socially regressive outcomes of protection policies. They can thereby mobilize more workers and social equity movements in opposition to environmental protection. Second, environmental movement organizations forfeit some active support by these groups for environmental reform with social justice (positive redistribution, or at least equitable distribution of burdens). Building environmentalist political legitimacy on relationships with economic elites is a highly restricting and contradictory action. While there may be temporary alliances in support of one or another environmental protection policy, the long-term trends between economic elites and environmental movements are undergirded by contradictory principles (Bryant & Mohai 1992; Hays 1969).

In almost no instances is a sustained, equalized coalition formed between environmental movement organizations and those of labor, lower working classes, minorities, or the poor, who represent a huge, though underrepresented, portion of the American population. Therefore, the environmental gains of the past twenty-five years have been limited and somewhat costly. The challenge to environmentalists now is to include a strong social agenda, as well as an environmental one, in their political goals. This agenda would reflect the social needs of a more diverse set of less powerful constituencies, who in turn would become political resources for the new environmental movement organizations. These less powerful groups cannot offer movement organizations much financial support or even, in most cases, the capacity to spend large amounts of time on the organizations' administrative and litigative protests and negotiations. Yet these groups may have the potential to be mobilized for elections and for some crucial public protests. The benefit to the more middle-class movement participants is political support in return for political leverage with treadmill elites in distributive conflicts. Labor groups may thus trade off their support for community pollution abatement in return for environmentalists' support for enhanced workplace safety or tariffs on foreign imports. Poverty groups may help picket city hall in protest over toxic waste dumps in return for environmentalists' support of their fears about incinerator operations in poor neighborhoods (Bullard 1992).

One reason why the movement is apparently unable to limit the expansionist tendencies of the treadmill is the environmentalists' conspicuous failure to link their ecological agendas with the socioeconomic needs of workers, minorities, and the poor. In effect, environmentalists have formed an uneasy alliance with some representatives of the treadmill to achieve a limited form of political legitimacy (Mitchell 1980). Because many environmental organizations have formed alliances that juxtapose the dominant expansionary interests of the treadmill and movements seeking to limit this expansion, the ecological protection potential of these movements is rather restricted. At the same time, this alliance produces a growing body of antagonists to environmental protection, since the less powerful are essentially marginalized in this alliance (Bullard 1993).

Nevertheless, the potential for a truly legitimized and actually sustainable environmental movement in the future remains. The core difference between the historical past and the foreseeable future of environmental movements lies in the ratio of social to environmental targets of the environmentalists' agenda (Hays 1969, 1985). But this shift is a major one, which will require more than just a mere adjustment of the movement organizations' tactics. It will require a new strategy, and perhaps new leadership and quite different modes of recruiting, socializing, and mobilizing old and new constituencies. In the process, at least initially, environmental protection goals may become more modest, as efforts shift to creating new movement relationships for an enduring environmental justice coalition. When not linked to the interests of the treadmill elites, environmental goals will be harder to achieve, for the forces mobilized against the attainment of these goals will be greater and more vociferous (Bullard 1992, 1993).

This discussion presents two sobering realities for environmental movement organizations: (1) no other coalition partner will be as uniformly committed to the ecological goals of environmental movement organizations, and (2) to achieve coalitions with any other partner, environmentalists must modify the primacy of strictly environmental protection goals and negotiate with the social and economic agendas of other partners. This will necessitate the development of attractive economic alternatives to current treadmill development trajectories.

If environmentalists form new and enduring coalitions with labor, community, or social equity movement groups or organizations, they actually have a greater chance of dominating the agenda, through political veto power over economic elites and their government supporters. This requires, in return, mobilizing environmentalists to support labor, community, or social equity goals as part of the environmental agenda of environmental justice. This model represents a quite different political process, one that is absolutely saturated with enduring conflicts. This model is one of enduring vigilance, repeated mobilization, painful negotiations of priorities, and sustained conflict with dominant economic and political institutions and their representatives (Bullard 1992, 1993; Bryant & Mohai 1992). In the absence of any of these traits, backsliding will occur rather rapidly, since it is unlikely in the foreseeable future that ecological use-values will ever replace expansionary exchange-values as the dominant political and economic culture.

The current environmental movement organizations are limited for a number of reasons. Specifically, many environmentalists have entered environmental movements after little previous political or social experience with dissent. Thus, the reluctance of environmentalists to engage in serious resistance to economic and political elites is understandable. Many of these environmentalists sought to avoid political conflicts, and environmentalism was a way of becoming active without entering into major conflicts with powerful elites, many of whom they have at least weak ties to and with whom they share many values. Conversely, they are more remote from a broader mass of the citizenry, engaged in "dirty work"— blue-collar, semiskilled, or marginal—and whose concerns are less about culture and the environment and more about economic survival.

Moving towards an emphasis on environmental justice will require many shifts within and between environmental constituencies. Many old participants would be likely to drop out of the movement organizations, and new minority, female, and social equity participants would be incorporated. These are not easy changes. But the alternative of remaining at the present levels of socioenvironmental change is a commitment to a very limited agenda. It is one that greater segments of the population will increasingly resist, for this type of scarcity becomes magnified by shifts in the world economic system, which will impose even more limits on organized labor and the poor. Resistance is likely to grow from economic elites as well, except for those industries whose products are themselves forms of environmental protection technology. In either case, conflicts with regard to environmental protection will grow. But only where these environmental industries are active will it be possible to build enough of a political base to challenge the dominance of the treadmill enthusiasts within the policy arena. Such sustainable resistance to the treadmill will necessitate greater government responsiveness, if only to achieve political legitimacy in the eyes of its constituents.

This possibility must also be tempered by the fact that environmental protection will have to be negotiated in conjunction with social distribution, which may even entail temporary withdrawals of some environmental protection policies that have placed an undue burden on the working class, minorities, and poor. One means by which this shift may occur is through the intervention of a declining middle class (Barlett & Steele 1992; Ehrenreich 1990; Galbraith 1992). Recent distributive evidence confirms that the acceleration of the treadmill in recent decades has increasingly redistributed wealth and income away from the professional-technical-middle management levels of the middle-middle class. Many members of this group are at risk of drifting into the working class, while only a small portion are moving up into the upper-middle class, which is increasingly resembling the upper class itself. The displaced middle class, which is educated and somewhat environmentalist, will increasingly have a dual interest in challenging the treadmill. For not only does the treadmill consume the environment, but it is increasingly consuming the U.S. middle class that emerged after World War II as well (Ehrenreich 1990). The outcomes of a new direction for the environmental movement will be variable, but they should lead to an enhanced form of environmental protection and socioenvironmental justice.

SELECTED REFERENCES

ALBRECHT, STAN
  1977   "The environment as a social problem." Ch. 15 in Armand L. Mauss, editor, *Social Problems as Social Movements*. Philadelphia: J. B. Lippincott Co.
BARLETT, DONALD L. & J. B. STEELE
  1992   *America: What Went Wrong?* Kansas City, MO: Andrews & McMeel.
BARRINGER, FELICITY
  1991   "In capital, no. 2 river is a cause." *New York Times*, November 30th.
BROWN, PHIL & E. J. MIKKELSON
  1990   *Toxic Waste, Leukemia, and Community Action.* Berkeley: University of California Press.
BULLARD, ROBERT D.
  1992   *People of Color Environmental Groups Directory.* Riverside, CA: Department of Sociology, University of California, Riverside.
  1993   *Confronting Environmental Racism: Voices from the Crossroads,* (ed), Boston, MA: South End Press.
BRYANT, BUNYAN & P. MOHAI, EDITORS
  1992   *Race and the Incidence of Environmental Hazards: A Time for Discourse.* Boulder, CO: Westview Press.
BURTON, DUDLEY J.
  1986   "Contradictions and changes in labour response to distributional implications of environmental-resource policies." Pp. 287–314 in A. Schnaiberg, N. Watts, and K. Zimmermann, editors, *Distributional Conflicts in Environmental-Resource Policy.* Aldershot, England: Gower Publishing.
COONTZ, STEPHANIE
  1992a   *The Way We Never Were: American Families and the Nostalgia Trap.* New York: Basic Books.

DIETZ, THOMAS & R. W. RYCROFT
1987   *The Risk Professionals.* New York: Russell Sage Foundation.
DOWIE, MARK
1992   "The new face of environmentalism: As big environmental organizations dodder, the movement's energy shifts to the grass roots." *Utne Reader,* July/August: 104–111.
DUNLAP, RILEY E. AND ANGELA G. MERTIG, EDITORS
1992   *American Environmentalism: The U.S. Environmental Movement, 1970–1990,* Bristol, PA: Crane Russak.
EHRENREICH, BARBARA
1990   *Fear of Falling: The Inner Life of the Middle Class.* New York: Harper Perennial.
FITZGERALD, FRANCES
1979   *America Revised: History Schoolbooks in the Twentieth Century.* Boston: Little, Brown.
GALBRAITH, JOHN KENNETH
1992   *The Culture of Contentment.* Boston: Houghton Mifflin.
GOULD, KENNETH A.
1988   "The politicization of science in the environmental impact statement process." *Wisconsin Sociologist* 25 (4):139–143.
1991a   "Money, management and manipulation: Environmental mobilization in the Great Lakes Basin." Doctoral dissertation, Department of Sociology, Northwestern University, Evanston, IL, June.
1991b   "The sweet smell of money: Economic dependency and local environmental political mobilization." *Society and Natural Resources* 4:133–150.
GOULD, KENNETH A. AND ADAM WEINBERG
1991   "Who mobilizes whom?: The role of national and regional social movement organizations in local environmental political mobilization." Paper presented at the annual meetings of the American Sociological Association, Cincinnati, August.
GROVES, RICHARD H.
1992   "Origins of Western environmentalism." *Scientific American,* July:42–47.
HAYS, SAMUEL P.
1969   *Conservation and the Gospel of Efficiency: The Progressive Conservation Movement, 1890–1920.* New York: Atheneum Books.
1985   "From conservation to environment." In *Environmental History,* edited by Kendall E. Bailes. New York: University of America Press.
KRAUSS, CELENE
1992   "Women and toxic waste protests: Race, class and gender as resources of resistance." Paper presented at the annual meetings of the American Sociological Association, Pittsburgh, August.
MCCARTHY, JOHN D. & M. N. ZALD
1977   "Resource mobilization and social movements: A partial theory." *American Journal of Sociology* 82 (6):1212–1241.
MILBRATH, LESTER W.
1984   *Environmentalists: Vanguard for a New Society.* Albany: State University of New York Press.
MITCHELL, ROBERT C.
1980   "How 'soft', 'deep', or 'left'? Present constituencies in the environmental movement." *Natural Resources Journal* 20 (April):345–358.
MORRIS, ALDON D.
1984   *The Origins of the Civil Rights Movement: Black Communities Organizing for Change.* New York: Free Press.

MORRISON, DENTON E.
1986   "How and why environmental consciousness has trickled down." Pp.
        187–220 in A. Schnaiberg, N. Watts, and K. Zimmermann, editors, *Distributional Conflicts in Environmental-Resource Policy.* Aldershot, England:
        Gower Publishing.
NEWHOUSE, JOHN
1992   "The diplomatic round: Earth summit." *The New Yorker,* June 1:64–78.
SCHNAIBERG, ALLAN
1975   "Social syntheses of the societal-environmental dialectic: The role of
        distributional impacts." *Social Science Quarterly* 56 (June):5–20.
1977   "Obstacles to environmental research by scientists and technologists: A
        social structural analysis." *Social Problems* 24 (5):500–520.
1980   *The Environment: From Surplus to Scarcity.* New York: Oxford University
        Press.
1983   "Soft energy and hard labor? Structural restraints on the transition to
        appropriate technology." Pp. 217–234 in Gene F. Summers, editor, *Technology and Social Change in Rural Areas.* Boulder, CO: Westview Press.
1986   "The role of experts and mediators in the channeling of distributional
        conflicts." Pp. 348–362 in A. Schnaiberg, N. Watts, and K. Zimmermann,
        editors, *Distributional Conflicts in Environmental-Resource Policy.* Aldershot,
        England: Gower Publishing.
1992   "Recycling vs. remanufacturing: Redistributive realities." Working paper
        WP-92-15, Center for Urban Affairs & Policy Research, Northwestern
        University, Spring.
SCHNAIBERG, ALLAN, KENNETH A. GOULD & ADAM WEINBERG
1992   "Losing the environmental battle but winning the legitimacy war: A
        revisionist analysis of 'the environmental movement'." Paper presented
        at the annual meetings of the American Sociological Association, Pittsburgh, August.
WEBSTER, DONOVAN
1992   "Sweet home Arkansas: In Bill Clinton's backyard, a determined band
        of down-home activists proves the power of Green politics." *Utne Reader,*
        July/August: 112–116.
ZALD, MAYER N. & J. D. McCARTHY
1980   "Social movement industries: Competition and cooperation among movement organizations." *Research in Social Movements, Conflicts, and Change*
        3:1–20.

8. Opting Out or Waiting to Enter?: The Underdeveloped Countries

UNDERDEVELOPMENT AND THE NATIONS OF THE SOUTH: THE ABSENCE OF A TREADMILL?

The world today is very different from the world of the eighteenth and nineteenth centuries. This statement may appear to be incredibly obvious and simple, but if we accept it as true, we will be forced to revise most of the common notions of Third World development and modernization. For if the world of today is different from that of the past, we cannot expect nations struggling to develop at the end of the twentieth century to have the same experiences as those nations that developed in centuries gone by. If development in the present time must be experienced differently from development in the past, the developing nations of the South, if they are to achieve development at all, will inevitably do so in ways that are new, different, and largely unprecedented (Chilcote 1984). The differences between the world of the past and the world of the present (and future) include complex changes in the state of the world economy, technological innovation, and the natural environment (Amin 1974, 1976).

"In fourteen hundred and ninety-two, Columbus sailed the ocean blue." (After that, all hell breaks loose.) In the centuries before Columbus, the center of world commerce, industry, art, and science was in the East. The peoples of the nations surrounding the Indian Ocean and the China Sea were involved in an elaborate system of world trade. Goods produced in one region were transported by ship or by caravan to other regions, where they would be exchanged for local goods or exotic imports from yet more distant lands. Columbus's accidental landing in the West Indies of the New World was in reality a failed attempt to find a Western route to the Far East. He simply did not expect the continents of North and South America to be there.

Shortly after Columbus's remarkable, though mistaken, journey, Vasco da Gama chose to take the simpler route to the East, following the coast of Africa, rounding the Cape of Good Hope, and arriving as the first European voyager to sail into the Indian Ocean. The Portuguese had come in search of the wealth of the Indian Ocean trade and so proceeded to plunder that wealth with great abandon. The conquest of East Africa's Swahili coast, the west coast of India, and points even further east disrupted the Indian Ocean trading network. In conquering the region, the Portuguese destroyed the basis on which the wealth that attracted them rested. Although Portuguese colonies remained for centuries to follow (some even to this day), the fortunes of these early explorers waned. Thus began the underdevelopment of the South.

Although the colonial histories of Africa, Asia, and Latin America vary in time and nature, all share the negative social, economic, and environmental impacts of the colonial experience (Bunker 1985; Groves 1992). The *conquistadores* plundered the wealth of the pre-Columbian civilizations of Latin America. French, Dutch, and English settlers displaced and decimated the populations of North America, while Africa and Asia were treated to a second round of colonial exploitation in the eighteenth and nineteenth centuries. The fabled "barbarism" of Africa evolved from British perceptions of the continent following the impact of the earlier Portuguese conquest. The continent itself was carved up by European powers in the "scramble for Africa" in 1895.

The colonialists' primary goal was to enrich themselves and their nations by removing anything of value from the South and repatriating that wealth to the North. The plunder of the wealth of the South was essential in subsidizing the development of Europe and the industrial revolution (Rodney 1982). The center of world commerce, science, art, and trade had shifted north to Europe and North America, producing the world economy that we are familiar with today. In many ways, this continuing subsidy helped form the basis for the modern treadmill of production. Expanding industrial investment in the North was funded from colonial profits, and this industrial-military expansion facilitated still more colonial ecosystem withdrawals.

What we refer to here as the South has been commonly referred to as the Third World. When Western political theorists developed a system of categorization for the nations of the world in the twentieth century, they designated the capitalist West as the First World, the communist East as the Second World, and the impoverished unaligned nations of the rest of the globe as the Third World (Horowitz 1972). Since the collapse of communism in the East and the new alliances between East and West, these political categories have lost much of their meaning. While some rough correlation between these designations and levels of wealth remains, it is probably more analytically useful to think of the world as being roughly divided into two basic parts.

The North is relatively wealthy, industrialized, technologically advanced, and militarily powerful. The South, with the exception of Australia and New Zealand which are more properly understood as Northern nations in geographic "exile," is characterized as being relatively poor, technologically less complex, agrarian, militarily weak, and, ultimately, economically dependent on the North. The South is also home to the overwhelming majority of the world's people. It contains the bulk of the world's land area as well as the bulk of the world's species and other natural resources (Seligson 1984).

Since the end of World War II, the majority of the colonies of the South have achieved the status of independent, sovereign nations, either through revolutionary rebellion or European disinterest. Most of the nations of the world are now located in the South. Being relatively (and absolutely in many cases) impoverished, most of these new nations have sought modernization or development as their primary goal. Although these terms are fuzzy in their precise meaning, broadly speaking they imply an overall increase in economic power, military might, and technological capacity to withdraw ecosystem elements (Evans 1979; Frank 1979).

In order to achieve development, these nations have attempted to move away from their traditional social, economic, and political arrangements, and their relationship to the natural world, toward what the West has portrayed as modernity. In the decades immediately following World War II, traditional societies were characterized by the West as being rural, tribal, agricultural, and authoritarian. They were typified by low levels of energy and natural resource consumption and low gross national product (GNP). In the West they were (and are) viewed as old-fashioned, backward, and ultimately inferior in comparison to the North. Western development experts contrasted this picture with the modernity of the nations of the North. Those nations were typified by high levels of urbanization, industrial economies, and democratic political systems. They had achieved tremendous technological complexity, high levels of energy and other natural resource consumption, and high GNP. As such, those who lived there held them to be advanced, modern, and ultimately superior to their impoverished Southern neighbors (Emmanuel 1972).

MODERNIZATION DRIVES: THE FUTILE SEARCH FOR A SOUTHERN TREADMILL

In attempting to achieve greater levels of modernization, the governments of Southern nations sought to reproduce the treadmill of production that existed in the nations of the North (Horowitz 1972). The governments and corporations of the North strongly encouraged modernization, for such changes would create new markets for the sale of Northern goods, new labor pools to be used in production, and new opportunities for profitable investment. The primary mechanism through which such efforts were manifested was the transfer of modern Western industrial technologies from North to South. It was believed that transplanting industrialization would lead to the emergence of other aspects of modernity such as democracy, urbanization, and ever increasing levels of wealth. Modernization theory, which was supported by Western governments, Western industries, and international development agencies, held that, by making initial investments in high-technology electrical power generation and industrial facilities, the process of modernization experienced in the West in earlier centuries could be replicated in the South (Horowitz 1972; Portes & Walton 1981). Nations of the South were encouraged to take loans to invest in these technology transfers. Experts predicted that the resulting industrial development would shortly produce enough wealth in each nation to repay the debts incurred, leaving enough wealth remaining in the South to invest in further industrialization (Mazrui 1986). Unfortunately, the experts were wrong (Redclift 1984).

Modernization theory promoted the belief that the South could mimic the development process experienced by the North. What it failed to account for were the dramatic changes in global circumstances that had occurred in the intervening century or two. It also failed to account for the environmental degradation resulting from development in the North and the impact that a replication of that process in the South would have on global resources and the global environment (Redclift 1984). This in turn could have negative impacts on the North as well as the South.

Modernization theory guided Western foreign policy and development strategies for decades, resulting in a variety of undesired social, economic, political, and environmental outcomes (Portes & Walton 1981). Some of the reasons for these undesired outcomes are as follows:

- It was assumed that the industrial nations of the North would have a modernizing impact on the South. However, history has shown that, in many instances, the North's impact was to reverse modernizing trends in the South. As you have seen, the impact of Portuguese colonialism in the Indian Ocean region destroyed a very modern, complex, and sophisticated system of international trade. Other interactions with the North yielded similar results. The British bombarded Chinese ports to force open new markets for their lucrative opium trade. The result of British opium sales in China was the gradual collapse of Chinese social structures, thus reversing the trend toward modernity in the region that had led all others in the development of the arts, sciences, and technology.

- The desire of the colonial powers to develop the South as a source of raw materials and new markets distorted development in the South by gearing these societies to meet Northern rather than local needs. The wealth of the South was used to finance the further development of the North, therefore impoverishing the South and precluding local development (Rodney 1982). The quest to extract natural resources from the South also promoted previously unparalleled levels of environmental destruction. Wildlife was depleted to provide furs, skins, feathers, ivory, and other animal products for Northern consumers. Forests and grasslands were converted to cash crop agricultural production, providing lumber, coffee, tea, sugar, bananas, rubber, cocoa, textiles, and other goods for markets in the North. Such transformation of the local environments was promoted with little or no understanding of local conditions. As a result, these agricultural enterprises often had devastating impacts on local soils and watersheds. Minerals were mined and transported to Europe and North America, leaving the terrain of the South scarred and useless. None of these extractive enterprises produced capital for development of the regions from which they were taken. They also left the South with infrastructures designed to take wealth out of the South rather than to promote reinvestment in local development (Slater 1974). Cities were developed on coasts to promote the transport of raw materials northward. Railroads and roads were constructed to bring goods from the interior to the ports. The built environment was in this way established to promote Northern, not Southern, development.

- What the societies of the North thought of as characteristics of modernity often proved to be idiosyncrasies of those societies, not attributes of development (Horowitz 1972). The wide geometric grid of streets in Northern cities was reproduced in the South to replace primitive networks of seemingly haphazard winding narrow roads, the Northern style being considered more modern (Alexander 1983). However, wide streets in temperate Europe served to maximize exposure to sunlight. In the tropical and arid climates of the South, maximizing exposure to sunlight resulted in insufferably hot and unpleasant living conditions. Similarly, straight roads constructed in a gridlike pattern may have appeared to be rational in the North, but in the South, seasonal weather patterns create powerful wind tunnels in these streets. A winding network of narrow streets provides a buffer against the winds and shade from the sun. It rarely occurred to colonialists and development "experts" that people in the South might actually have known what they were doing.

- In addition, the global context of development is very different for the South in the twentieth century than it had been for Europe in earlier centuries. European industrialists in the eighteenth and nineteenth centuries did not have to compete in a global market with already vast and powerful industrial economic actors. In contrast, the South entered into this competition already far behind the North's economic and technological leaders. Imagine a small entrepreneur living in East Africa seeking to develop a new business. She sees a local market available to her that might create the demand for her new product. She may even have enough capital to begin a small-scale manufacturing enterprise. However, she enters into this market having to compete with large multinational corporate producers located in the North. Despite the lower cost of local production, local labor, and local marketing, the multinationals, having vast markets and a vast amount of capital, can afford to undercut her price and force her out of the market. Once she goes out of business, the multinationals can then raise the price to regular market levels and resume making local profits, which are returned to the North. This example serves to illustrate the enormous differences in the economic context of development experienced by the South in the twentieth century.

• As you can see, what is good for Northern capital-investing multinational corporations is not necessarily good for Southern development goals. In order to protect the local small company mentioned above, the East African nation would have to prevent the multinationals from entering its market or place tariffs on the imported product. Militarily and economically powerful nations in the North vehemently oppose such measures as protectionist and antithetical to free trade. The power of the Northern nations and corporations is often too great for relatively weak nations to oppose (Seligson 1984).

Another example of this conflict of interests can be found in the history of Ghana's aluminum smelting project. Ghana is a small nation on the west coast of Africa. Northern governments, Northern corporations, and international lending and development institutions encouraged Ghana's government to invest in the aluminum industry. Ghana has a rich supply of bauxite, the material from which aluminum is derived. A Northern corporation, in cooperation with the Ghanaian government, constructed a modern aluminum smelting plant there. It was hoped that the plant would encourage the development of local bauxite mining, aluminum can manufacturing, and beef production (which was to be canned in Ghana and exported to Northern beef consumers). However, the corporation involved already owned an interest in bauxite mines in Jamaica. It also owned ships to transport that bauxite. Rather than developing a local mining industry, the corporation found it cheaper to ship ore from Jamaica to Ghana, thus precluding the emergence of an indigenous mining industry. In addition, the local people did not want to sell their beef for canning, so rather than canning Ghanaian beef, the industry imported beef, which it already owned, thus precluding the development of a Ghanaian beef export industry. The only local input into the Ghanaian aluminum smelter was cheap labor and the capital investment of the relatively impoverished Ghanaian government. In the end, the nation was left in deep debt to the North, with only a few relatively low-wage jobs to show for the investment. The profits from the enterprise were largely retained by the Northern-based corporation (Mazrui 1986).

The international scope of capital and industry in the late twentieth century thus hinders Southern development in a way that European nations in prior centuries did not experience. The irony here is that, had the project gone as Ghana had planned, the result would have been local development, but at great expense to the local environment. Mining produces a variety of ecological problems, including the clearing of forest, contamination of water supplies, and often toxic tailings piles. Cattle ranching promotes the clearing of forests and indigenous species, land degradation, and soil erosion. It also takes land out of agricultural production of food for indigenous peoples.

• As this illustration has demonstrated, Northern development schemes often fail to account for the global context in which they must operate. They also often fail to incorporate local environmental conditions. Modernization theory promoted the belief that by transplanting industrial technologies to Southern nations, development could be seeded. The foundation of any modern industrial technology is energy. Therefore, electric power generation was (and is) often seen as the most essential element in modernization. The South is littered with huge, centralized, expensive hydroelectric power dams that the South was encouraged to invest in. Unfortunately, cheap electric power does not necessarily result in industrial investments; other factors often outweigh the benefits of cheap power in industrial equations. In addition, lack of knowledge about local conditions often leads foreign engineers to design and construct projects that are ill suited to the local natural environments.

For example, the Oskombo dam on the Volta River in Ghana was constructed as the foundation of an elaborate post-independence industrial development scheme, which included the aluminum smelting operation described above. The dam flooded a huge portion of Ghana's interior, submerging farm land, forests, and the species that inhabited them. Unfortunately, Northern engineers had measured rainfall in abnormally wet years. They failed to consult the farmers of Ghana, perhaps feeling that Western experts had nothing to learn from "backward" African peasants. The dam that the experts constructed generates almost no electricity because the water behind it fails to rise to the level needed to turn the turbines (Mazrui 1986). Similar engineering failures can be found in nearly every nation of the South. They produce little in the way of economic development, but the loans that paid for their construction still cost these poor nations billions of dollars in debt servicing. That money is sent north to the wealthiest nations on earth (Oxaal et al. 1975).

- These engineering failures are the result of limited knowledge of local environments. Modernization theorists failed to recognize the significant differences between the environments of the North and the South, as well as the differences between the various nations of the South. Although the contrasts between the desert nation of Egypt and the tropical rainforests of Brazil may seem obvious to us, modernization theory held that development would, could, and should be the same in all nations. Both Brazil and Egypt host huge hydroelectric dams, built by Northern engineers, that have produced little economic growth but massive ecological harm. Nevertheless, nations of both the South (like China) and the North (like Canada) continue to destroy irreplaceable ecosystems with questionable hydropower development schemes.

Clearly, modernization theory ignored the negative environmental impacts that the treadmill had produced in the North. The long-term socioenvironmental costs of depleting nonrenewable natural resources was not included in cost-benefit analyses. The rampant exploitation of fertile lands, forests, fisheries, and mineral resources promoted by the treadmill produced dramatic ecological disorganization, while providing few real socioeconomic benefits. In addition, a rapid increase in the number of poor in the South exacerbated ecological pressures. Forests were removed to provide timber for export, firewood, construction materials for homes, and to bring new land into cultivation to provide luxury crops for the North while feeding expanding southern populations. Deforested land used for intensive agriculture was eroded and rapidly depleted of essential nutrients, thus dramatically reducing its productivity. Land degradation and deforestation now represent serious ecological constraints on economic development plans throughout much of the South (South Commission 1990).

Modernization theory was obviously an extremely simplistic and naive approach to economic development. Its underlying assumptions produced flaws that ultimately undermined most of the projects that it prescribed, and caused irreversible ecological damage in the process. The most significant assumption was that there is a singular linear treadmill path to a single point known as development. Nations are different; ecosystems are different; cultures are different; and goals are different in every region of our small but diverse planet. It is impossible for each nation to follow the treadmill of production. Moreover, it is unlikely that all nations desire the same outcomes for their societies (Frank 1979).

Modernization theory denies the possibility of alternatives to the treadmill path to economic development. Yet the global economy and the global ecology require such alternatives. The failure of earlier modernization efforts has necessitated a search for alternative means by which to achieve diverse ends. Alternative social and physical technologies are needed to produce economic development and to produce it in ways that are ecologically benign and sustainable in the long run. The nations of the South have learned this lesson from painful and costly experience. As we in the North find ecological limits imposing on our own development trajectories, many have turned to the South for alternative paths. However, just as the trajectories of the North did not work in the South, it may be that the techniques developed indigenously in the South may fail in the North.

APPROPRIATE TECHNOLOGY: A SOUTHERN ALTERNATIVE TO THE TREADMILL OF THE NORTH?

Since the publication of E. F. Schumacher's book, *Small Is Beautiful: Economics as If People Mattered* in 1973, Western environmental activists and technology theorists have looked to the underdeveloped nations of the South for practical examples of appropriate technologies and sustainable economics (see Chapter 9). Schumacher's vision of technological appropriateness, which he presented in *Small Is Beautiful*, germinated from his experiences in India, where he was exposed to a society that appeared to be functioning within ecological limits. He interacted with the relatively low-tech, labor-intensive, cottage-industry-style forms of production employed there. These interactions impressed on him the notion that it was possible to meet the material and spiritual needs of people without destroying the ecological base on which all life depends.

Upon returning to the highly industrialized West, Schumacher developed a theory which argued that the long-term solutions to the environmental crisis in modern industrial societies could be found in a transition to the production techniques being utilized in the developing nations of the South. He proposed that such a transition to lower tech, more labor-intensive, smaller scale production would allow the nations of the North to provide an acceptable standard of living for their people, while decreasing their dependence on increasingly scarce nonrenewable natural resources. He went on to propose that, in addition to the environmental benefits of such a transition to a more appropriate technology of production, this dramatic sociotechnological change would also produce a set of new social relations that would be more personally and spiritually fulfilling for participants than modern Western high-tech, capital-intensive, large-scale production.

Schumacher provided few clues as to how such a transition to sustainable economics might be achieved in the context of growth-oriented industrial capitalist societies. Nonetheless, his message was well received among many environmentalists in the North (Schnaiberg 1982, 1983). His alternative social and technological complex was promoted by those critics in the wealthy nations of the North seeking to find a way out of an apparently self-destructive socioeconomic system. They viewed the efforts of Third World nations to achieve better standards of living through the means they had available to them as an alternative development trajectory. Such environmentalists perceived these developing nations as leaders in the struggle to preserve the natural world (Schnaiberg 1983). Whereas before the nations of the South had been encouraged to replicate the social, political, economic, and technological systems of the North, Schumacher now encouraged industrial Northern societies to replicate the systems in place in the South (Dickson 1975; Schnaiberg 1982, 1983). In this way, he turned the common notions of development and modernity on their heads, promoting development as an idea whose time had passed, and ecologically sustainable underdevelopment as the wave of the future (Redclift 1984).

Closer examination of the social and economic goals underlying Third World technological implementations reveals the irony in Schumacher's vision. What Schumacher perceived as Southern efforts to live within ecological limits could actually be better understood as frustrated efforts to break their economies free of those limits. Whereas he proposed a voluntary transition to less industrialized technological complexes in the North, the historical utilization of appropriate technologies in the South resulted from a lack of economic alternatives and the failure of modernization schemes to produce the sought-after treadmill of production (Dickson 1975).

The nations of the South can be broadly categorized as those societies experiencing a lack of technological complexity, a shortage of capital for investment, and an abundance of underutilized labor. Under such circumstances, the nations of the South could not implement the technologically complex, extraordinarily expensive systems of the treadmill of production. Finding themselves without the means by which to participate in the treadmill, the populations of these nations found it necessary to make do with what they had. What they had was primarily an abundance of labor power and a relatively rich supply of natural resources. What they sought was not protection of their ecosystems, but expansion of their material standards of living.

If necessity is the mother of invention, it is also the mother of Southern appropriate technology. With little chance of being able to emulate the development trajectories of the North, many of the nations of the South developed a technological structure that could make use of those things they had rather than one that required those inputs they did not have.

If the peoples of these nations found their techniques of production to be rewarding and fulfilling, those rewards and that fulfillment existed only in contrast to the chronic poverty and threat of starvation that is typical of subsistence agriculture. The fact that it might have looked good to the alienated, critical members of Northern societies was irrelevant (Harvey 1989).

Given the opportunity to utilize labor-saving industrial technologies, many of those Third World peoples involved in the backbreaking toil of low-tech production would certainly have taken it. Given the opportunity to increase their level of material wealth and comfort through the acquisition of Northern industrial consumer goods, many would have struggled to attain it. Given the opportunity to have leisure time, weekends, quitting time, and paychecks that could be used to fill this time with "fun-filled" experiences, certainly many would have opted for it. However, the truth of the matter is that these opportunities were essentially unavailable to the people of the South. They did not choose to be spiritually fulfilled by endless days of local-level low-tech labor, rather than be oppressed and alienated by modern treadmill production and consumption. They chose their path as an alternative to the endless monotony and insecurity of attempting to cajole the earth into providing enough food to sustain them and their families until the next harvest. Rather than being the leaders of an environmental revolution, they were (and are) the impoverished followers trying to gain what crumbs they might from the industrial world treadmill that surrounds them (Evans 1979; Castells & Laserna 1989).

If the dissatisfied peoples of the North were to make a transition to low-tech, small-scale, labor-intensive, environmentally-sustainable techniques, they would do so contrary to the efforts of Third World peoples, not in harmony with them. The impoverished populations of the South are struggling to attain the luxury and security that we in the North have come to take for granted (Redclift 1984). We in the North, at least some of us, are struggling now to regain our continuity and interconnectedness with the natural world, which we have sacrificed for our own comfort and security. If Schumacher's vision of a technological and social transition were to be realized in the North, it would be realized in stark contrast to the transition in the South, where the harsh realities of nature still impel the people who must seek out their survival in it to break free of ecological limits and have their day in the dimmed, but still wondrous, sun.

The perception of a trajectory exists only in relation to the direction and velocity of the viewer. If Schumacher saw an alternative path of sociotechnological development in the efforts of Third World peoples, it was only because he was passing them heading toward the point from which they had eagerly departed (Redclift 1984).

ALTERNATIVES TO THE TREADMILL:
CHINA AND TANZANIA

A few nations in the world have invested much time, energy, and money in efforts to achieve a different type of development. Rather than accepting the urban, industrial, high-tech, competitive, ecologically destructive development goals promoted by the North (Amin 1974, 1976), these nations have defined the ends to which they aspire in very different terms at one time or another. Different goals require different means to achieve them. The experiences of two nations, China and Tanzania, serve to illustrate the promises and obstacles encountered in efforts to be different in a world that has promoted sameness. As we will see, even nations attempting to achieve alternative development paths can fail to take account of the social, cultural, and ecological factors that necessitate the emergence of unique schemes designed specifically for their unique conditions.

The United Republic of Tanzania and the People's Republic of China have each struggled to implement communal systems of agricultural production, in an attempt to achieve nontreadmill conceptions of development. Both nations sought to develop communal agriculture as a means of insuring a minimum standard of living for all their peoples and sufficient surplus to invest in social services and productive enterprises. Such a development path is substantially different from that followed by most other nations in the global community. Tanzania's alternative development path, focused primarily on agrarian transformation, was inspired largely by the development of the People's Communes in rural Maoist China (Hyden 1980). Despite apparent similarities between the two agrarian nations of the South, differences in both the social and environmental circumstances prevailing in each nation at the time of rural transformation have actually led to quite different results. Whereas the Chinese government was able to mobilize the rural peasantry and implement communal production, the Tanzanian government was largely incapable of mobilizing the peasants for communal agriculture. Tanzania's Chinese-inspired model for the communalization of rural production proved to be inappropriate to the realities of peasant life in Tanzania (Hyden 1980). In order for Tanzania to fully implement a communal organization of agriculture, the Chinese model would have had to be extensively modified to account for the unique environmental and social conditions of rural producers in Tanzania. Until such modifications are made, Tanzania's alternative development effort will continue to flounder as the government attempts to implement an agricultural system that is largely inappropriate to the social and environmental conditions prevailing in rural Tanzania.

The difference between the Chinese and Tanzanian governments' ability to implement a communal system of agricultural production stems largely from differences in the nature of peasant production systems which the new systems were intended to replace. The important differences between the pretransformation Chinese and Tanzanian peasant forms of production result from the interaction of social and environmental factors that are unique to each nation. The high degree of independence enjoyed by Tanzanian rural producers is partly due to the rain-fed nature of Tanzanian agriculture. In contrast to China, where environmental pressures have necessitated a complex system of irrigated agriculture, Tanzania's agriculture depends primarily on seasonal rains. Because rain is a resource that cannot be controlled by a social class or government, reliance on that resource helps Tanzania's peasants to resist integration into a larger social framework. As long as a sufficient amount of rain falls, rural producers in Tanzania can farm wherever arable land is available, with or without government approval.

In contrast, a system of irrigation networks, as exists in China, requires some central control over a vital resource. The use of large-scale irrigation systems requires peasants to work in cooperation. Reliance on a regulated water supply also forces Chinese peasants to be subject to some authority other than nature (Wittfogel 1957). When the Chinese government took control of the irrigation networks and vastly extended them, it created a situation in which a large portion of the Chinese rural population was directly dependent on the government for their supply of water. Establishing control over a necessary resource for farming has given the Chinese government significant leverage in promoting its policies among the rural population (Hsu 1982). In contrast, the Tanzanian government has no such leverage.

In addition to allowing for control by a central authority, reliance on a system of irrigation promotes peasant interdependence and cooperation. Because much of China's rural population has been dependent on irrigation for many generations, they are somewhat accustomed to relying on the cooperation of other peasants in their productive enterprise. The fates of many Chinese farmers are bound together by their reliance on an irrigation system utilized by an entire community. The rural producers in China are therefore accustomed to a much lower degree of freedom from one another than are the rural producers of Tanzania (Hsu 1982; Hyden 1980). The rain-fed nature of Tanzanian agriculture, combined with a relative abundance of arable land in most regions, has served to promote peasant autonomy rather than peasant cooperation.

China's system of irrigation networks has been developed in response to increasing population pressures on a limited amount of arable land. The country's extremely high person/land ratios indicate that land scarcity is chronic. The lack of uncultivated arable land in China greatly reduces the potential for peasant independence. Since the central government ultimately controls all the land that is cultivated, Chinese peasants had little opportunity to achieve subsistence levels of production outside of the commune system. In contrast, Tanzania, despite some regional land scarcity, is largely land abundant. The existence of readily available arable land outside of the formal agricultural system allowed Tanzanian peasants to produce independently of the communes. The availability of arable land promoted the Tanzanian peasants' exit option, permitting autonomous production beyond government control (Hyden 1980).

The differences between Tanzania's and China's person/land ratios have also had an impact on the relative intensity of agricultural production. Because China has had to feed large populations from a relatively small amount of arable land, intensive agriculture has been necessary. Agricultural production in Tanzania, however, has not been very intensive owing to the relatively low person/land ratios. Therefore, although schemes to raise the level of agricultural production in China may appear to be directly linked to human survival, farmers are likely to view schemes to increase agricultural production in Tanzania as unnecessary. Farmers in Tanzania have traditionally produced only enough to insure their own continued survival. Unlike the patterns of intensive cultivation, production substantially above subsistence levels has been unnecessary for Tanzania's peasants. As a result, rural producers in Tanzania are likely to be skeptical of government programs describing the need for so much extra work.

Conversely, China's peasantry has been producing above subsistence levels for centuries. Throughout the dynasties, China's peasants had been taxed harshly by other social classes, requiring them to produce above subsistence for the purpose of extracting rural wealth (Hsu 1982). Although the Chinese government abolished this taxation by the landowning elites, it was quickly replaced by government taxation, thus maintaining the practice of extracting surplus production. Therefore, while production above subsistence levels for extraction by the government was an established norm in China, in Tanzania it was a relatively new concept introduced by colonial rulers without much success. The Tanzanian peasantry remains largely unconvinced of the need for increased levels of production.

The reluctance of Tanzania's peasantry to change their techniques is largely a result of their level of production. Peasants producing at or near the level of subsistence are conservative because taking a risk by changing techniques means risking starvation. Any government policy aimed at altering the variables that a subsistence farmer must calculate to survive not only presents a risk of death, but also requires the peasant to become dependent on the government for the information necessary to survive. Peasant experiences with development experts provides reason enough to be cautious. As a result of the precarious position of subsistence farmers, the Tanzanian peasantry is highly resistant to any changes in their existing agricultural production process.

In summary, the *Ujamaa* system of collective agricultural production would have had to be altered to reflect the realities of peasant life and local ecology in Tanzania. Although the Chinese communal agricultural system provides a good working model, the vast environmental differences and differences in peasant circumstances between China and Tanzania require that Tanzania extensively modify China's agrarian technology to make it suitable to the Tanzanian situation. Until such revisions are implemented, Tanzania's agrarian system will remain an example of the transference of an inappropriate foreign technology (Hyden 1980).

WORLD CONTEXTS OF APPROPRIATE TECHNOLOGY: PRECURSOR OF SUSTAINABLE DEVELOPMENT?

The alternative development paths both China and Tanzania have embarked on have come under extreme pressure from the world economy around them. The ability of the nations of the South to implement alternative development paths utilizing appropriate technologies to achieve ecologically sustainable development is structurally inhibited by socioeconomic forces beyond their control. The recent decision by China's leaders to abandon alternative development schemes in favor of a market (treadmill) economy clearly illustrates this point. Similarly, recent negotiations between the International Monetary Fund (IMF) and the government of Tanzania point toward a greater reliance on market forces, retreating from one of the modern world's few remaining national alternative development paths. In *Small Is Beautiful,* Schumacher identified this crisis in modern Western production as the suffocation and debilitation of human nature, the breakdown of the physical environment that supports human life, and the exhaustion of nonrenewable natural resources. Thus, the need for a more appropriate technology (AT) of production in the North is rooted in environmental concerns and a distaste for the existing treadmill of production. This concept of AT therefore includes techniques such as solar, wind, and geothermal production of energy, and a cottage-industry-style organization of labor.

In the South, however, the application of a fairly well-defined notion of AT, as conceived in the North, evolved differently. The perception of a need for more appropriate methods of production in the South has not been based primarily on concerns for the stability of the ecosystem, nor on a distaste for particular types of labor (Redclift 1984). In the developing nations of the South, the concept of appropriate technology for production stems from the constraints on these nations owing to their position in the world economy. The South is technologically dependent on the North, and the transfer of technology from North to South is an issue of major concern to the South. The notion of appropriateness becomes important in deciding which types of technology the various nations of the South should adopt. Each Southern nation must rely heavily on the transfer of technology from the North and does not have the economic power to purchase whichever technologies individual nations may prefer; the decisions of Southern nations as to what productive technologies to use are, therefore, greatly influenced by the desire and willingness of Northern governments, international development agencies, and multinational corporations to export certain types of technology. In the South, the notion of appropriate technology emerged in response to the failure of modernization theory, which had guided earlier technological imports.

Both Northern and Southern notions of appropriate technology developed out of a common dissatisfaction with the most modern and sophisticated technology available, although for somewhat different reasons. Whereas Northern AT evolved from a distaste for the social and environmental impacts of modern industrialization, Southern predispositions toward AT have resulted from the failure of modern technology to produce just this rapid and rational economic development that its exporters had promised (Redclift 1984; Reddy 1979; Robinson 1979). The notion of appropriateness was adopted in an attempt to promote the transfer of technologies that would meet the needs of the recipient Southern nations rather than the needs of the Northern technology exporters.

The types of technology that Southern nations will find most desirable are largely dependent on the social and economic goals of the individual nations. These social and economic goals are, in turn, determined primarily by the social and economic circumstances of these societies. Most nations of the South have a surplus of available human labor in relation to the employment capacity of the existing productive systems. There is a chronic shortage of capital. A dominant social goal of many Southern nations is, therefore, an increase in the employment capacity of their productive technology at the lowest possible cost. The goal of increased employment often comes into conflict with the desire of the North to export its expensive labor-saving technologies. These technologies are fundamentally inconsistent with a shortage of money and an abundance of labor (Reddy 1979). The determination of what technology is most appropriate to the nations of the South is therefore often based on the desire for maximum employment, constrained by the availability of labor-intensive technologies.

Just as the determination of what technology is appropriate to the nations of the South is affected by those nations' social goals and the economic goals of the Northern technology exporters, so is it affected by the economic goals of Southern nations (Gould 1987). Most Southern nations are attempting to increase their productive capacities to achieve greater power in the global economy. A main condition in determining the appropriateness of a technology, then, is the absolute productive capacity of the technology. In a conference held in Teheran, Iran, in 1979 on appropriate technology for Third World development (prior to the revolution there), the absolute productive capacity of a given technology emerged as the single criterion by which appropriateness was determined (Robinson 1979). This definition of appropriate technology is far removed from that presented by E. F. Schumacher. The Teheran conference was dominated by Western economists, which probably accounts for their willingness to equate appropriate technology with efficiently productive technology, in terms of overall output. The determination of appropriateness varies from nation to nation, and, although economic growth through increased production is a dominant concern, most Southern nations base their determination on a mixture of economic and social goals, such as distribution of wealth within the nation and employment.

In contrast to Schumacher's conception of AT, environmental concerns affect the definition of appropriateness in the South less than do economic concerns. Like Schumacher's, the Southern definition of appropriate technology includes notions of autonomy through the use of local resources (Reddy 1979). However, in this context, environmental integrity has not been primary. Many Southern nations are seeking to decrease their dependency on the North through greater use of local resources, both material and human, and this concern often plays a part in the determination of appropriateness. The need for such self-reliance was made apparent by the history of development projects like the Ghanaian aluminum smelter mentioned earlier. However, the degree to which this concern affects definitions of appropriateness depends on development objectives. Furthermore, the long-range renewability of local resources often plays only a minor part in determining appropriateness in the South, except where the exhaustion of an economically important resource is considered imminent.

What is considered to be a distinct category of an alternative to the treadmill technologies in the North thus became a relativistic concept devoid of objective meaning in the context of the South. Any technology could be considered an appropriate technology depending on the objectives and values of those making the determination (Gould 1987). This conceptualization of AT in the South makes the term virtually meaningless as a category of treadmill alternatives. In many instances, though, some environmental considerations have been included in the development, implementation, and evaluation of alternative technological systems in the South (Robinson 1979). The examples that follow serve to illustrate the criteria used in determining the appropriateness of technological systems, including those pertaining to the environment.

Green Revolution in India

One example of an alternative technological application in the South is the Green Revolution in India. The goal of this development scheme was to increase agricultural production in the South to alleviate food shortages and stimulate development in rural areas. Agricultural production was to be increased through the introduction of hybrid seeds producing extremely high yields, in conjunction with the application of more modern farming techniques such as the use of chemical fertilizers and advanced irrigation methods. The Green Revolution would not be defined as AT by Northern environmentalists, for the technology involved calls for greater reliance on fossil fuels and industrial chemicals, greater centralization of control over production, and more capital-intensive techniques. This scheme increases dependency on nonrenewable resources through the use of petrochemical-based fertilizers and pesticides. However, the new agricultural technology utilized in the Green Revolution has succeeded in increasing agricultural output, which makes it appropriate to the specific goal of making more food available to the Indian population. This technology has also resulted in a general, though uneven, increase in the incomes of agriculturalists and has stimulated development in rural areas to some extent (Frankel 1971).

Apparently, only one element of this appropriate technology for increasing food production would also be considered AT in the North. That element is the increased requirement for physical labor in production. The hybrid seeds used to increase agricultural output require multiple harvests, which has put an increased demand on human labor. The introduction of chemical fertilizers has also made weed control a more urgent problem and therefore also requires more physical labor. The fact that the technology of the Green Revolution is both more capital-intensive and more labor-intensive makes the polar opposition between capital- and labor-intensive techniques that is commonly referred to by Northern environmentalists somewhat less useful. Thus, the labor intensity of a given technology is not necessarily related to environmental integrity.

Rural Development in Post-Earthquake Guatemala

Another application of alternative technologies is the three-point program of rural development in post-earthquake Guatemala begun in 1976. The first part of this program involved a scheme to use locally available materials for the construction of more earthquake-resistant traditional rural homes. The use of expensive concrete was replaced by volcanic materials and lime which occur naturally throughout rural Guatemala. The capital-intensive purchase of concrete was replaced with labor-intensive gathering of local building materials, thereby lowering the cost of construction and increasing the autonomy of rural Guatemalans (Caceres 1980). This project achieved the goals of the Guatemalan government, while also meeting some of the criteria for AT established in the North. However, a question remains as to the degree to which the local volcanic materials utilized can be considered renewable. If it is foreseeable that these building materials may be exhausted locally, this alternative housing construction project may be excluded from Northern notions of ecological sustainability.

The second part of the Guatemalan development scheme was the introduction of Vietnamese-style latrines producing fertilizer to replace defecation in local fields (Caceres 1980). The goal of the Guatemalan government in initiating this project was to reduce the risk of disease from poor sanitation, while making available useful fertilizer for rural agriculture. This project allows for local and independent production of fertilizer from renewable resources while solving a health problem at the same time. However, the project also calls for the construction of woodsheds to enclose each latrine. This could lead to local deforestation and then soil erosion and a reduction of agricultural output. In addition, a question remains as to the origin and durability of the tanks. The latrine project does, however, meet the primary goal of reducing the risk of disease from poor sanitation.

The third part of Guatemala's post-earthquake development project was the introduction of the *poyo de lorena,* or mud stove. Mud stoves are traditional in Guatemala, but these new stoves are more complex and far more energy efficient. The government initiated this project to help ease the shortage of wood fuel in rural Guatemala (Caceres 1980). The average rural family spends much of its annual income and time on the purchase and transportation of wood (Wharton 1980). The new stoves are made of locally available materials and can be constructed on the spot as they are needed. The new technology simply channels the heat from a wood fire through a mud base utilizing as much of the heat as possible and directing it to predesigned spaces where pots are to be placed. The stoves are made from local renewable materials, construction is decentralized and labor-intensive, and the goal of the project is greater environmental integrity through more efficient usage of renewable fuel. The real problem with this project is in getting people to adopt it. The time that it saves people in gathering and transporting scarce wood is partially absorbed by the extra time that it takes to construct, maintain, and use the new stoves, which are quite complex and somewhat fragile. As is true for most Northern, environmentally "friendly" AT projects, a major task before implementation is to get people to see how they benefit directly from an environmentally sound technology when it may require greater labor on their part.

Rural Development in Sri Lanka

Another example of applied alternative technology was a program of the Sri Lankan Divisional Development Council. One aspect of this program was the organization of local blacksmiths to produce light engineering works. The goal of this project was to rehabilitate traditional artisans and redistribute wealth from manufacturing to the rural areas from the industrial urban sector. The scheme involved the organization of artisans into collective factories located in rural regions where windmills, two-wheel tractors, and hydroelectric equipment were produced (Gunawardhana 1980). Although this program ultimately collapsed as a result of competition from capital-intensive multinational corporate production (much like our hypothetical East African firm), the scheme was appropriate to the goals of utilizing local artisans for larger scale production and redirecting some wealth to the rural areas. The question of whether or not this plan was consistent with the goals of Northern environmentalists depends largely on which previously existing type of production it is compared to. The local blacksmith plan was more decentralized and labor-intensive than urban factory production. However, it was more centralized and capital-intensive than production by individual artisans. Since the output of these collectivized artisans competed with urban factory production, it is probably fair to say that it represented an AT alternative to production as maintained by the multinational corporations. However, this element of relativism in the Northern notion of AT is worth noting.

Another aspect of Sri Lanka's rural development plan was the collectivization of traditional ceramic pottery production. The ideas behind this project were also greater utilization of the productive capacity of rural artisans and a redirection of wealth from the cities to the rural areas. Local artisans who produced pottery were brought together in centrally located production centers where local materials were made available to large groups of artisans. By doing this, the government also relieved the problem of individual artisans tunneling under their plots of land for clay, which often resulted in injury to the artisans from the collapse of these tunnels (Gunawardhana 1980). The production in collective factories competed with the production of aluminum pots by multinational firms in the cities. Ultimately, that competition resulted in the abandonment of the local potters project. The scheme was appropriate given the limited goals of the Sri Lankan government, although they failed to provide the necessary protections for the project. Both the blacksmith and potter programs were inappropriate to the goal of revitalizing the local artisans, inasmuch as the government did not provide market protections for these industries. The lack of market protections allowed the programs to be undermined by competition from the more modern production technologies of the treadmill.

Soap-Making in Mali

Soap-making has been a traditional source of income for West African women. Locally produced soap in parts of Mali, however, dissolves quickly and is often too caustic. The product from Mali's one soap factory does not meet national demand for soap, and imported soap is too expensive for rural residents. In response to this situation, one women's cooperative has established a local soap-manufacturing enterprise. The women introduced soap-boiling tanks to replace cold process soap-making. The local women experimented with numerous combinations of different types of oil and fillers until they developed a laundry soap equal in quality to the more expensive factory-produced soap. The soapworks produces approximately 2000 bars of soap each week, and is managed and staffed entirely by women (Lawland 1980).

This successful rural enterprise meets both Northern and Southern criteria for appropriateness. The women's soapworks utilizes locally available renewable materials, is small in scale, and is labor-intensive rather than capital-intensive. It produces for a market that is inadequately served by capital-intensive factory production, and its product is of much higher quality than that of previous local production (Lawland 1980). It also proved appropriate to the women's goal of preserving their central economic function within the society, which is often threatened by the introduction of new industrial technologies. Furthermore, the women were able to achieve this goal while remaining within their cultural gender roles.

TECHNOLOGIES AND SOCIAL RELATIONS

As discussed above, the Southern concept of appropriate technology bases the definition of appropriateness on a technology's usefulness in achieving specified economic and social goals. A major problem with this concept is that the social and economic goals of a nation often come into conflict. Moreover, as with the treadmill system itself, AT's environmental outcomes are often of only peripheral interest (except where planners are dealing with scarce natural resources). This problem can be viewed in part as a conflict between the forces and relations of production. One element that both Southern AT programs and Northern AT proponents have in common is that both tend to concentrate on changes in the forces or technologies of production while ignoring the related social and ecological effects resulting from the existing relations of production (Schnaiberg 1982, 1983). As Stokes and Anderson (1990) have recently argued, both societies suffer from the "disarticulation" between aggregate national goals and the distribution of social welfare to their citizen-workers. Perhaps the clearest example of this from the cases cited above is in the Green Revolution program in India.

The economic goal of the program was to increase agricultural output, and this was achieved. However, the social goal of increasing the wealth of farmers in relation to that of the urban sector was achieved only in part and to the detriment of many small farmers. The introduction of expensive hybrid seeds that require expensive chemical fertilizers greatly increased economic differences among farmers in India (Frankel 1971). Large landowners were able to use the new technology because the program was designed for larger scale production as implemented in the North. Small landholders were forced out as a result of competition with the greatly increased output of the already larger scale agriculturalists. The newly created class of wealthy peasants bought the small holdings of poor peasants and hired them to work as wage-laborers on farms of increasing size. The fact that the new agricultural technology required more human labor allowed the landless peasants to be used by the new landed elite. The social impact of the Green Revolution was to impoverish the majority of small-holding peasants and make them landless farm workers, while allowing a few large landholders to accumulate more wealth and land. The reason for this result is that the technology involved was developed without consideration of the social and ecological circumstances in rural India and instead was based on Northern-style large-scale agribusiness techniques. The Green Revolution thus has also produced numerous ecological problems, including soil degradation, fresh water contamination, and species depletion in India, just as treadmill agriculture has produced similar problems in the North.

The technological changes promoted in Guatemala's post-earthquake development program likewise focused primarily on changes in the technologies of production (Caceres 1980). The alterations made in the technologies actually required only minimal changes in social relations. Although the transfer to locally available building materials has shifted the process of materials acquisition from a capital-intensive to a labor-intensive endeavor, the actual process of constructing rural homes has remained unchanged.

In contrast to the Guatemalan development plan, the Divisional Development Council of Sri Lanka attempted to rehabilitate rural artisans primarily through changes in the relations of production. Both the blacksmith and potter projects involved bringing isolated artisans together for communal production in order to produce more complex light engineering works. While the technologies of production remained essentially unchanged, production was altered by an increased division of labor and factory-style organization of the production process (Gunawardhana 1980). The process thus addressed was allocation of human rather than natural resources.

Changes in the technologies of production must be suited to existing and desired relations of production in order to minimize conflicts between economic and social and environmental goals. To a large extent, this process involves striking a balanced compromise between economic growth, social equity, and ecological sustainability, in cases where these goals are valued (Leonard et al. 1989). The compromises that result from this process will be determined by the relative importance of these goals in national political agendas, constrained by the technological options available. Because "increased inequality is a necessary effect of advanced technology's use in developing countries," any compromise between growth and equity must involve calculations as to the socioeconomic and ecological costs of increased inequality, as well as the socioeconomic costs of adopting lower tech industry (Redclift 1984:105). In such calculations, not only growth, but also the structure and benefits of growth are of central importance. Whatever the result of such a compromise is, progressive political movements in the South seek to induce national governments (or communities) to "articulate" (Stokes & Anderson 1990) likely negative social changes resulting from the introduction of new production techniques, in order to avoid worsening inequalities.

A technology that appears to promote the desired relations of production as well as the desired economic growth must also be appropriate to the internal socioeconomic and environmental circumstances of a given nation. Any technological change, no matter how utopian in its projected impacts, must first be implementable. If the internal circumstances of a nation will present major obstacles to the implementation of a new technology, this must be considered in determining the cost and feasibility of adopting new techniques. The experience of Tanzania's program of agrarian transformation serves as an example of the difficulties encountered when a new production technique is appropriate to the social and economic goals of a nation, but inappropriate to the existing environmental and socioeconomic circumstances of the people who are asked to adopt it.

EXTERNAL VERSUS INTERNAL CONSTRAINTS ON TREADMILL ALTERNATIVES

Another conflict that emerges from an examination of appropriate technologies for sustainable development is between internal self-sufficiency and production for export. Much of the South is presently pursuing the dual goals of increasing its share of production for the world market and becoming more internally self-sufficient. In 1975 the United Nations Industrial Development Organization (UNIDO) held a conference in Lima, Peru, to discuss appropriate industrial technologies for Southern development. At that conference, UNIDO set a development target of a 25 percent share of world industrial production in the South by the year 2000 (UNIDO 1979). UNIDO determined that in many areas of production, AT-type production techniques are efficient and preferable for producing goods to be consumed by the populations of Southern countries. AT-based industries are therefore considered appropriate where the use-value of products is emphasized for local populations. However, where production is for export, they determined that the most modern and sophisticated technology should be utilized. Advanced technologies are therefore considered appropriate where the exchange-value of products is emphasized. Since the Lima conference concluded that the primary goal of Southern industry should be to increase production for export (emphasizing the exchange-value of products), the message to the nations of the South was that non-AT production is most appropriate to the collective goals of the South.

Any developing nation that adopted the UNIDO policy on appropriate technology would, by necessity, become more dependent on Northern multinational corporations. They would have to import large indivisible technological packages which, in turn, require the adoption of organizational structures developed in the North (Redclift 1984). The UNIDO recommendations ignored the increasing income disparities, growing unemployment, rural impoverishment, mass migration to urban slums, increasing import bills, worsening balance-of-payments crises, increasing technical dependence, decreasing self-reliance, increasing vulnerability to major fluctuations in international trade, and increased environmental degradation that are all associated with the introduction of modern treadmill production methods (Reddy 1979).

This UNIDO definition in terms of production for export leaves the nations of the South with no choice among technologies. The pragmatic impact of this use of the term *appropriate technology* is the support of those small-scale projects that Southern nations may pursue to meet the basic needs of their people, while focusing their real development efforts on meeting the needs of the North, as is consistent with the logic of the treadmill.

Another problem related to the conflict between production for export and production for internal self-sufficiency is the problem of scale and competition. The production techniques used in Sri Lanka's Divisional Development Council program collapsed under pressure from multinational-based competition. Although small-scale local production was sufficient to meet the requirements of the society for the goods produced, multinationals were able to undercut the price of these goods and therefore made AT-type projects seem inefficient. It appears that AT-based production systems must be protected from competition from treadmill production if the goal of the production system is more than just the lowest possible price per unit. Because the private sector focuses on efficiency goals, it becomes the responsibility of national governments to insure that equity goals are not precluded by the multinationals' preponderance of economic power. Otherwise, any large multinational corporation will be able to undercut AT-based production long enough to force the alternative out of the market (Schnaiberg 1982, 1983).

The clear examples of successful appropriate technological applications in the South are cases where either the scale of operation is small enough so that no treadmill-based competition has been attracted to the market that is served, or the treadmill production is insufficient to meet demand in a specific region. One such project is a solar water desalinization still installed on Source Philippe, a small island off the coast of Haiti, where deforestation resulted in a lack of sufficient clean water (Lawland 1980). In this project, a Canadian firm built a simple solar still from locally available materials that can easily be maintained by the small population of the island. The population of the island was only 250 people; therefore, the local market for fresh water was too small for a large corporation to profit from establishing an expensive desalinization plant there. The UNIDO view that AT-type production is appropriate only for production for internal self-sufficiency on a small scale appears to merely reflect the economic principles of the treadmill, which guide multinational corporate investment. According to these principles, AT-type production is appropriate only where the goods and services produced for a specific market cannot yield a sufficient profit to attract multinational corporate investment.

In the case of soap-making in Mali, the market for soap was sufficient to attract treadmill corporate production in the nation's capital, but that production was incapable of meeting the demand for soap in certain rural areas. The success of the women's soap production project is due largely to the fact that the women involved intentionally directed their enterprise toward meeting a need that was insufficiently met by treadmill production. If treadmill production expands enough to provide comparable goods at a comparable price, the women's soapworks will likely be forced out of the market despite the positive social consequences of the enterprise. From the experiences of these projects, it appears that the future role of AT may be confined to filling the gaps left behind by expanding multinational corporations.

APPROPRIATE TECHNOLOGY AS AN ADJUNCT TO THE TREADMILL

In addition to the use of the appropriate technology concept in the context of Southern development examined above, there also exists what may be perceived as grass-roots AT in the informal urban sectors of the South.

This grass-roots AT is really AT by necessity. In most Southern nations, mass migration to cities that cannot accommodate the increasing population has resulted in the establishment of spontaneous squatter settlements. In these settlements, houses are constructed by the residents out of whatever materials are available locally. This type of housing is appropriate in the sense that these people are otherwise homeless and no other provisions for their housing are available. These squatter settlements also meet some of the criteria of Northern environmentalists. Construction of squatter homes involves a reuse of waste materials, and therefore requires almost no additional resource extraction from the natural environment. Many of these settlements locate near garbage dumps to provide easy access to raw materials. These settlements are also appropriate in that they are usually located near urban centers—since their residents seek employment primarily in these urban areas it reduced the need for energy expenditures for transportation. However, these squatter settlements are often located on ecologically marginal lands, which are particularly susceptible to environmental degradation (Leonard et al. 1989). These marginal lands often include steep hillsides which are vulnerable to extreme erosion, endangering the local ecology and the people who must live with the threat of sudden death from mud slides in heavy rains.

Some Southern governments, such as that of Tanzania, are also beginning to view this type of housing as appropriate in terms of the cost of providing shelter. Even with the provision of minimal services such as fresh water supplies, this type of housing is far less expensive than government housing projects, which are often unpopular with the intended residents. Just as AT-based production is being used to fill the gaps where treadmill production cannot operate with sufficient profit, AT-based construction in squatter areas is being used by the people to fill the gaps where governments cannot provide adequate shelter.

Informal sector occupations in Southern cities also utilize "appropriate" technology out of economic necessity. In order to earn a living in the cities where there are too few jobs to provide employment for the majority of residents, urban dwellers produce goods and services for each other, and those in the formal sector, by utilizing whatever resources are available. Services such as food carts to provide meals for those earning regular wages utilize a low level of technology, are small in scale, and are labor-intensive. Poverty makes capital-intensive enterprises in these areas impossible. In these instances, people have no alternative but to use AT-type enterprises to earn a living. This type of AT, however, is not utilized only by those in the informal sector. The goods and services that these enterprises provide are used by those employed in the formal sector, because the cost of these goods and services are generally lower than those provided by the formal sector. As a result, the informal occupations lower the cost of living for those in the formal sector and, therefore, informally provided goods and services help to subsidize capital accumulation within the formal sector. In this way, these occupations not only fill the gaps left behind by the formal sector, but also stimulate the expansion of the treadmill by providing cheap goods and services.

The Wahiya and Zabaline ethnic groups help to subsidize formal sector development in Cairo, Egypt, by recycling waste materials for sale to local industries. The Wahiya act as brokers, paying for trash collection rights and charging fees to the Zabaline for the right to pick it up. The Zabaline derive a large portion of their income from collecting and sorting waste into marketable components. Paper, cloth, glass, tin, plastic, bones, and other organic matter are separated and sold as raw materials to a wide range of local industries. Hundreds of workshops and factories in Cairo depend on the Zabaline for raw materials (D'Avanzo 1980). The role of the Zabaline is another example of how AT by necessity supports the treadmill. The Zabaline are able to survive without putting pressure on the government to provide jobs and services, while at the same time, reducing the pressure on the government to furnish elaborate waste disposal services. In addition, they provide local industry with a source of cheap raw materials without which many local industries and workshops would not be able to operate (D'Avanzo 1980). From this perspective, it appears that some forms of AT may be promoted by the treadmill as a way of utilizing unemployed workers in support of the treadmill's development, as well as to provide goods and services where non-AT enterprises would be unprofitable.

In the South, AT will thus be used in dualistic development policies to relieve certain disparities within nations rather than as an alternative to modern industrial production. In most Southern nations, a great disparity exists between the amount of goods and services available to rural and urban residents (de Janvry 1981; Castells & Laserno 1989). It appears that AT will be implemented in rural areas to reduce demands on the modern urban sectors. AT-based production of energy and necessary commodities in rural areas will allow treadmill development efforts to concentrate on the production of goods for export to the North, while satisfying the needs of the rural areas at a minimal cost. This use of AT is likely to be viewed as temporary, for the expanded regular treadmill industrial sector will eventually enter the rural markets served by AT production. This is consistent with the observation that, for tactical political reasons, some support of AT ideas and research may be necessary to minimize the costs of doing business or governance (Schnaiberg 1983). This should not be confused with accepting these ideas: they are instances of co-optation as the preferred path of treadmill proponents, in contrast to outright resistance to economic and environmental change (Schnaiberg 1983).

Utilization of AT in rural areas may also reduce migration to already overcrowded cities by allowing for the provision of more goods and jobs locally. In addition to reducing pressures on strained urban services, this would also reduce ecological pressures on environmentally marginal land. AT-based production in rural areas could also direct a little more wealth toward this sector, thereby slightly reducing conflict between rural and urban residents. As a result of the bias against employing females in treadmill production, rural-to-urban migration often involves a disproportionate number of young men seeking jobs. Many treadmill enterprises involve the production of goods traditionally produced by women. As a result, treadmill production is displacing women from their otherwise central economic role. As with soap-making in Mali, women may respond by developing AT-based enterprises to maintain their economic function. In this way, dualistic development based on the rural application of AT is gender stratified. A dualistic development policy based on rural use of some AT-based production looks like AT for the masses and the treadmill for the formal sector urban elites. The real beneficiaries of such a program will be national governments and multinational corporations, who may be able to pacify the masses with AT-produced goods and services, while reaping the profits from treadmill expansion and production for export northward.

As mentioned above, AT-based production may also be used to alleviate the tension within Southern cities between the formal and informal economic sectors. By promoting the existing AT-based spontaneous housing and employment in the informal urban sector, national governments may be able to reduce demands on, and provide support for, modern formal sector industrial development. Besides providing cheap housing, goods, and services to the urban poor, AT-based occupations reduce the pressure on national governments to provide formal sector jobs for the people. Those who find employment in the informal sector can help subsidize treadmill expansion by providing cheap goods and services for the formal sector. They also demonstrate that they can get along without government efforts to provide formal employment. Informal urban sector enterprises also support industrial development by providing a training ground for entrepreneurship at no cost to national governments. Therefore, if the formal urban sector expands, these AT entrepreneurs can be easily assimilated into treadmill production. In this way, the Southern urban poor, living by their wits as a result of the treadmill system's inability to provide for their needs, actually serve as a multifaceted support base for that very system.

The native inhabitants of the Ecuadorian Amazon have lived in harmony with their natural environment for centuries. Appropriate technology and sustainable economies are not new concepts for them. Many of Ecuador's Amazonian Indians have continued to provide for their basic needs without destroying the ecosystem on which they depend, despite the encroachment of the modern industrial treadmill of production in other parts of the nation. While these native peoples were maintaining their "appropriate" economy, increasingly the nation of Ecuador became economically dependent on the treadmill's world economy, as a supplier of oil to fuel the treadmill industry in the North. Ecuador, one of the poorest nations in South America, draws half of its tax revenues from the export of oil on the world market. However, the rapid depletion of already tapped oil reserves threatens the continuation of this nonrenewable resource extraction-based economy. If new domestic oil reserves are not made available, by the year 2000 Ecuador will be unable to export oil, which would result in the collapse of its already marginal economy.

The remaining economically attractive Ecuadorian oil reserves are located in the Amazon. Cesar Verduga, Ecuador's minister of government, admits that the introduction of oil extraction would destroy the Amazon's fragile ecology. It would also destroy the homes and economies of Ecuador's native Amazonian peoples. The increased political militancy of Ecuador's Indian minority is emerging as a major economic factor in the nation's development. Recently, a coalition of Amazonian Indians and local environmentalists led a successful campaign to stop oil company plans for oil development in Ecuador's Amazon. Another such coalition is now waging a similar campaign to thwart another oil extraction project. Increasing Indian militancy, heightened by the five hundredth anniversary of Columbus's arrival in the New World, has led Ecuador's government to promise the transfer of formal title to 4305 acres of traditional homelands to native peoples.

Not surprisingly, such increases in native land rights and political power have aroused strong opposition. Andres Borja, president of the Association of Highland and Eastern Ranchers, has stated that "The Indians got too much land. . . . It is completely out of proportion for a group that barely adds up to 20,000 people." Native land titles present serious obstacles to the expansion of treadmill forest clearing to support export-oriented beef production. In addition to rejecting oil extraction and cattle ranching, Ecuador's Amazonian natives also oppose export-oriented farming. Jose Maria Cabascango, a leader of the Confederation of Indigenous Nationalities of Ecuador, has stated, "We should only produce food for our own consumption, not to earn dollars." Such an overt rejection of the national and global treadmill economy, in favor of sustainable and appropriate self-sufficiency, has angered Ecuador's new president. President Sixto Duran Bellen, an advocate of free-market development, is unhappy with Indian opposition to Amazonian oil development. When asked how he would respond to such political obstacles, he ominously replied, "I'm impatient."

MODERNIZATION, APPROPRIATE TECHNOLOGY, AND TREADMILL REFORM

It has been widely held that AT could be used in the South to achieve greater national autonomy, provide for the needs of indigenous populations, and alleviate the strain on already degraded ecosystems (Robinson 1979). This ideal replaced the earlier drive for modernization. Although this scenario could be possible (under drastically altered geopolitical circumstances), it seems very unlikely that AT will serve this purpose in the South (Redclift 1984). In some instances, certain variations on AT are being used to increase reliance on local rather than imported resources. Moreover, some nations are using the concept of appropriateness and its successor, "sustainability," to provide themselves with options in technology transfers from the North. However, Northern-style AT in the South is most likely to be applied only as a structural supplement to standard treadmill technologies (Chase-Dunn 1989).

Some Northern environmentalists have indicated that AT is the antithesis to expansionist, ecologically destructive corporate industrialism (Schnaiberg 1982, 1983). However, the use of AT within the larger definition of appropriate technology and "sustainability" that is being used in discussions of Southern development contradicts that notion. Small-scale, decentralized, labor-intensive, environmentally sound technology in the South is actually working in support of increased percentages of world industrial production through standard industrial development. In the context of the South, AT has been largely considered appropriate only to provide goods and services to those people within nations who are not benefiting directly from treadmill production. Even in nations that have experimented with fairly large-scale AT-type development programs, the main thrust of national technological development has remained on capital-intensive, centralized, industrial technology, dependent on depleting nonrenewable natural resources for production for export in the world market, with very few exceptions.

The most important factor preventing the South from pursuing an AT-based sustainable alternative to the treadmill's development trajectory is the tremendous pressure exerted on these nations by the world economy to participate in the world market. Southern nations are constrained not only by the types of technology that the North is offering to transfer, but also by the patterns of consumption in the North (Chase-Dunn 1989; Dos Santos 1970). The need to acquire capital, which is now concentrated in the North, drives Southern nations to produce what the North requires. The nations of the South are therefore forced to develop in a manner that will meet the needs of Northern overconsumers rather than Southern underconsumers (Redclift 1984). In this way, the South has become the developmental shadow of the North, with little control over its role in the world economy or the direction that its future economic development will take (Dickson 1975). Furthermore, competition between Southern nations to supply the North with the goods that it desires promotes the adoption of productive technologies that are best at satisfying the consumption demands of the North (Gould 1987). As a result, nations that choose to strike a compromise between economic goals, social goals, and ecological sustainability, may find themselves no longer competitive in the world market.

Those national governments that are most willing and able to deny or suppress social equity and environmental goals while maintaining high levels of output may ultimately prove to be the fastest developers (Deyo 1989; Harvey 1989). It may be that these nations will find AT-based production most useful in reducing the cost of social control through the provision of cheap goods and services for the masses, while the main development trajectories remain focused on meeting the needs of the North. Unless Southern nations focus their national development objectives on self-sufficiency rather than on production for export, AT can only play a peripheral role in Southern development. It is not clear that such self-sufficiency is feasible; nations such as China and Tanzania have attempted to do so without long-term success. It may be that Northern consumption patterns must be altered before the South can redirect development trajectories toward production for meeting Southern rather than Northern needs. What Northern environmentalists can do to improve the environmental, economic, and social conditions in the developing world is, therefore, to work to change the patterns of resource consumption in their own nations.

SELECTED REFERENCES

ALEXANDER, LINDA
  1983 "European planning ideology in Tanzania." *Habitat International* 7 (1/2): 17–36.
AMIN, SAMIR
  1974 *Accumulation on a World Scale.* New York: Monthly Review Press.
  1976 *Unequal Development.* New York: Monthly Review Press.
  1990 *Maldevelopment: Anatomy of a Global Failure.* London: Zed Books.
BROOKE, JAMES
  1992 "Ecuador gives title to big Amazon area." *New York Times,* October 9.
BUNKER, STEPHEN G.
  1985 *Underdeveloping the Amazon: Extraction, Unequal Exchange, and the Failure of the Modern State.* Urbana, IL: University of Illinois Press.
CACERES, ROBERTO
  1980 "A new approach towards rural development: Appropriate technology and the earthquake of 1976 in Guatemala." In J. de Schutter and G. Bemer, editors, *Fundamental Aspects of Appropriate Technology.* Delft: Delft University Press.

CASTELLS, MANUEL & R. LASERNA
  1989 "The new dependency: Technological change and socioeconomic re-
         structuring in Latin America." *Sociological Forum* 4 (4): 535–560.
CHASE-DUNN, CHRISTOPHER
  1989 *Global Formation: Structures of the World-Economy.* Cambridge, MA: Basil
         Blackwell.
D'AVANZO, TOM
  1980 "Social structure and solid waste: An adventure in problem analysis." In
         Robert J. Mitchell, editor, *Experiences in Appropriate Technology.* Ottawa:
         Canadian Hunger Foundation.
DE JANVRY, ALAIN
  1981 *The Agrarian Question and Reformism in Latin America.* Baltimore, MD:
         Johns Hopkins University Press.
DEYO, FREDERIC C.
  1989 *Beneath the Miracle: Labor Subordination in the New Asian Industrialism.*
         Berkeley, CA: University of California Press.
DICKSON, DAVID
  1975 *The Politics of Appropriate Technology.* New York: Universe Books.
DOS SANTOS, THEOTONIO
  1970 "The structure of dependence." *The American Economic Review* LX (2):
         231–236.
EMMANUEL, ARGHIRI
  1972 *Unequal Exchange: A Study in the Imperialism of Trade.* New York: Monthly
         Review Press.
EVANS, PETER B.
  1979 *Dependent Development: The Alliance of Multinational, State and Local Capital
         in Brazil.* Princeton, NJ: Princeton University Press.
FRANK, ANDRE GUNDER
  1979 *Dependent Development and Underdevelopment.* New York: Monthly Review
         Press.
FRANKEL, R. FRANCINE
  1971 *India's Green Revolution: Economic Gains and Political Costs.* Princeton, NJ:
         Princeton University Press.
GOULD, KENNETH A.
  1987 "The devolution of a concept: 'Appropriate' technology in a third world
         context." Paper presented at the annual meetings of the Midwest Socio-
         logical Society, Chicago, March.
GROVES, RICHARD H.
  1992 *Conservation and the Gospel of Efficiency: The Progressive Conservation Move-
         ment, 1890–1920.* New York: Atheneum Books.
GUNAWARDHANA, C. A.
  1980 "Appropriate technology in Sri Lanka." In J. de Schutter and G. Bemer,
         editors, *Fundamental Aspects of Appropriate Technology.* Delft: Delft Univer-
         sity Press.
HARVEY, DAVID
  1989 *The Condition of Postmodernity.* Oxford, England: Basil Blackwell.
HOROWITZ, IRVING L.
  1972 *Three Worlds of Development: The Theory and Practice of International Stratifi-
         cation.* Second edition. New York: Oxford University Press.
HSU, ROBERT C.
  1982 *Food for One Billion: China's Agriculture since 1949.* Boulder, CO: Westview
         Press.

HYDEN, GORAN
1980   *Beyond Ujamaa in Tanzania: Underdevelopment and an Uncaptured Peasantry.* New York: Heinemann.
LAWLAND, TOM A.
1980   "An analysis of factors affecting the successful continuity of a solar distillation plant in the West Indies." In J. de Schutter and G. Bemer, editors, *Fundamental Aspects of Appropriate Technology.* Delft: Delft University Press.
LEONARD, H. JEFFREY, M. YUDELMAN, J. D. STRYKER, J. P. BROWDER, A. J. DEBOER, T. CAMPBELL, & A. JOLLY
1989   *Environment and the Poor: Development Strategies for a Common Agenda.* New Brunswick, NJ: Transaction Books.
MAZRUI, ALI A.
1986   *The Africans: A Triple Heritage.* Boston: Little Brown.
OXAAL, IVAR, T. BARNETT & D. BOOTH, EDITORS
1975   *Beyond the Sociology of Development.* Boston, MA: Routledge & Kegan Paul.
PORTES, ALEJANDRO & JOHN WALTON
1981   *Labor, Class, and the International System.* New York: Academic Press.
REDCLIFT, MICHAEL
1984   *Development and the Environmental Crisis: Red or Green Alternatives?* New York: Methuen.
REDDY, AMULYA KUMAR N.
1979   *Technology, Development and the Environment: A Re-appraisal.* New York: United Nations Environment Programme.
ROBINSON, AUSTIN, EDITOR
1979   *Appropriate Technology for Third World Development.* New York: Macmillan.
RODNEY, WALTER
1982   *How Europe Underdeveloped Africa.* Washington, DC: Howard University Press.
SCHNAIBERG, ALLAN
1982   "Did you ever meet a payroll?: Contradictions in the structure of the appropriate technology movement." *Humboldt Journal of Social Relations* 9 (2) (Spring/Summer):38–62.
1983   "Soft energy and hard labor?: Structural restraints on the transition to appropriate technology." In Gene F. Summers, editor, *Technology and Social Change in Rural Areas.* Boulder, CO: Westview Press.
SCHUMACHER, E. F.
1973   *Small Is Beautiful: Economics As If People Mattered.* New York: Harper & Row.
SELIGSON, MITCHELL A., EDITOR
1984   *The Gap between Rich and Poor: Contending Perspectives on the Political Economy of Development.* Boulder, CO: Westview Press.
SLATER, D.
1974   "Colonialism and the spatial structure of underdevelopment: Outlines of an alternative approach, with special reference to Tanzania." *Progress in Planning* 4 (2): 137–162.
STOKES, RANDALL G. & A. B. ANDERSON
1990   "Disarticulation and human welfare in less developed countries." *American Sociological Review* 55 (1): 63–74.
UNIDO [UNITED NATIONS INDUSTRIAL DEVELOPMENT ORGANIZATION]
1979   *Monographs on Appropriate Industrial Technology.* Nos. 3, 4, 6, 8, and 9. New York: United Nations.

WHARTON, DONALD
  1980 "Designing with users: Developing the Lorena stove Guatemala." In
        Robert J. Mitchell, editor, *Experiences in Appropriate Technology*. Ottawa:
        Canadian Hunger Foundation.
WITTFOGEL, KARL A.
  1957 *Oriental Despotism: A Comparative Study of Total Power*. New Haven, CT:
        Yale University Press.

9. Ecological Sustainability: Of What? For What?

ECOLOGICAL SUSTAINABILITY: ROOTS AND RATIONALES

Economic Growth and Ecological Limits

In the United States, as well as most nations of the world, socioeconomic policies are generally predicated on the assumption that unlimited economic expansion is desirable, possible, and necessary. Both Democrats and Republicans continue to pay homage to the notion that growth is good and to prescribe economic growth as a panacea for nearly all social and economic problems (Needleman 1991). Accordingly, political rhetoric on the national, state, or local level will almost always include an emphasis on economic growth. Political debate in the United States focuses not on the validity of the assumption that unlimited growth is desirable and possible, but rather on the appropriate policies to foster such economic expansion. Political discourse rarely seeks to examine the assumptions underlying the treadmill of production, but instead centers on how to accelerate the treadmill. Such policy debates in modern industrialized capitalist societies assume as a given that the best way to reduce poverty, create jobs, increase revenues, and provide social programs is to expand the economic base on which the society rests. Rather than seeking to divide pieces of the pie more equitably, government seeks to expand the size of the pie, the assumption being that an expanding pie will result in larger pieces for all, at both the top and bottom of the social stratification system.

Historical evidence clearly demonstrates, however, that an expansion of the pie does not necessarily result in larger pieces for all. In fact, the size of the pieces going to the wealthiest individuals is often inflated, while simultaneously the size of the pieces accruing to the most impoverished members of society are shrinking (Barlett & Steele 1992; Phillips 1989). Since 1981 the economy of the United States has experienced periods of growth and contraction. The pie has gotten larger, and the pie has gotten smaller. What has remained constant, however, is the expansion of the wealth of the wealthiest and the contraction of the wealth of the poorest (Barlett & Steele 1992). Such a radical maldistribution of wealth has even led some American politicians, including President Clinton, to initially propose distributing all additional future tax increases to the rich and lowering middle class tax rates, in keeping with his middle class support in the 1992 elections. After taking office, however, his proposal shifted to have increased tax rates for both upper and middle classes, with a larger increase for the rich.

What is almost never considered is the validity of the assumptions underlying the treadmill. Rising unemployment results in calls for expanding the nation's manufacturing base and investment in industrial production to bolster America's competitiveness in the world economy (Reich 1991). Both major American political parties insist that investing in modernizing the nation's factories, thereby expanding production, will prevent jobs from being lost to other nations. In addition, organized labor has been repeatedly asked or coerced into accepting declining incomes, job security, and benefits in order to increase the wealth of managers, so that they may reinvest in industrial modernization (Galbraith 1992). Workers are asked to accept the "reality" that they must take less from the treadmill in order to avoid losing jobs to workers in the South, whose poverty compels them to work for even less money than workers in the North (Reich 1991).

Such policy trajectories contain a number of startling ironies, some obvious, and some more subtle. The most obvious irony is that workers are told that they must take less in order to make more. They are encouraged to believe that, by agreeing to make less money relative to managers, they will be aiding American competitiveness in the world market, creating new domestic jobs, and thereby expanding the economic pie, supposedly making their share of that pie larger in the long run. It should be apparent, however, that making less money is not a good way of making more money. Accepting lower wages, fewer benefits, and less job security is hardly a reliable strategy for insuring higher wages, greater benefits, and increased job security. In addition, reducing the wealth of workers and increasing the wealth of investors and managers is an inefficient mechanism for building a broad base of domestic economic demand for consumer goods (Blumberg 1980).

Lower paychecks are likely to result in lower demand for the variety of products that the middle class might purchase. Lower demand is likely to result in even further loss of domestic manufacturing jobs, and even fewer and smaller paychecks, which in turn will reduce domestic demand even further. The domestic demand that will be increased by such a negative redistribution of wealth is demand for very expensive luxury products consumed by the tiny percentage of the population at the highest end of the stratification scale. Hence, the trickle-down strategy for expanding the American economy that was put in place in 1981 has resulted in a downward spiral for the economy, higher unemployment, lower wages, and a loss of the manufacturing base, while producing huge and unprecedented windfalls for the already wealthy (Barlett & Steele 1992;

Phillips 1989). Retention of domestic manufacturing jobs now depends on preserving the privilege of the wealthiest in order to maintain demand for luxury goods and to retain the small number of wage-labor positions that such demand creates. Yacht manufacturing has remained, while radio, TV, and VCR manufacturing has departed (Reich 1991).

A less obvious, but equally important, irony emerging from the ideology of ever expanding economic growth has to do with the nature of technological innovation. A primary goal of technological innovation since the earliest emergence of the industrial revolution has been to reduce demand for labor and replace it with capital. As we have seen in Chapter 8 in regard to the nations of the South, technological modernization results in substituting labor-intensive techniques with capital-intensive techniques. Technological progress therefore translates into replacement of jobs with machines. Those who control the trajectory of technological innovation through economic power over the corporate, university, and government institutions that produce scientific and technological change seek to reduce long-term labor costs through replacement with short-term investments in technological substitutes. The entire complex of modern technological innovation is fueled by the desire to reduce labor inputs (Reich 1991). This technological trajectory manifests itself in a variety of ways, from kitchen appliances designed to "save time" in the home, to remote controls designed to eliminate the need for people to get off of their couches to change channels, to robotic assembly lines designed to increase production while reducing labor costs. Politicians, corporate investors, and university scientists are all engaged in promoting the further development of labor-saving technologies. (Ronald Reagan sold labor-saving kitchen appliances in his TV advertisements for General Electric in the 1950s. In the 1980s he sold robotics and star-war technologies in his role as president in TV advertisements for trickle-down economic growth strategies.)

For managers, technology has a number of important advantages over wage-labor. Machines do not get sick, become pregnant, strike, demand higher pay, require retirement pensions, or organize politically. Nor do they vote against political incumbents or organize into unions if they perceive their political and economic interests to be threatened. They also do not require public assistance from the government when they are replaced by a new generation of labor-saving, capital-intensive technologies (Galbraith 1992). For politicians and corporate managers, machines are more reliable, more malleable, and less costly than workers.

What this implies for workers is that strategies to increase American competitiveness in the world economy through technological modernization are necessarily contrary to their own interests (cf. Reich 1991). Accepting lower wages and fewer benefits to increase the wealth of managers, so that they may invest in the modernization of the American manufacturing base, will ultimately allow managers to replace them completely with machines. When the primary goal of technological innovation is to reduce the demand for human labor, modernization of industry to bolster international competitiveness means creating higher unemployment. As in the nations of the South, technological modernization in the North results in a decreased employment capacity for the affected economies (Barlett & Steele 1992). Politicians and corporate managers who extol the virtues of modernization and implore workers to assist in the modernization effort through the granting of economic concessions are in reality asking or coercing workers to collude in their own displacement. Modernization may make American-based corporations more competitive in the global economy, but it does so at the expense of domestic jobs, domestic paychecks, and domestic consumer demand. In addition, replacing labor-intensive techniques with energy-intensive techniques is likely to put greater strain on the world's limited nonrenewable energy resources (Redclift 1987).

Human Economies and Natural Resources

Increased demand for nonrenewable energy resources brings us to the primary ecological fallacy underlying the assumption of unlimited economic expansion. Human economies are ultimately dependent on natural resources. All human societies depend on their natural resource base for the production of goods. The earth is the resource base of any technological complex. Our technological systems, from the most labor-intensive subsistence agriculture to the most capital-intensive robotic supercomputer manufacturing, depend on the resources provided by natural ecological systems.

The ideology of economic expansion assumes never-ending growth. Endless growth requires an endless supply of resource inputs and an endless capacity for absorbing ecological additions. The problem with such assumptions is that a system that requires continuously increasing environmental additions and withdrawals is ultimately dependent on a finite planet, with a finite resource base and a finite capacity to absorb ecological additions. Dependence on a finite resource base precludes endless growth, endless withdrawals, and endless additions. Therefore, the global ecosystem must ultimately impose limits to economic growth. If economic expansion is constrained in the long run by these ecological limits, then any socioeconomic system predicated on the assumption that infinite economic expansion is possible, desirable, and necessary must ultimately fail. Thus, if ever increasing global poverty and unemployment are not sufficient to bring the assumption of economic expansion into question, the collapse of the global ecosystem on which all life depends will (Brown et al. 1991).

The Dimensions of Sustainability

The reimposition of ecological limits stems primarily from two environmental barriers to the continuation of our current development trajectory. The first barrier is ecological scarcity. The depletion of nonrenewable natural resources will ultimately result in our running out of key inputs for our industrial technological complex. The second barrier stems from the negative impacts of externalizing the costs (both economically and ecologically) of industrial and municipal wastes. The pollution of our natural resource base threatens both the continuity of the environment as a source of vital inputs (such as fresh water) and the health of all organisms, including humans. In addition, rapid population growth exacerbates the rapidity with which these two barriers become evident, because such growth often increases both ecological withdrawals (depletion) and ecological additions (pollution). The emergence of major depletion and pollution problems at the end of the twentieth century has brought into question the viability of our technological systems and the validity of the economic assumptions on which those systems are predicated.

An important critique of current technological and socioeconomic trends has been based on the notion of sustainability (South Commission 1990; World Commission on Environment & Development 1987). Is our current technological and economic structure sustainable in the long run? In order to understand the problem that we are faced with at this point in human history, we need to examine the ways in which our current trajectory is vulnerable to problems of depletion and pollution, which we outline below (Redclift 1987).

DEPLETION

Energy Demand Reliance on nonrenewable energy resources insures that these resources will eventually be completely depleted. Increasing demand depletes these resources at an ever increasing pace. Economic growth necessitates greater levels of consumption by greater numbers of people. Energy conservation efforts can only buy us a bit more time. Therefore, the ideology of growth moves us closer and closer to the day when no fossil fuel resources will remain. When that day comes, if we have not developed alternative technologies for energy supplies, the entire socioeconomic and industrial-technological complex of global society will collapse (Frahm & Buttel 1982). Such a collapse will be the single most cataclysmic event in all of human history. Very few in the North will survive.

Raw Material Inputs Our current systems depend on a finite supply of other nonrenewable natural resource inputs, such as a wide variety of metals. Increasing levels of consumption by increasing numbers of people deplete the supply of these resources increasingly quickly. The greater the economic growth, the faster the rate of depletion. Such depletion makes these resources increasingly scarce and, therefore, increasingly expensive. The greater the cost of these natural resource inputs, the more incentive there is for industries to search for substitutes. In most instances, resource substitutes are less well suited for the process for which they are required. Eventually, these nonrenewable substitutes are also depleted. Each round of substitution results in increased costs, increased scarcity, and a decreased natural resource base on which society depends. In the long run, such continuous substitution will result in both economic collapse (as key industrial processes become too expensive to perpetuate) and ecological collapse (as the simplified ecosystem must rebalance at a less productive, varied, and rich state). Both forms of collapse will take a huge toll on human and other populations (Brown 1991).

POLLUTION

Chemical (Toxic) Industrial Wastes   The addition of toxic chemical wastes to the environment reduces the capacity of ecosystems to support life and yield utilizable natural resources. The disruption of ecosystems tends to simplify the environment, making it less productive. Chemical additions have resulted in the extinction of certain species locally, thus reducing the genetic diversity of local ecosystems. Contamination of fresh water resources has resulted in a variety of negative health impacts on humans and other species. Such contamination necessitates increased resource expenditures to treat, transport, and store fresh water.

Municipal Waste   Much of the recent reemergence of environmental concerns in the public arena stems from new problems associated with the disposal of municipal garbage. The closing of local landfills, contamination of aquifers, local resistance to the siting of both new landfills and incinerators, and regional conflict surrounding the transport of municipal waste have all contributed to the current garbage crisis. This crisis has resulted in a variety of proposed solutions, including the options of reducing, reusing, and recycling waste products (Schnaiberg 1992a, 1992b).

If the pollution and depletion problems briefly outlined above make our current economic and technological trajectory ultimately unsustainable, how can we begin to redirect our society toward the goal of sustainability?

SUSTAINABILITY GOALS VERSUS TREADMILL-SUSTAINING PRESSURES

As we have seen in Chapter 8 regarding the notion of appropriate technology, the various definitions and conceptualizations of terms such as sustainability are extremely important in developing new trajectories (Farvar & Glaeser 1979; Frahm & Buttel 1982; Glaeser 1984; Shiva 1989). In Chapter 8, the different conceptualizations of the meaning of *appropriate* were shown to lead in very different socioeconomic and technological directions. The ambiguity that emerged from that variety of definitions was largely responsible for the failure of the appropriate technology movement in the 1970s to achieve a significant restructuring of modern technological complexes.

In the 1990s sustainability has been invoked in much the same way as appropriateness was in an earlier decade, that is, as a means by which to reassess socioeconomic and technological systems in terms of their long-term viability within the constraints of ecological limits (Court 1990). Having found that our current trajectory must ultimately collapse under the dual ecological pressures of depletion and pollution, we can utilize the notion of sustainability as a criterion with which to judge the appropriateness of a socioeconomic or technological system for achieving long-term economic, social, and ecological stability (cf. Redclift 1987). However, in order to operationalize the concept of sustainability, it is crucial that we define it clearly. Otherwise, sustainability will go the way of appropriateness, devolving in a sea of ambiguity and cross-purposes into a meaningless construct signifying nothing, as Chapter 8 documented.

In fact, given the social and economic power of the treadmill as the basis of our modern societies, our first response to the reemergence of ecological scarcity has been to search for means by which to sustain the treadmill. Governments, managers, and workers all have their economic futures tied to the continuation and acceleration of the treadmill of production. It is not surprising then that the initial reaction to the idea that the treadmill will not be sustainable in the long run will be to attempt to make minor adjustments to the treadmill to get around ecological limits, at least in the short run. The least costly, least disruptive, and least structural changes will be applied first (Redclift 1987).

The environmental slogan "reduce, reuse, recycle" presents three very different approaches to achieving sustainability. They are listed in order of their environmental benefits, reduction being the most beneficial and recycling the least beneficial. This rank ordering also reflects the depth and breadth of structural change that each response requires, the greatest change being associated with the notion of reduction and the slightest change with recycling. It is therefore not surprising that our society's initial response to the reimposition of ecological limits has been to enthusiastically support recycling as a panacea for environmental problems (Schnaiberg 1992a).

In the 1960s and 1970s, when the notion of ecological limits to growth still appeared to be more theoretical than tangible, governments, industries, and consumers largely rejected the idea of recycling as an unnecessary and radical response to environmental disorganization. The litter problem brought government and industry to support fines meant to discourage disposal of municipal waste anywhere other than the sanctioned dumps. As those dumps filled in the 1980s and as local communities opposed efforts to site new dumps, the cost of waste disposal increased. By the 1990s the social, economic, and ecological limits to waste disposal had become much more tangible than they had been in the 1970s. Faced with increased disposal costs, governments and industries came to embrace recycling enthusiastically, where just twenty years earlier they had rejected it out of hand (Schnaiberg 1992b).

Recycling is now the primary thrust of the response of government, industry, consumers, and even many environmental organizations, to the reemergence of ecological limits. Recycling requires very little change in the economic strategies of government and industry or in the current technological trajectory. Those minor changes that it does require fall mainly on consumers, who must wash, sort, and transport their recyclables for reuse by the corporation that produced them. While postconsumption recycling does have some impact on the levels of natural resource extraction required to keep the treadmill in motion, that impact is the least of the three options proposed in "reduce, reuse, recycle," and it has the most regressive social and economic impacts.

Another attempt at sustaining the current production system involves in-plant industrial waste recovery. This effort involves recovering industrial chemicals and reusing them for further industrial production. Some industrial producers have adopted this strategy because, like consumer-based recycling, it cuts industrial production input costs. Rather than purchasing new chemical inputs, the industry makes the most use of already paid-for chemicals. The cost of the slight modification of the production facilities that this requires is often passed on to consumers in the form of higher product prices. The corporation also gains public relations benefits by being portrayed (by itself, government, and environmental groups) as environmentally friendly. As a result, corporations such as 3M are touted as environmental leaders, while continuing their contribution to the treadmill of production at a cost-savings. Although such minor adjustments to the technology of the treadmill do reduce the amount of toxic chemicals entering the environment in the short run, in the long run increased profits will be used to expand industrial facilities (Catton 1980). Thus, the savings will result in getting more production and consumption from the same amount of chemical environmental degradation, accelerating the treadmill. The acceleration of the treadmill will mean more consumer-generated waste, more industrial energy resource consumption, and more environmental degradation, all at a lower cost to the industry (Commoner 1972).

In many ways this is similar to the impact of the call for increased fuel efficiency for automobiles. At first, increasing the number of miles that a consumer can travel on one gallon of gasoline might appear to be a reasonable approach to reducing carbon monoxide additions and fossil fuel withdrawals. However, in most cases, the increased fuel efficiency gets translated into more miles of travel, not into fewer gallons of gasoline purchased (Commoner 1977). Consumers who can now travel farther for the same amount of money choose to do so, rather than travel only as far or as much as they did previously. Instead of saving money on transportation costs and saving the environment through a reduction of pollution and depletion, people often simply take advantage of their increased range of travel. As a result, fuel-efficient automobiles do not have a significant impact on the environment, except for reducing some local smog problems. We simply get more mileage from the same levels of depletion and pollution. This may increase the short-term sustainability of the economy, but it does little to increase the sustainability of the environment. In addition, increased mileage may allow people to live farther from work, travel farther to shop, and take longer distance vacations. All of these activities involve an increase in natural resource usage: roads must be constructed or expanded, subdivisions encroach on relatively untouched ecosystems, and parking lots and malls get larger and larger (Mumford 1967). What at first appears to be a partial solution to environmental problems turns out to be simply another means to preserve the existing socioeconomic and technological complex, accelerating the treadmill and increasing the velocity at which we overshoot ecological limits (Catton 1980; Commoner 1977).

One way of documenting this is to consider how Americans have changed their driving patterns since the start of the "oil crisis" in 1974. In 1975, the average mileage per gallon obtained from autos in the United States was 13.52. By 1988, legislation had produced a fuel efficiency of 19.95 miles per gallon (U.S. Federal Highway Administration 1987, 1989), almost a 50 percent improvement in fuel efficiency. However, from 1975 to 1988 the fuel consumed by automobiles only decreased from 76.4 to 71.7 billions of gallons, about 6 percent of a decline. The reason for this is that automobile driving increased from 1040 to 1439 billion miles, an increase of almost 40 percent! We see in these statistics little evidence of any disinvestment in the energy-inefficient private automobile as a key element in American transportation.

Other efforts aimed at sustaining the treadmill of production are also focused on energy, inasmuch as fossil fuel depletion is the most threatening natural resource withdrawal limit to the treadmill. Many efforts are being aimed at exploiting a wider variety of energy sources as a means of spreading the depletion process over a wider variety of natural resources, thereby forestalling the day when the complete exhaustion of any one key resource results in economic collapse. Energy resource substitution seeks to achieve short-term treadmill sustainability by substituting more abundant resource inputs for less abundant ones. For example, since the oil shocks of the 1970s research and development efforts have focused on the production of electric automobiles as a way of decreasing dependency on oil (Commoner 1977). Of course, electric cars must be charged from some source of electric power generation. Since the United States has a relative abundance of coal, electric cars could be charged from coal-burning power plants. This would reduce automobile consumption of oil by substituting coal as the ultimate power source. The development of electric cars will allow us to continue our current patterns of automobile use, without much concern for the depletion of oil reserves. No significant structural change in the treadmill of production would be required. Car companies would still produce private transportation vehicles, energy resource-extracting corporations would continue to extract and sell energy resources, governments would continue to build and maintain roads, and our current patterns of spatial arrangements (such as commuting to work, driving to nonlocal shopping malls, and long driving vacations) would require no alteration. Thus, the treadmill is sustained. However, electric cars still require the depletion of fossil fuel resources. In addition, more coal-burning power plants will be required, producing more greenhouse gases (emitted from more centralized sources). In the long run, the environment benefits very little from such technological tinkering. In the long run, a treadmill utilizing electric cars is as ecologically unsustainable as gasoline-based cars (Commoner 1977).

Yet another thrust in the effort to substitute one nonrenewable energy resource for another is focused on the expansion of nuclear power generation. In this approach to sustaining current production systems, nuclear power is substituted for fossil fuel usage, where possible. Of course, nuclear technologies involve some of the most pernicious environmental risks yet devised by humanity (Gofman & Tamplin 1971). One need only to look at Hanover, Washington; Fernald, Ohio; Oak Ridge, Tennessee; Port Hope, Ontario; Laguna, New Mexico; or the Argonne National Laboratory site in Illinois to see the extreme and unremediable hazards posed by nuclear technologies. After more than fifty years of development, no technology has yet been developed for the safe disposal of nuclear waste. The accidents at Three Mile Island and Chernobyl have clearly demonstrated the environmental risks involved in nuclear power generation. And, as others have demonstrated (Ophuls 1977), the limited time frame in which these power plants are operational requires continuously increasing the rate at which they are produced, leaving increasing numbers of decommissioned plants to be monitored and protected for thousands of years. In addition, the huge amounts of water that these plants require for cooling have led them to be located directly on our primary sources of fresh water.

Nevertheless, it is conceivable that the United States could follow the lead of France in substituting nuclear power with fossil fuels to reduce both the threat of fossil fuel depletion and the emission of greenhouse gases. The calculation as to how many Chernobyls equal how many coal-burning power plants in terms of negative environmental impacts will be left to others (Mazur 1991: ch. 8). Interestingly, it is a symptom of the treadmill that we are left to calculate how much genetic mutation is worth how many degrees of global warming. It would be possible to charge electric cars from nuclear power sources in order to maintain the economic and technological structures that are already in place, at least in the short run. Of course, in the long run, uranium resource supplies must also be depleted, and that depletion will accelerate as substitution for fossil fuels continues and as the energy demands of an increasingly larger and more consumption-oriented global population rise. But that depletion is likely to be far enough in the future to have the issue evaded in schemes to sustain the treadmill now. Finally, when forced to consider the possibility of exhausting uranium supplies or nondisposability of radioactive waste, the technologists and politicians engaged in efforts to perpetuate the treadmill will resort to the fantasy technology of nuclear fusion, which we are told will provide inexhaustible supplies of safe, clean, and cheap energy. That is what an earlier generation of technologists and politicians said about nuclear fission just fifty years ago (Gofman & Tamplin 1971).

Similar efforts to create and sustain the treadmill were also developed much earlier in our history than nuclear technologies. The rapid deforestation of North America in the nineteenth century led a generation of conservationists to promote sustained-yield management of forests in order to get around the ecological limits imposed by overconsumption of a renewable resource (Hays 1969). Unlike fossil fuels, forests can renew themselves naturally, or they can be farmed like any other agricultural product. Therefore, finding a way to insure a continual supply of wood for future human demand does not require the invention of brave new technologies. Natural forests can be (and are) clear-cut, and they are replaced with uniform rows of commercially valuable species of trees to be harvested and replanted at regular intervals. Such a system can guarantee a usable "crop" of wood each year. At the same time, however, it does so at the expense of the natural environment. Complex natural ecosystems are replaced by mono-crop agriculture, resulting in the extinction of a wide variety of flora and fauna. Just as a corn field bears little resemblance to a wild prairie, a tree farm bears little resemblance to a natural forest. The extremely simplified managed environment cannot support the genetic diversity that natural forests harbor. The ecologically barren forests that replace natural diversity in managed tree farms can be seen throughout the United States, from lumber company forests to national forests. They can also be seen throughout the world. Sweden, often touted for its high level of environmental concern, is famous for its ability to provide sustainable-yield forestry. However, closer examination of the Swedish ecology reveals that over 90 percent of its native forest is extinct. North American tree species have replaced native Swedish species. Native plants and animals have been exterminated, sacrificed for an economically-sustainable industry. The Swedish treadmill is sustained at the expense of the Swedish environment.

Finally, another scheme to sustain the treadmill in the face of ecological limits is the economic notion of "burning the rocks." As depletion of key mineral resources continues, the demand for these minerals increases relative to the decreasing supply. The market price of these minerals is inflated as increases in demand accelerate and supplies dwindle. The higher the price that the market will bear for such minerals, the more economically feasible it becomes to mine ever poorer ores. Of course, at some point, the market value of the mineral will become meaningless if no one can afford to create real economic demand for it. However, many economists argue that the free market will make it profitable to extract trace amounts of minerals from ever larger volumes of rock, thereby tapping the so-called crustal abundance of minerals. As the price inflates, mineral-extracting corporations will find that it pays to "burn the rocks" to extract minuscule amounts of precious minerals. This approach to sustaining the economy, taken to its logical conclusion, recommends that, in the face of ecological scarcity, we would be wise to tear down the Rocky Mountains to remove a few tons of precious minerals. The environmental implications of such a solution are obvious. Eventually, we would have to strip-mine the entire planet, destroying the global ecosystem on a massive scale. Of course, the energy inputs required to do this would be enormous. It will take quite a few fusion reactors to tear down the Rocky Mountains and burn them for their trace mineral content. Even if such massive environmental destruction could be made possible by the development of a fantasy energy technology, eventually we will run out of rocks to burn as well. At that point, a global population of 6 + billion would have to live floating on the sea as we mined the final layers of the earth's terrestrial crust. Long before that we will have already mined the garbage dumps left by earlier generations in order to extract the precious materials buried within them.

As we have seen, a sustainable socioeconomic and technological complex based on an essentially unaltered treadmill of production could be run on increasingly abundant nuclear fission reactors, with the reactors built near population centers. We could drive electric cars (if we could afford them), and mine huge quantities of nearly worthless rocks to get trace amounts of minerals. We could cook and heat with renewable wood taken from our sustained-yield tree farms (although we would have to clear the remaining natural forests of the world to meet demands). We would, of course, have to pay higher prices for all our consumer goods, even as production costs dropped owing to the internal recovery of chemicals and our provision of free recyclable inputs to producers. (Remember, modernization costs are passed on to workers and consumers.) We will recycle almost everything, which will require us to spend most of our "leisure" time cleaning, sorting, and transporting raw material inputs for the industries around us. Ironically, in this way industry would make truly efficient use of us as workers. We would work eight hours a day for the corporation in the factory. Much of the rest of the day, we would subsidize industry with our domestic labor. Whatever time remains would be devoted to shopping for the products being manufactured (Schor 1991).

This is one model for a potentially sustainable economy. It requires minimal social, economic, or technological change. Neither the economic nor the technological complex is altered substantially. Production and consumption patterns don't change much either, except that the numbers of poor people will likely increase dramatically (just as they are currently increasing). Technologies are not replaced by many new innovations. Of course, it will produce a very harsh, dead environment to live in. Most life on earth will have to be sacrificed, except when a species is economically valuable. Most natural ecosystems will have to be destroyed. And the economic aspirations of the billions in the South will have to be crushed. But it could be done in the name of treadmill sustainability, if only for another few hundred years (Redclift 1987).

PRESERVING THE ENVIRONMENT FOR OTHER SOCIAL USES

Don't despair: there are other models for a sustainable society based on very different conceptualizations of what sustainability means, what we want to sustain, and who we want to sustain it for (e.g., Evernden 1985). Alternatives to perpetuating the unaltered treadmill are conceivable, even if powerful forces are mobilized against such alternatives. One alternative conceptualization of sustainability seeks to preserve part of the natural environment for other social uses. These alternative uses of the environment are not purely economic in character. They include recreational activities such as hiking, walking, camping, boating, fishing, hunting, bird watching, swimming, and picnicking. Alternative social uses also include somewhat less tangible benefits such as aesthetic appreciation, relaxation, peace of mind, and spiritual rejuvenation. Although these less tangible benefits are difficult to quantify in economic terms, they are no less important in this conceptualization of sustainability than those that can be conceived to be part of a recreation industry economy. In fact, despite the lower emphasis on purely economic uses of natural resources manifest in this alternative conceptualization of sustainability, the alternative social uses included in this view can be easily construed as being integral to a tourism and recreation economy.

Such alternative use economies can be found throughout the United States and the world, with many regional and national economies largely dependent on these uses of the environments for their survival. Many of the island nations of the Caribbean depend on the attractiveness of their natural environment—their clean beaches, mountains covered with lush vegetation, and clean coastal waters—to support their socioeconomic systems. Similarly, regions of the United States, especially those that are more peripheral to the industrial economy, depend on tourism and recreation for large shares of their economic activity (Gould 1991). The sea islands of the Carolinas, the mountains of southern Appalachia, the coasts of south Florida, the lakes of Minnesota, the ski slopes of Colorado, and many other regions rely on their natural resource endowments to provide attraction for tourists and recreational travelers.

Even the deindustrializing areas of the Great Lakes are seeking to find new, less environmentally destructive underpinnings for their local economies. Where once the Great Lakes may have been seen primarily as an industrial sewer, the economic necessity of finding alternative ways to utilize local natural resources is leading to new visions of the lakes as recreational opportunities (Gould 1991). Such economic and conceptual restructuring necessitates the preservation or remediation of local environments to allow for new uses. As a result, in some areas industrial outfalls are being replaced with marinas.

Clearly, what may at first appear to be a turn away from an exclusive emphasis on economic sustainability may in fact be a turn toward sustainable economies. Although framing alternative social uses in such a utilitarian fashion may appear to unnecessarily reorient these alternatives back toward economic conceptualizations of natural resources, it is important to remember that such sustainable economies rely on a demand for alternative uses. Without interest in the recreational and quality-of-life benefits of the natural environment, tourism and recreation economies could not exist. It is therefore necessary to promote and maintain societal interest in these alternative social uses of natural systems. Such interests allow localities to achieve economic sustainability in ways that are less damaging to natural systems than the industrial economies outlined in the previous section.

This alternative view of sustainability requires that we reduce our negative impacts on the environment in order to permit the economic manifestations of this alternative conceptualization to flourish. Treading more lightly on the environment will require much more structural change in our society's economic and technological relationships with the natural world. Remember that in the slogan "reduce, reuse, recycle," reduction is the approach that requires the greatest degree of social structural change. If recycling is aimed primarily at sustaining the existing socioeconomic structure, some reuse and reduction become necessary when seeking to sustain the natural environment for other social uses. It is important that we remember the distinction between sustaining the current socioeconomic and technological trajectories, and seeking to achieve economic and environmental sustainability by altering those trajectories. Sustaining the present economy is qualitatively different from constructing a sustainable economy in social variations in reimposing ecological limits (Schnaiberg 1992a, 1992b).

A view of sustainability that includes using natural systems for social purposes other than sustaining the current economic trajectory requires that environmental considerations be included in the previously purely economic calculus that views the natural world as essentially a stock of natural resources to be exploited for industrial production. Although the view of the environment is still utilitarian in terms of protecting natural systems only to provide for human needs, human needs are conceived more broadly here than in our first conceptualization. Here, they include those needs that are not purely material. Economic benefits must be attached to using the environment for other social ends in order to provide incentives for residents of potentially attractive recreation areas to maintain the integrity of the local environment in the face of the forces of the treadmill. It is easy for those living in urban areas to promote and support the preservation of the environments in places where they don't live but would like to exploit for their own enjoyment. However, those who actually reside in these economically more peripheral areas are not as ready to sacrifice the economic benefits of industrialization for more environmentally benign resource uses (Burton 1986). Most suburban and urban dwellers already have access to the economic benefits associated with the treadmill of industrial production. They also are overwhelmed by the social and environmental costs of such urban-industrial complexes. As a result, they seek temporary escape from the negatives by traveling to less developed areas, with the intention of returning shortly to the world of material gains. Of course, many of the poor inner-city residents do not receive the material gains of the urban-industrial complex. While bearing the bulk of the social, economic, and quality of life costs, they do not have the means by which to take temporary retreat in other, less oppressive environments.

People worldwide who live in less developed areas cannot afford to preserve the natural world around them for the enjoyment of others without some economic means to support their own material well-being and accumulation. It is unjust and naive to expect those in less developed areas to accept their relative poverty for either the recreation of the wealthy or the health of the environment. People in less developed areas will resist the efforts of the urban elite to dictate patterns of natural resource uses in their regions, which would ultimately deepen their level of structural marginality. If others are to be expected to preserve the natural world for the benefit of those who prosper from degrading it, at the very minimum these others must be given a means by which to reap economic benefits from their efforts. The development of tourism and recreation economies is one method of achieving some of these benefits, with minimal costs to nonlocal environmental users.

Tourism and recreation economies benefit the natural world by creating structural economic alternatives to extractive or other ecologically destructive enterprises. This is as true in the less developed parts of the world as it is in the deindustrializing regions. Such ecologically more sustainable economies give people an economic stake in some level of environmental preservation. In many instances, it also promotes the preservation of traditional crafts, such as in Native American reservations and some nations of the South. However, sustainable economies that seek to preserve the natural world only in ways that provide for other social uses of natural resources still produce many negative environmental impacts. Although such a conceptualization of sustainability is far less destructive to the environment than the continuation of the unmodified treadmill, the economies based on other social uses are not environmentally benign.

One need only look at Miami Beach, Florida; Cancún, Mexico; Gatlinburg, Tennessee; or Aspen, Colorado, to see that unmitigated expansion of tourism and recreation economies tends to destroy the very basis on which they emerged. Unspoiled beaches with beautiful scenery rapidly devolve into crowded strips of sand with views of nothing but high-rise hotels. Mountain tranquility metamorphoses into endless strips of fast-food emporiums, condominium developments, and traffic snarls. Trout streams become endless lines of hooked worms and empty beer cans. For the majority of places of unspoiled natural beauty, discovery by urban and suburban residents spells destruction if access to these areas is not somehow restricted. Not long ago, the islands of the Caribbean were relatively far away, separated from the American masses by ocean, high air fares, and limited accommodations. Today these islands have been transformed into reproductions of Miami Beach as access has increased. Similarly, Yosemite Valley was once a remote "Shangri-La" of natural splendor. It is now a fast-food "Mecca" with pretty views.

In addition to the environmental problems of overdevelopment, tourism and recreation also tend to overload local infrastructures. In the Caribbean, as in American national parks, sewage and sanitation systems cannot expand rapidly enough to handle the increases in human and consumer wastes. Fresh water supplies are contaminated and depleted, garbage dumps proliferate, and untreated sewage destroys marine ecosystems. Overuse also brings with it increases in local air and noise pollution, as cars, planes, helicopters, personal watercraft, and snowmobiles converge on an area. Furthermore, the removal of "souvenirs" depletes the local environment and destroys cultural historical artifacts (as tourists create demand for black coral or take home "a piece of the rock" from ancient structures). Similarly, hunting and fishing, if left unchecked or unstocked, deplete local fauna populations. A preference for particular sport species may create demand for the alteration of local ecosystems in favor of more uniform and reliable "killing fields." Finally, mass tourism increases the overall demand for energy resources for transportation, accommodations, eateries, and amusements. This increased demand accelerates the rates of energy resource depletion, as well as the production of greenhouse and ozone-depleting gases. (Remember that the rapid development of Florida, the American Southwest, and tropical resort spots from Hawaii to the Ivory Coast was accelerated by the development of air-conditioning technology, which is an energy-guzzling, prime source of chlorofluorocarbons.) However, despite these negative environmental impacts, if managed well, tourism and recreation economies are still more ecologically benign than many industrial and extractive economic developments (cf. Evernden 1985).

If restricted access is necessary to preserve these areas from overdevelopment by the very people who flock there to escape overdevelopment, a mechanism to limit use must be developed. Within the socioeconomic confines of the treadmill, the primary mechanism for limiting access in an age of relatively abundant transportation technologies is monetary cost. Those physically accessible tourism and recreation spots that are not buried under high-rise hotels and fast-food chains are too expensive for all but the treadmill elite to enjoy. The agents who benefit the most from the destruction of the natural world are also those who have the means to preserve small portions of it for their own alternative social uses, relegating the rest of society to the utilization of rapidly denuding areas. If pricing is the mechanism by which access to the natural world is restricted, only those with the largest stake in destroying it will be able to enjoy that which they have left undamaged (Schnaiberg 1994). Although this may adequately achieve the limited environmental goals of sustainability for other social uses, it fails to achieve the social goals of making those alternative uses available to the majority. It attains some environmental integrity at the expense of environmental justice (Schnaiberg 1994). To achieve both the environmental and social goals of this alternative development trajectory, access must be limited by more egalitarian methods, such as lotteries, first come first served, licensing, or rotation plans. The limited alternative mechanisms for distributing access to these other social uses graphically illustrate the hegemony of the logic of the treadmill in allocating natural and social resources.

In addition to the negative environmental impacts, a number of social impacts are associated with tourism and recreational uses of natural systems which may be offensive to our sense of socioenvironmental justice. Especially in the impoverished nations of the South, the food produced to provide tourists with luxurious feasts takes land out of use for subsistence agricultural production to feed local populations. Even if this loss of farms is offset somewhat by the creation of local jobs, local populations become more dependent on the cash economy, where previously they may have been self-sufficient in terms of their food supply. The jobs that are created, whether in the United States or in the South, tend to be low-wage, low-skill, servant positions, requiring self-sufficient farmers to become waiters and maids dependent on tips from wealthy overconsumers. This is distorting to local economies and demeaning to local populations. The other jobs promoted by tourism are often illicit positions, such as prostitution and drug dealing. The negative social and health impacts of both activities are rather obvious. In addition, although it creates demand for cash crop agricultural products in some regions, land devoted to coca, marijuana, or poppy production removes land from food production. Finally, "souvenir hunting" is often just a pretty term for the looting of cultural artifacts.

These negatives may be offset somewhat by the decreased health risks, especially to industrial workers and the poor, associated with the alternative of an industrial manufacturing economy. Therefore, as a move from the industrial treadmill toward broader social uses of the environment, the emergence of a larger tourism and recreation sector of the economy may be seen as social and environmental progress (if local wages can be kept relatively high). However, as a move from subsistence agricultural self-sufficiency, such a change could be construed as ecologically and socially regressive, depending on the evaluative criteria operationalized in the analysis. It is important to remember that even a society concerned with preserving the environment for other social uses depends on an economic base to provide the wealth to be used to purchase, or fund through governments, access to these other uses. If that economy is primarily industrial, many negative environmental and social impacts associated with sustaining the treadmill will continue. The primary benefit of this conceptualization of sustainability is in bringing other social uses into the societal accounting in treadmill cost-benefit analyses (Schnaiberg 1980: ch. 7).

PROTECTING ECOSYSTEMS FOR OTHER SPECIES: SUSTAINABLE ECOLOGY

Although clearly an improvement over the unmodified treadmill, protecting the environment for other social uses is still an overtly anthropocentric view of nature (Evernden 1985). Such a view still values the environment primarily as a set of resources for humans to do with as they please.

They may decide to save flora and fauna for their own enjoyment rather than destroying it for their own material enrichment, but flora and fauna and the complex web that interconnects them are valued only in terms of human need and human desires. A more deeply ecological view would seek to preserve the natural world on its own merits, conceptualizing the human interaction with nature as a set of obligations rather than a set of rights (Evernden 1985). Such a move toward sustainable ecology, where the preservation of natural systems is primary and the rights of other forms of life are respected, would require drastic structural changes in our social, economic, and technological systems. To preserve ecosystems for other species, without regard to the potential value of those ecosystems to human economies, we must dramatically reduce the impacts of human societies on the environment. Such reduction will require much sacrifice of the material standards of living which the majority of those in the North and the elite minority in the South have become accustomed to. We will, however, make great gains in terms of the other social uses of natural systems discussed in the previous section. We will have to live within very restrictive ecological limits. The luxuries of private cars, unconstrained energy use, high-technology medical care, and the material benefits derived from a plethora of industrial chemical processes will be lost. People will have to become more locally self-sufficient for their needs and less acquisitive in their desires. In instances where human economies conflict with the requirements of ecosystems, economies will have to be adjusted.

Operationalizing sustainability as an ecological ethic requires many material sacrifices. For example, it will necessarily mean that we reduce the quality of our environmental impacts (types of human withdrawals and additions), the quantity of our impacts (populations benefiting from those withdrawals and additions), or both. We can choose to dramatically reduce either the world's human population, through famine, war, lack of health care, "final solutions," or family planning, or the levels of withdrawals and additions that each individual requires. With this full ecological imposition of limits, painful tradeoffs between population size and levels of consumption must be addressed at all levels of social, economic, and technological decision making (Schnaiberg 1981). Such an implementation of ecological sustainability will also necessitate some very painful distributive questions. Whom, and how many, should be allowed to consume what and for how long? Should we reverse our current thrust toward extending the life span of humans? Should we, as we do now, restrict high levels of resource consumption to a privileged few while the majority live in perpetual poverty at near-starvation levels of consumption? Should forced sterilization be implemented? If so, who should be sterilized—the masses of the poor or the privileged elite? Should grizzly bears that attack humans be rewarded rather than killed or relocated? Should humans that encroach on grizzly bear territories be shot?

ENDANGERED SPECIES AND SUSTAINABLE DEVELOPMENT: ENVIRONMENTALISM GONE LOCO

As the world witnesses the most rapid and extensive extinction event in human history, many international bodies and national governments have attempted to protect the remaining population of specific endangered species. In Chile, one such endangered species is the *concholepas concholepas*, a tasty mollusk known in Asia as "Chilean abalone" and locally as the "loco." The loco is found exclusively off the coast of Chile and southern Peru and is considered a delicacy by locals, as well as by the more affluent populations of Hong Kong, Taiwan, and Singapore. Unsustainable rates of loco extraction have resulted in the collapse of the loco population. In 1988 it was discovered that loco stocks had dropped from 208,000 to 28,000 in a single year. This dramatic population decline led Chilean authorities to impose a ban on loco extraction in an effort to preserve the species. However, far from ending the loco trade, the ban actually accelerated extraction.

Following the ban, "loco gangs" emerged to traffic in the protected species. The ban on loco extraction caused the world market price for the mollusk to soar. The illegal sale of locos to Asian markets is now estimated to be a $70 million (U.S. dollars) a year industry. Local fishermen can earn up to five times their usual income by engaging in illegal loco extraction. The usual income for Chilean fishermen is about U.S. $250 a year. In this instance, as in many others, the socioeconomic circumstances of individuals in a global economy have determined their willingness to protect the environment. As one local fisherman put it, "Why shouldn't fishermen in this country be able to make a decent living?" After all, "It's not like they're selling drugs, it's just fish. And if people are willing to pay, what's the problem?"

The loco ban is producing many of the same social impacts that have emanated from bans on drugs. The loco trade is also proving as difficult to control as drug smuggling, despite the imposition of fines and jail terms. Although over 200 loco traffickers have been arrested since 1990, the industry is still expanding. Enforcement is nearly impossible, with 169 inspectors managing fishing along a 3000-kilometer coast. The *locotraficantes* are highly organized, encompassing all stages of production, from local extraction, through processing, to distribution on the world market. Attempts to thwart this illicit business have even resulted in death threats to judges in Chile as well as to Chilean officials in Asia.

The government has recently determined that the only way to stop this trade and prevent the extinction of the loco is to encourage fishermen to commit themselves to sustainable development and environmental awareness. In October 1992 the Chilean National Fisheries Service decided to allow fishermen to extract locos, but only those larger than 10 centimeters, while imposing bans only between January and May, which is the peak period of loco reproduction. Chilean officials are also working with the United Nations Food and Agriculture Organization to develop methods of commercially farming locos. In addition, the Chilean government has established 26 loco-management zones, in cooperation with local fishermen, to educate impoverished coastal residents about the ecological hazards of over-fishing. This sustainable development scheme appears to be having some success. Here, as elsewhere, it has proved necessary to provide an ecologically sustainable local economy in order to achieve the goal of protecting a species' intrinsic right to continue to exist.

Although many deep ecologists (Evernden 1985) have promoted such a conceptualization of ecological sustainability, very few have been willing to confront the essential social, economic, political, and technological questions arising from the problem of how to achieve these ends. The political spectrum of deep ecological responses to the problem of implementation ranges from the eco-fascist, to the eco-anarchistic, to the eco-metaphysical. Some (Ophuls 1977) have suggested a benign dictatorship of the eco-sensitive, who would make the difficult choices and hand them down to a world of politically powerless people. But how would such leaders be chosen, and how would they enforce their rulings? Others have suggested that we all get "back to the land," living as self-sufficient subsistence agriculturalists. But how would we prevent people from utilizing the environmentally destructive technologies we have developed? And how would we support such subsistence agriculture without denuding the world's forests? (In China, relatively low levels of consumption and large populations destroyed the great forests thousands of years before the industrial revolution.) Yet others have suggested that by raising the consciousness of every human being, we will achieve a voluntary eco-poverty and voluntary eco-family planning. Any of these mechanisms will be difficult in a world in which, from the richest to the poorest, we are seeking ways to increase our material standards of living, even if we do so by writing books about the need for environmental sensitivity. How do we get from unmitigated environmental destruction to unmitigated environmental integrity? Do we even want to?

CAN WE DO IT ALL? CAN WE DO IT AT ALL?

Clearly, the higher the degree of environmental protection we attempt to attain, the greater the disruption of the treadmill, and the deeper and broader the social, economic, and technological changes we will need to implement. Just as recycling does the least good for the environment but is the most easily implementable, so too will it be easiest for us to continue down the road of sustaining the treadmill at the expense of the natural world. Moving from recycling to reuse will produce much greater environmental gains, but it will require greater material sacrifices and greater structural change in our economies. It will also evoke greater levels of resistance from the treadmill elites (Schnaiberg 1980: ch. 9).

To reuse is the first step toward reducing our levels of material consumption. We will still manufacture and purchase the products we do now, but we will have to produce them to last and use them for much longer. When people in industrial economies reuse their old cars instead of buying new ones, profits to elites decline, industrial workers lose jobs, and their families are impoverished or they go on the public dole. If we reuse all the products that we now habitually replace, because of either changing fashion or built-in obsolescence, the level of economic activity will drop precipitously, and the treadmill will slow down. When these changes occur because of economic rather than environmental considerations, we call it a recession. Although it may be possible to make some gains in the public political arena by appealing for environmental protection, it will be less likely to prove effective when framed as an appeal for a voluntary economic recession. However, when framed as a measure to preserve the environment for other social uses, where the majority of the population will be able to take advantage of these uses, some sacrifice of growth could become politically acceptable. Such an appeal will be less effective if it is grounded on the intrinsic rights of nonhuman species rather than on the desirability of preserving the environment for other social uses. To sacrifice some growth so that we can go fishing is one thing; to sacrifice growth and restrict fishing is quite another.

To move from extensive reuse to extensive reduction will be even more difficult. Reuse raises deeper distributive questions than recycling, and reduction moves these distributive questions to the forefront. Will we all reduce equally? To equal levels? Will some have to reduce more? Relatively or absolutely? By reusing, consumers may be able to save money while still retaining access to a wide variety of products. If consumers can be weaned from their socialization to expect new and improved product fashions, they may even find that more durable goods are a benefit to more than just the natural environment.

Reduction, however, implies giving up access to many consumer products that have severe negative environmental impacts. Living simply so that others may simply live may have some limited appeal on a voluntary basis, but involuntary reductions of material standards of living are likely to be met with all the enthusiasm of urban dwellers in Pol Pot's Cambodia. In addition to the virtual elimination of private automobiles, electronic goods, and fossil fuel heat, the extreme economic restructuring required by such changes will leave millions unemployed. If reuse implies fewer jobs as the treadmill of production slows, reduction implies sweeping plant closings as the treadmill grinds to a halt. Most industrial workers and their families may find themselves ill equipped to live off the land as subsistence agriculturalists as they migrate from the urban industrial centers. Of course, the government may "assist" in relocating urban workers to rural work "camps," but this is unlikely to be achieved on a voluntary basis. Reduction will necessitate a voluntary economic depression. Policies promoting a depression and mass relocation to government-sponsored agrarian work camps are not likely to gain much public support in the political arenas of the industrialized nations, and they are too similar to the status quo to gain much support in the South.

To move from eco-fantasy (utopian or dystopian, depending on your point of view) to eco-political reality, what can we reasonably expect to accomplish in terms of altering the treadmill of production in order to achieve some measure of environmental protection and sustainability in the next twenty to fifty years? The changes required to sustain the existing economic treadmill should be relatively easy to accomplish. Such changes are based on the internal logic of the treadmill itself and do not represent a threat to the current distribution of power. They may produce a greater gap between rich and poor as pricing is used to distribute increasingly scarce natural resources, but such restratification is already firmly in progress. Both recycling and resource substitution have already become socially and politically acceptable means by which to sustain the current economy by increasing the burden on the working class and the poor. The wealth and power of the privileged elite are not threatened by implementing this notion of sustainability. Therefore, the elites have promoted such socially regressive nonstructural environmental alterations of the treadmill.

As we have seen, sustaining the treadmill may appear to produce some limited environmental gains in the short run. But in the long run, the treadmill will consume the natural world just as surely as it is doing now. To achieve more lasting environmental goals, some structural modification of the treadmill will have to be achieved (Redclift 1987; Schnaiberg 1980: ch. 9). The most promising political basis on which to achieve fundamental support for accepting the economic costs of greater levels of environmental protection is an appeal based on the desirability of making other social uses of the natural world. This approach may offend the sensibilities of many deep ecologists (Evernden 1985), but it remains the best hope for real environmental benefits in the near future. The greatest gains are likely to be made in those arenas where institutionalizing some concern for preserving the environment for other social uses least threatens jobs and economic growth. The greater the disruption of the economy, the harder it will be to make the necessary modifications to the treadmill.

Difficulty does not imply impossibility. However, the greater the potential resistance, the more social resources and political savvy that environmental goal attainment will require. To force the treadmill to yield to concerns for preserving the environment for other social uses will require a great deal of coordinated political activism and the development of realistic economic alternatives for the dislocated activities and actors. Environmentalists will have to recognize and address the real socioeconomic tradeoffs involved in treadmill modification, using sound political persuasion and sound economic planning (Redclift 1987). Mechanisms to distribute the economic costs of environmental protection more equitably throughout the stratification spectrum will have to be developed if environmentalists are to gain the support of the majority of the domestic and global population, which is either poor or working class. To underestimate or to ignore the potentially regressive social impacts, the depth and breadth of the tradeoffs, or the resistance of those powerful actors whose interests may be threatened is to invite political defeat.

To press for voluntary reduction on a mass scale based on concern for the intrinsic rights of ecosystems, species, and individual nonhuman organisms is also to invite defeat in the public political arena. It may be possible to achieve some of this in a very limited way, restricted primarily to the protection of "sexy mega-species" like whales, pandas, and gorillas. The best hope for making gains based on sustaining the environment for its own sake will be to raise consciousness on a mass scale through success in achieving sustainability for other social uses. We must eco-walk before we can eco-run. Successful institutionalization of other social use goals could result in a greater number of people seeing the validity and necessity of deeper ecological views. Putting people back in touch with nature may allow greater recognition of nature as an important value regardless of human usage. However, people are always likely to put people first in human political systems, especially when the tradeoffs between social use and ecological integrity are greatest. In the near future, there are simply too many human problems, too many human interests, and too many politically and economically distasteful tradeoffs for relatively abstract environmental goals to be pursued with great enthusiasm by political leaders and the majority of their constituents. It is best then to focus on what is reasonably achievable, at least as a first step toward ecotopian visions.

SELECTED REFERENCES

BARLETT, DONALD L. & J. B. STEELE
   1992   *America: What Went Wrong?* Kansas City: Andrews & McMeel.
BLUMBERG, PAUL
   1980   *Inequality in an Age of Decline.* New York: Oxford University Press.
BROWN, LESTER R., EDITOR
   1991   *The WorldWatch Reader on Global Environmental Issues.* New York: W.W. Norton.
BROWN, LESTER R., C. FLAVIN, & S. POSTEL
   1991   *Saving the Planet: How to Shape an Environmentally Sustainable Global Economy.* New York: W.W. Norton.

BURTON, DUDLEY J.
   1986 "Contradictions and changes in labour response to distributional implica-
        tions of environmental-resource policies." Pp. 287–314 in A. Schnaiberg,
        N. Watts, and K. Zimmermann, editors, *Distributional Conflicts in Environ-
        mental-Resource Policy.* Aldershot, England: Gower Publishing.
CATTON, WILLIAM R., JR.
   1980 *Overshoot: The Ecological Basis of Revolutionary Change.* Urbana, IL: Univer-
        sity of Illinois Press.
COMMONER, BARRY
   1972 *The Closing Circle: Nature, Man and Technology.* New York: Alfred A.
        Knopf.
   1977 *The Poverty of Power: Energy and the Economic Crisis.* New York: Bantam
        Books.
COURT, THIJS DE LA
   1990 *Beyond Brundtland: Green Development in the 1990s.* London: Zed Books.
EVERNDEN, NEIL
   1985 *The Natural Alien.* Toronto: University of Toronto Press.
FARVAR, M. & GLAESER, B.
   1979 *Politics of Ecodevelopment.* Berlin: International Institute for Environment
        and Society, Wissenschaftzentrum-Berlin.
FRAHM, A. M. & FRED BUTTEL
   1982 "Appropriate technology." *Humboldt Journal of Social Relations* 9 (2),
        (Spring/Summer):11–37.
GALBRAITH, JOHN KENNETH
   1992 "The tyranny of the contented: Because most voters are financially com-
        fortable, our government ignores economic suffering." *Utne Reader* Sep-
        tember/October: 64–65.
GLAESER, BERNHARD
   1984 *Ecodevelopment: Concepts, Projects, Strategies.* Oxford: Pergamon Press.
GOFMAN, JOHN W. & ARTHUR R. TAMPLIN
   1971 *Poisoned Power: The Case against Nuclear Power Plants.* Emmaus, PA: Rodale
        Press.
GOULD, KENNETH A.
   1991 "Money, management, and manipulation: Environmental mobilization in
        the Great Lakes." Dissertation, Department of Sociology, Northwestern
        University, Evanston, IL, June.
HAYS, SAMUEL P.
   1969 *Conservation and the Gospel of Efficiency: The Progressive Conservation Move-
        ment, 1890–1920.* New York: Atheneum Books.
MAZUR, ALLAN
   1991 *Global Social Problems.* Englewood Cliffs, NJ: Prentice-Hall.
MUMFORD, LEWIS
   1967 *The Myth of the Machine: Technics and Human Development.* New York:
        Harcourt, Brace Jovanovich.
NEEDLEMAN, JACOB
   1991 *Money and the Meaning of Life.* Garden City, NY: Doubleday.
OPHULS, WILLIAM
   1977 *Ecology and the Politics of Scarcity: Prologue to a Political Theory of the Steady
        State.* San Francisco, CA: W. H. Freeman.
PHILLIPS, KEVIN
   1989 *The Politics of Rich and Poor: Wealth and the American Electorate in the Reagan
        Aftermath.* New York: Random House.

REDCLIFT, MICHAEL
1987 *Sustainable Development: Exploring the Contradictions.* New York: Methuen.
REICH, ROBERT B.
1991 *The Wealth of Nations: Preparing Ourselves for 21st Century Capitalism.* New York: Alfred A. Knopf.
SCHNAIBERG, ALLAN
1980 *The Environment: From Surplus to Scarcity.* New York: Oxford University Press.
1981 "Will population slowdowns yield resource conservation? Some social demurrers." *Qualitative Sociology* 4 (Spring): 21–33.
1992a "Recycling vs. remanufacturing: Redistributive realities." Working paper WP-92-15, Center for Urban Affairs & Policy Research, Northwestern University, Spring.
1992b "The recycling shell game: Multinational economic organization vs. local political ineffectuality." Working paper WP-92-16, Center for Urban Affairs & Policy Research, Northwestern University, Spring.
1994 "The political economy of environmental problems: Consciousness, conflict, and control capacity." In Riley Dunlap and William Michelson, editors, *Handbook of Environmental Sociology.* Westport, CT: Greenwood Publishing.
SCHOR, JULIET B.
1991 *The Overworked American: The Unexpected Decline of Leisure.* New York: Basic Books.
SHIVA, VANADANA
1989 *Staying Alive: Women, Ecology, and Development.* London: Zed Books.
TOBER, JAMES A.
1981 *Who Owns the Wildlife? The Political Economy of Conservation in Nineteenth Century America.* Westport, CT: Greenwood Publishing.
U.S. FEDERAL HIGHWAY ADMINISTRATION
1987 *Highway Statistics Summary to 1985.* Washington, DC: U.S. Government Printing Office.
1989 *Highway Statistics 1988.* Washington, DC: U.S. Government Printing Office.
VINCENT, ISABEL
1992 "Fishermen find lucrative business in shady trade." *The Globe and Mail,* [Toronto, Canada], November 21.
WORLD COMMISSION ON ENVIRONMENT & DEVELOPMENT
1987 *Our Common Future.* New York: Oxford University Press.
WORSTER, DONALD
1973 *American Environmentalism: The Formative Period, 1860–1915.* New York: John Wiley & Sons.

EPILOGUE: *International Words and Deeds*

10. *The Road to* and *from Rio: Sustainable Development versus the Politics of the Treadmill*

THE VIEW FROM RIO: DILEMMAS IN EVALUATING ENVIRONMENTAL CHANGES

A book like this customarily ends with a concise statement of where we are with regard to the state of environmental problems and solutions and what can be done to improve this situation. As we have noted earlier, the recent United Nations Conference on Environment and Development was a morass of confusion and contradiction in its attempt to answer these two questions. Both governmental and nongovernmental conferences proceeded simultaneously, with quite different perspectives and policies. With well-earned humility, therefore, we will not seek to answer these questions here, important as they are. Rather, we will try to explain why these questions are so difficult to answer both now and in the foreseeable future.

Evaluating the state of environmental problems and the effectiveness of society in dealing with them is difficult largely because these are intensely political as well as scientific questions. In this section, we note three levels of difficulty:

1. limitations in the scientific data available for various kinds of environmental problems and policies.
2. problems of comparing various kinds of environmental impacts and policies.
3. political differences in the criteria used to evaluate each impact or policy.

Let us start with the ecological dimension of these analyses. Suppose that we had unlimited natural scientific research resources and could document everything about the biosphere. Would that enable us to answer the question of whether environmental problems are becoming worse or improving? The answer, alas, is "No." Why? The core reason is simple: the "objective" scientific data would have to be evaluated by the analyst, and that would require a social and a political definition of "better" and "worse."

Take any of the range of environmental issues we have treated in the

227

preceding chapters. Is the toxic waste problem becoming better? To answer that, we would need data on every form of toxic waste, and how it is handled and distributed across ecosystems. We don't actually have such complete data. In fact, current estimates in the United States may account for only 10 percent of the actual toxic wastes released into the American environment. But assume we did have this full set of data. Suppose that for 50 percent of these wastes, there is some agreement that methods of reduction, reuse, and recycling together have reduced their total emissions by 25 percent. For the remaining 50 percent of toxic wastes, assume that these have risen by 25 percent in a given period. A policy analyst would then have to compare and contrast the total "impacts" of the two sets of toxic wastes in order to determine if the toxic waste problem was getting better or worse. That would require enormous assumptions, or inferential leaps, for two reasons.

First, we never have full documentation of all the ecological and health impacts of any toxic waste (see Chapter 7). Moreover, there appears to be a systematic treadmill bias in what we do record. Researchers avoid studying many toxic byproducts of major economic growth sectors, because leaders of these treadmill sectors tend to oppose such study (Schnaiberg 1980: ch. VII).

Second, even if we did have them available, we would have to make political and social judgments about the social severity of any given increased impact, in order to compare it with the effect of some decreased impact (Spector & Kitsuse 1987). This would require a magical metric, so that we could compare losses of habitats for animal and plant species, extinctions of some species, increases in various human illnesses, and raised levels of mortality for young versus middle-aged versus elderly citizens. These would then have to be compared with the protections, gains, and decreases in negative impacts in these same categories. Within the period of modern environmentalism, there has been a recurring demand for just such an overview metric, with creative fantasies about natural resource units, reduced person-years of life expectancy, science courts, energy-entropy equations, and the newest entry, sustainability (Schnaiberg 1980: chs. VI & VII). All of these seek to raise the discourse to a level of scientific authority, which has itself been increasingly under attack by sociologists of science. These analysts note that scientists themselves construct models of the world and do not merely discover them (e.g., Mulkay 1991). In addition, they also construct models which would only serve to reinforce their own authority (e.g., Wright 1992).

Third, and perhaps most subtly, there is a problem of a frame of reference for evaluating toxic and other ecological hazards, as well as policies designed to reduce such hazards. This factor, which we could call the "fully-only" debate, is the most basic, enduring, and difficult political dynamic in evaluating social and environmental change. The corporate executives, engineers, and public relations spokepeople for Active Petroleum Corporation and Basic Chemical Company (see Chapter 3) use measures of historical change in evaluating ecological hazards and environmental protection policies. They will present objective data to argue how fully they have changed their ways of operating. Their corporate balance sheets and reports to stockholders will note, among the following, fully how much more they spent for toxic waste processing in 1994 compared to 1993. They might also note that they produced only 75 percent of the toxic wastes in 1994 than they had in 1993. Consulting Associates might note that fully 25 percent more of their consulting time in 1994 was spent on environmental clean-up operations, compared to 1993. From these objective reports (giving them the benefit of the doubt) the following inflated political rhetoric emerges: "we are good environmental citizens," and, "we have done fully as much as we possibly can to respond to environmentalists."

This same scenario from these fully-environmental corporations may be viewed quite differently by some environmental movement organizations, their scientific allies, and some environmental agencies such as the Environmental Protection Agency (EPA) This is because their frame of reference is quite different: they are measuring change relative to a standard of future environmental protection. That is, their question is: how close has this corporation come to having little or no impact on its ecosystems? Note that this is a different yardstick from that used by corporations to measure recent changes in environmental hazards and environmental protection. Typically, these ecological and social analysts find that these corporations have only reduced their emissions by 25 percent from 1993 to 1994, and that they have only spent 25 percent of what they should spend additionally in 1994 to reduce to insignificance their emissions from 1993 levels.

This means that the same information is processed in diametrically different ways by these two social groups, and each is correct in their perception. Figure 10.1 on p. 230 llustrates this process in a graphic fashion.

We can also illustrate this analytic uncertainty, by drawing on our automobile fuel usage example from Chapter 9. Table 10.1 on p. 230 estimates 1988 automobile fuel demands under various real and hypothetical conditions. These conditions include combinations of the actual fuel efficiency improvements in autos from 1975 to 1988, as well as estimates of what would have happened if hypothetical driving restrictions had been added to a national energy policy, along with the legislation mandating higher fuel efficiency. These driving restrictions, which would have seriously challenged many treadmill features of private automobile use, would have mandated no increase in total driving from 1975 to 1988 (a difficult policy to enforce, we acknowledge).

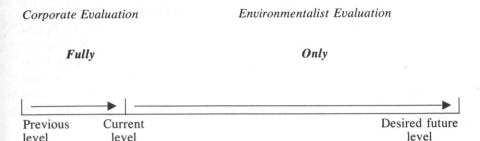

FIGURE 10.1 The Fully versus Only evaluation of environmental policy changes

There are two quite different reference points from which we can review the estimates of Table 10.1. We could compare the fuel consumption estimates to the historical automobile demand in 1975. From this perspective we can interpret cell (d) to indicate that we saved "fully" 30 billion gallons, compared to what would have happened *if there had been no gains in fuel efficiency*. This is a typical type of evaluation offered by corporate officials. Conversely, as we suggest in Figure 10.1, we could instead refer to the fuel savings that a policy, which included and/or substituted driving restrictions, might have potentially generated. Here, we would interpret cell (c) as indicating that we have saved "only" 4.3 billion gallons, far below the potential gains of 24.3 billion gallons that cell (a) suggests would have occurred *if we instituted both fuel efficiency and driving restrictions*. This is a typical type of evaluation made by environmental movement organizations.

Thus, as analysts who are aware of all three levels of problems in assessing the environmental problem, we are reluctant to make any summary evaluations of the nature of current and prospective ecological and

TABLE 10.1   Alternative Estimates for Fuel Consumed by Automobiles in 1988, and Fuel Savings (in Parentheses) from the 1975 Start of the "Energy Problem"

		Behavioral Restrictions on Driving?	
		YES	NO
	YES	(a) 52.1 billion gals. (*24.3* billion gals. saved)	(c) 71.7 billion gals. (*4.3* billion gals. saved)
Technological Controls on Fuel Consumption?	NO	(b) 76.4 billion gals. (*0* gals. saved)	(d) 106.4 billion gals. (*30* billion gals. saved)

health hazards. It is our political judgment, in the light of scientific data, that there are very serious local, regional, national, international, and global ecological problems. Readers who seek to make their own judgments should consult sources such as *The Environmental Almanac, Environmental Indicators, State of the World, World Resources,* and *The Earth Care Annual.* These contain evidence of both positive reductions in ecosystem disorganization (e.g., in pesticides) and negative increases in such disorganization (e.g., tropical rainforest destruction).

Overall, however, our central argument in this book is that the trend is towards increased scale and scope of ecosystem disorganization, unless the treadmill of production is seriously decelerated or dismantled. This is the next summary position we will outline here.

THE ENDURING QUALITY OF ENVIRONMENTAL TENSIONS

Our title of this book indicates our belief that the nature of our problems with the natural environment is enduring. But they are not necessarily unchanging or unchangeable in the future. In the modern period of environmentalism, we have seen a dramatic increase in public consciousness about ecological limits and in the mobilization of citizens in a wide variety of environmental movement organizations. Together with these popular and even populist changes, modern governments have established new forms and mechanisms for some restrictions on economic markets. This has represented some movement away from an economic synthesis of the conflicts between economic expansion and ecological protection, towards a somewhat managed scarcity approach to balancing economic growth through treadmill acceleration, and tinkering with the treadmill structure to slow the rate of increase in ecological withdrawals and additions.

But the core logic of the treadmill is strongly anti-ecological. Indeed, as Barlett and Steele (1992) have cogently argued, it is also strongly antisocial. The political and economic agreement to create social welfare by accelerating the treadmill has been an enduring feature of the twentieth century, especially following the two world wars. From the broadly utilitarian perspective of delivering the greatest good(s) to the greatest numbers, this treadmill seems to have done its task with some efficacy from 1918 to 1963. Beyond that, as Commoner (1972) noted two decades ago, the economic productivity of capital, the core dynamic allocative mechanism of the treadmill of production, began to decline. Social analyses in the following two decades (e.g., Barlett & Steele 1992; Blumberg 1980; Phillips 1989; Schor 1991) affirm that the treadmill of production is running faster and delivering fewer social benefits to ever wider segments of the U.S. and world populations for each accelerative spurt of the treadmill. This implies that the social productivity of the treadmill has slowed even more in the past two decades (Goodwin 1992).

These two analyses of the changing economic and social efficacy of the treadmill are coupled with the central argument of this book: that ecological productivity is also declining. That is, fewer social welfare benefits are being generated for each withdrawal from or addition to ecosystems. If we stopped our summary at this point, the attentive reader would properly ask: "then why are we retaining our commitment to the treadmill of production, since it works so badly?"

Throughout these chapters, our response has been that the treadmill works very well for a variety of social groups and organizations. It delivers historically unprecedented rates of profit to one set of capital owners, as indicated in the recent decade by a substantial increase in the number of U.S. millionaires (as contrasted with an equally substantial increase in poverty and homelessness). It is precisely those groups for whom it works so well, who have maintained or expanded their political power to induce governments to deepen their commitments to the treadmill (Galbraith 1992). In recent presidential elections in the United States, the candidates have competed over *how* to accelerate the treadmill rather than *whether* to dismantle it (Phillips 1989). Candidates in both parties obtain support from segments of the society which derive considerable benefits from maintaining the treadmill (Barlett & Steele 1992).

The remainder of the population derives a complex and volatile mixture of benefits and costs from the acceleration of the treadmill. As Schor (1991) has noted, the United States has broadened its consumption of goods, but at the cost of diminished leisure and many social goods, including family time and environmental protection. As long as the political, social, and cultural institutions of modern society are heavily dependent on and supportive of the treadmill logic and structure, the tensions between the treadmill and the ecosphere will continue to expand.

It is not clear how high these tensions, or others in the social and political arena, must rise before some serious reconsideration of the treadmill will occur. At each point, those social agents with a variety of exchange-value or market interests (through investments, wages, or tax revenues) will defend the treadmill and attack those who question its logic. What is clear is that the treadmill has become the "only game in town," especially after a nominally different (cf. Feshbach & Friendly 1991) system of socialist options had virtually disappeared by the dawn of the 1990s. In the absence of a serious restructuring of the markets of the treadmill, this "victory of the treadmill," a geopolitically important change, may turn out to be a Pyrrhic victory. But such restructuring will be resisted in an enduring series of skirmishes and perhaps major conflicts, since some members of every society are highly satisfied by the treadmill's operation, and all members of every society seek some satisfactions that the treadmill has historically offered to many citizens in the modern world (Galbraith 1992).

CONFLICT AND COALITION

Why Is Conflict Unavoidable?

As you have seen throughout this book, the future of environmentally and socially sustainable development is dependent on the outcomes of a variety of current and future conflicts. The contradictions between the logic of the treadmill of production and the logic of natural ecosystems necessitate that conflicts will emerge in any attempt to preserve and protect natural systems in the face of ever increasing demands on resources emerging from treadmill acceleration. This is both the good news and the bad news. It is bad news primarily because many of us would prefer to believe that we can simultaneously avoid conflict and protect the environment. Many of us find the very idea of conflict distasteful and the notion of enduring conflict even more unpleasant. However, the good news is that, by demonstrating an ability and willingness to engage in conflict on a variety of levels, we can make an important contribution to the success of ecologically and socially sustainable development trajectories.

In addition, any conflict presents both constraints and opportunities. The constraints emerge from the resistance to change that a variety of groups with varying interests in maintaining the treadmill will likely present. Any social action in defense of the environment must begin with a clear analysis and comprehension of the powerful forces that will be mobilized to thwart that action. The opportunities emerge from the fact that the very existence of conflict indicates that outcomes are uncertain. If outcomes are uncertain, change can always be accomplished, and there is no reason to accept the notion that the victory of the treadmill is a foregone conclusion (Phillips 1989).

Conflict also presents an opportunity to form coalitions between a wide variety of individuals and groups in support of social change. Forming a coalition is not an easy task. It can be expected that treadmill supporters will make strong efforts aimed at preventing and dividing coalitions. Coalition formation can also be expected to require difficult compromises with other groups and individuals seeking to dismantle the treadmill, for a variety of ecological and nonecological reasons (see Chapter 7). Coalition formation is, however, essential to achieve success in conflicts with the logic of the treadmill, and in the coalition formation process, new friends, new allies, new ideas, and new possibilities will necessarily emerge. If we are to make socioenvironmental progress, we must accept the idea that not only conflict but also coalition formation is good, productive, necessary, and normal. The trick will be to form the right coalitions at the right times and for the right conflictual issues (Staggenborg 1991).

International Conflict and Coalition

As seen in Chapter 8 and elsewhere throughout the book, a primary arena for future conflict over environment and development will be on the international level. The wide variation between the levels and types of ecological damage inflicted by the nations of the world guarantees that nations will come into conflict with one another over solutions to global environmental problems. Similarly, the wide variation among nations in terms of the distribution of benefits received from ecosystem withdrawals and additions will also necessitate conflict in the international arena (Buttel & Taylor 1992). In seeking solutions, conflicts will emerge from the international distribution of the costs and benefits of environmental protection. Some of the lines of cleavage for these present and future international conflicts are relatively obvious to us from this point in history. Others are more subtle and will emerge from the actions taken in the international arena in the immediate future.

One clear line of cleavage is the tension between the North and the South. As indicated in Chapter 8 and as evidenced by the Rio conference, the unequal distribution of environmental destruction, economic gains from that destruction, and costs of environmental protection between North and South will be the primary dimension of international conflict in the environmental and other arena(s) in the years ahead. The establishment of a new world order where the gains and losses of the last few hundred years of unequal development are frozen in place for perpetuity will not be acceptable to nations of the South as they attempt to provide for the needs and aspirations of their people. Global environmental protection will necessarily require a redistribution of wealth from rich to poor nations. This will produce conflict as industrialized nations attempt to preserve their privilege and power, and developing nations attempt to bring living standards up from bare subsistence levels (Buttel & Taylor 1992). The North will have to sacrifice more, simply because it has more to sacrifice. Such conflicts also present the potential for coalitions and North-South agreements. The South will be in an increasingly better position to negotiate the terms of exchange for increasingly scarce resources and for protection of Southern environments that will produce benefits for North and South alike (Hecht & Cockburn 1992).

Another point of conflict in the international arena will continue to be between North and North. Industrialized nations will tend to come into conflict with each other as they vie for relative positioning in an increasingly competitive and ecologically limited world economy. They will also continue to come into conflict over transnational flows of environmental hazards, such as the acid rain conflict between the United States and Canada, the European uproar over the Chernobyl accident in the former Soviet Union, and the contamination of shared bodies of water such as key European rivers, the North Sea, and the Great Lakes. They are also likely to come into occasional conflict over the assessment of the need to establish international treaties to limit certain activities such as whaling, chlorofluorocarbon production, and greenhouse gas emissions. Those nations contributing most to the problem will feel unfairly limited by other nations which will have to institutionalize fewer economic changes. The good news here is that, by forcing each other to become aware and sensitive to the transnational ecological impacts of their economic activities, these conflicts are likely to be catalysts for multilateral agreements and coalitions aimed at reducing specific activities that result in the more mobile ecological hazards. The Montreal Protocol and the U.S.-Canadian agreement on acid rain are but two examples of how these North-North conflicts have resulted in multinational environmental protection measures. By creating international limits on certain activities that apply to all industrial nations, the economic playing field has been leveled. As a consequence, nations can compete economically without the unequal advantage that might accrue to a nation that has failed to implement specific environmental limitations.

Yet other conflicts will continue to emerge between South and South. These conflicts are likely to develop along a number of lines. First, as ecological limits are reimposed on human economic activities, a certain amount of scrambling for position will probably take place among the nations of the South. Just as tensions have developed between North and South owing to differences in levels of economic power, contributions to ecological disruption, and the distribution of environmental protection costs, so will these dimensions cause some friction within the developing world. Redistributional issues are likely to emerge in the South between the more and less prosperous countries. As in North-South and North-North conflicts, equity and environmental efforts by one nation are likely to bestow benefits on neighboring nations. If those neighbors act as "free riders" (Olson 1965), using the ecological gains accruing from their neighbors' actions as an opportunity to expand growth policies domestically, either a renewal of the current race to expand production will occur or the economic gaps between neighboring nations will widen. Therefore, strong South-South coalitions must be developed, not only for empowerment in conflicts with the North, but also for ensuring cooperation rather than competition between Southern nations (South Commission 1990). Already a number of such coalitions have been formed, more or less successfully, around resource production (such as the Organization of Petroleum Exporting Countries), around regional development (such as the Organization for African Unity), and around equity issues (such as the alliance among the so-called frontline states in southern Africa). The more successful these South-South coalitions are, the greater the opportunity to avoid economic competition and to protect ecosystems across national boundaries.

National Conflict and Coalition

On the national level, conflict will center on two primary dimensions. The first will continue to be the contradictions between growth and environmental protection. As we have seen in Chapters 3, 4, and 5, most individuals and groups have an economic stake in continuing the treadmill. As ecological limits and economic recessions further impede the generation of wealth, we are likely to hear a renewed call for treadmill acceleration at the expense of the environment. The "environmental president's" failure to mention environmental issues in the 1992 State of the Union Address indicates how rapidly environmental concerns can fall off of the national political agenda. Those seeking to promote ecological goals will have to come into direct conflict with growth proponents. To succeed in these conflicts, coalitions will have to be made across the second dimension of national conflict. That dimension is the conflict between growth and social equity goals. Until recently, treadmill elites have been successful in pitting equity groups against environmental groups (Bullard 1993). Environmental groups, as seen in Chapter 7, have often proved willing to accept this position in relation to equity proponents. Success in opposing the treadmill of production will require new and sustainable coalition formation between environmental and equity groups. These coalitions will necessitate some difficult compromises. However, such coalitions, if formed, will prove a powerful force in promoting environmental justice values in opposition to the continuation and acceleration of the treadmill.

Regional Conflict and Coalition

Within nations, conflicts between and within regions are likely to occur. Some of this discord can already be seen in the tensions between midwestern states and the states of the northeast over the acid rain problem. In that conflict, economic gains made in the midwest through electrical power generation and heavy industrial production produced transregional environmental problems that primarily affected northeastern forests, lakes, and streams. Those ecological impacts resulted in economic losses as well, as tourism declined owing to the loss of trees and fish. While that issue pitted midwest against northeast, it also served as a catalyst for regional coalition formation among northeastern states who found themselves drawn together by mutual ecological interests. Those mutual interests further raised environmental consciousness regionally, which can be used to ecological advantage in other conflicts, such as that surrounding Hydro-Quebec's James Bay project in Canada.

Similarly, the contamination of the Great Lakes has served to bring the eight Great Lakes states together in an effort to protect this regional resource but not without a great deal of interstate conflict. The process of negotiating agreements on issues such as nutrient loadings to the lakes was full of conflict but eventually resulted in regional cooperation. The Council of Great Lakes Governors was formed largely in response to calls by southwestern states for an interregional diversion of Great Lakes water to the water-scarce cities of their region (Gould 1991). Here again, an interregional conflict served as a catalyst for regional coalition formation. Similar situations are bound to emerge in regions such as the Mississippi River basin, as states and municipalities attempt to clean up the river while distributing the costs of clean-up equitably.

Local Conflict and Coalition

On the local level, conflicts between growth proponents and environmentalists are likely to be particularly prevalent, as towns and municipalities find themselves in increasingly competitive situations owing to the mobility of capital both nationally and internationally (Gould 1991). As with nations and regions, competition to retain and attract economic investment will cause ecologically sensitive communities to lose economic ground to those communities that are more willing to accept hazardous industries and waste facilities. In such a situation, environmental advocates are likely to be attacked by local growth coalitions (Logan & Molotch 1987) as opponents of economic progress. The successful resolution of such conflicts will depend primarily on two types of coalition formation.

First, environmentalists will have to form grass-roots coalitions with equity groups to garner the breadth of support necessary to oppose the power of growth-oriented local officials and investors. Here again, environmental justice coalitions such as those appearing throughout minority communities in the southern U.S. (Bullard 1990, 1993) and elsewhere (Krauss 1992) will be essential. Second, intercommunity coalitions will be needed to thwart the tendency of nearby communities to compete for capital investment, both private and public. One community's refusal to accept a hazardous waste dump or industry is likely to simply send that investment to the next community down the road. The mobilization of grass-roots opposition between communities will make it possible to keep a hazard from being located in a wider region. Further coalition formation with yet more distant communities will make it impossible to locate hazards in an increasingly larger region, eventually causing the treadmill to yield to widespread intercommunity opposition to a particular industrial process or product (Schnaiberg 1992). In such a process, it will be essential that strong efforts be made to mobilize the least powerful communities to prevent all producers of hazards from seeking the poorest and most disenfranchised localities. That is where the redistributive dimensions of equity movements will be most important: sending resources to those at the bottom of the power hierarchy (Gould et al. 1993; Schnaiberg 1993).

Interpersonal Conflict and Coalition

The conflicts necessitated by the contradictions between ecological systems and the treadmill of production will even devolve down to the interpersonal level (as indicated in Chapter 6). At this level, we must remember that conflict does not always mean confrontation. Successful conflict resolution in favor of ecosystems on the interpersonal level will require much skill and patience. The types of interpersonal conflicts that are likely to emerge are those within families. You may experience conflict with your parent(s) over differences between their career expectations for you and your own career choices in light of your understanding of ecological limits. This kind of conflict may be particularly distasteful, but it is nonetheless wise to predict and prepare for it. Parents may not readily understand your concern with ecological sustainability, as your economic success is likely to be a primary concern for them. Helping them to redefine success may be a task in your future (Galbraith 1992; Saltzman 1991). Your success in your future path will be largely determined by their level of resistance.

Similar conflicts may also emerge between you and your peers, for people do not have equally sophisticated views of ecological problems. You may have to explain yourself at length as you try to get them to understand the career and lifestyle choices you make. This explanation may or may not be successful. This may be one way for you to find out who your real friends are, and why. You will also have to recognize that many of your peers are likely to make nonecological career and lifestyle decisions, and that they may appear to be enjoying the material fruits of your ecological sacrifices. Take heart. If you want to make a difference, you have to be different.

Finally, conflict may emerge as you negotiate your future with your present or future mate. Decisions about lifestyles, levels of material comfort, career structures and projections, and family size all present the possibility for conflict (Schor 1991). Again, it is important to remember that conflict need not always be confrontational. Coalition formation between you and your mate, you and your friends, and you and your parents

---

ECOLOGICAL PROMISES VERSUS ECONOMIC PRESSURES: ENDURING CHALLENGES TO "ENVIRONMENTAL" LEADERSHIP

One way of appreciating the enduring quality of conflicts that center around environmental policies is to examine the change of U.S. political administrations in 1993. After 12 years of capital accumulation policies, Americans elected a new, more "environmental" slate, Governor Bill Clinton of Arkansas and Senator Al Gore of Tennessee. Gore had been actively involved in the 1992 United Nations Conference on Environment and Development in Rio. As the author of a 1992 book, *Earth in the Balance: Ecology and the Human Spirit*, he thus became the United States' most publicly environmentalist leader in the national political arena since Theodore Roosevelt.

Paradoxically, the presidential campaign involved little debate about environmental policy, and the program proposed for the incoming administration is not strongly environmental. Domestic pressures from the recession, which simultaneously threatened jobs, wages, tax receipts, and public employment, could not be readily solved by modern policies of economic stimulation. Such tax-based subsidies would only aggravate the huge national debt generated by the previous administrations' underwriting of capital accumulation by treadmill elites. This policy disproportionately benefited the owners of capital rather than blue-collar and middle-class workers, increasing the accelerative pressures on the treadmill. Should the new administration's program fail to satisfy these disaffected blue- and white-collar workers who voted for new economic policies, it will be resisted by congressmen, who have to run for reelection in two years, as well as by the one-third of the senators who also face reelection in 1994.

Does this mean that the "human spirit" that the new vice-president alluded to in his book will be irrelevant for the future legislation program? Environmental movement organizations are prepared to defer some of their environmental policy pressures on the new administration. They hope that in the longer term, an environmental-friendly administration will shape economic policy while incorporating environmental protection as much as is politically possible. If this hope proves true, the net social system change would be a modification of rather than a dismantling of the treadmill.

---

may prove particularly difficult (Goodwin 1992; Reich 1991). Then again, success at bridging these conflicts may be particularly rewarding (Galbraith 1992).

Intrapersonal Conflict and Its Resolution

The final and most basic level of conflict may be that which is internal to yourself. Positioning yourself within the context of all these conflicts and coalitions is likely to require quite a bit of soul-searching. Not eve¹ level, type, or style of conflict and coalition is right for everybody. You will have to determine what you can and can't do, and how you want to approach the tasks at hand. You may find yourself conflicted over the gap between your material desires and your understanding of the ecological ramifications of satisfying those desires. You may also have to come to grips with difficult tradeoffs between social status and personal integrity. These are difficult conflicts, especially since a part of you identifies with both sides. You must decide who you are, who you want to be, and what you want to do in light of your understanding of the world around you and your place in it (Saltzman 1991).

Ultimately, you will have to decide whether to act on your knowledge and understanding in the face of current and future conflicts, or to acquiesce to the power of the treadmill. Without doubt passive acquiescence to the status quo is in many ways an easier road to travel. You must decide whether the path of least resistance is the path that you want to travel. Although blazing new trails is always difficult, it is also more rewarding. We can't promise you a road to glory, but we can guarantee that without people who are willing to take up the challenge, the treadmill will roll on, and the planet and all its inhabitants will pay the price.

CONCLUSION: THE FUTURE IS WIDE OPEN (WITHIN LIMITS)

The fact that the future of societal-environmental relations will inevitably be full of conflict means that the future offers us substantial opportunities for positive change. Each conflict, along each dimension, for every issue, and at every level, will eventually be resolved in ways that benefit either the environment or the treadmill. Concerted effort on the part of determined individuals, groups, communities, regions, and nations can help to achieve environmentally and socially sustainable outcomes in many of these conflicts (Barlett & Steele 1992; Galbraith 1992; Reich 1991).

Despite all this potential for positive change, it would be foolish, and ultimately self-defeating, to underestimate the powerful forces mobilized in support of the treadmill. The power and inertia of the treadmill represent constraints within which any future progressive change with regard to both social equity and ecological integrity goals will be achieved. There is no way to achieve these goals in conjunction with maintaining the core logic of the treadmill. Underestimating the power of the treadmill leads ʌloping unrealistic expectations as to what true opposition to it will ʌ's opponents. Equally important, underestimating the ability ʌ social change leads to developing unrealistically low what their efforts can actually achieve (Reich 1991;

With regard to future possibilities represented by the treadmill, we must accept the nature of the conflicts that will emerge and the social, economic, and political terrains on which these conflicts will occur. The lines of conflict have already been drawn by the historical evolution of the treadmill. But the outcomes of these future conflicts are not predetermined. Effective action *is* possible. The treadmill is not immutable. Both social consciousness and ecological changes afford new pressures and possibilities. In that sense, the future is truly wide open (Goodwin 1992; Reich 1991; Schor 1991).

SELECTED REFERENCES

BARLETT, DONALD L. & J. B. STEELE
1992 *America: What Went Wrong?* Kansas City, MO: Andrews & McMeel.
BLUMBERG, PAUL
1980 *Inequality in an Age of Decline.* New York: Oxford University Press.
BULLARD, ROBERT D.
1990 *Dumping in Dixie: Race, Class and Environmental Quality.* Boulder, CO: Westview Press.
BULLARD, ROBERT D., EDITOR
1993 *Confronting Environmental Racism: Voices from the Crossroads.* Boston, MA: South End Press.
BUTTEL, FREDERICK H.
1992 "Environmental sociology and global change: A critical assessment." *Society and Natural Resources* 5(3) 211–230.
BUTTEL, FREDERICK H. & H. NEWBY, EDITORS
1980 *The Rural Sociology of the Advanced Societies: Critical Perspectives.* Montclair, NJ: Allanheld, Osmun & Co. & London: Croom Helm.
COMMONER, BARRY
1972 *The Closing Circle: Nature, Man and Technology.* New York: Alfred A. Knopf.
1990 *Making Peace with the Planet.* New York: Pantheon Books.
FESHBACH, MURRAY & ALFRED FRIENDLY, JR.
1991 *Ecocide in the USSR: Health and Nature under Siege.* New York: Basic Books.
FRIEDLAND, WILLIAM, H. L. BUSCH, F. H. BUTTEL, & A. RUDY, EDITORS
1991 *Towards a New Political Economy of Agriculture.* Boulder, CO: Westview Press.
GALBRAITH, JOHN KENNETH
1992 *The Culture of Contentment.* Boston: Houghton Mifflin.
GOODWIN, RICHARD N.
1992 *Promises to Keep: A Call for a New American Revolution.* New York: Times Books.
GOULD, KENNETH A.
1991 "Money, management and manipulation: Environmental mobilization in the Great Lakes Basin." Doctoral dissertation, Department of Sociology, Northwestern University, June.
GOULD, KENNETH A., A. S. WEINBERG, & A. SCHNAIBERG
1993 "Legitimating Impetus: Pyrrhic Victories of the Modern Environmental Movement." *Qualitative Sociology,* (special issue), April.

HECHT, SUSANNA & A. COCKBURN
1992 "Rhetoric and reality in Rio." *The Nation*, June 22: 848–853.
KRAUSS, CELENE
1992 "Women and toxic waste protests: Race, class and gender as resources of resistance." Paper presented at the annual meetings, American Sociological Association, Pittsburgh, August.
LOGAN, JOHN R. AND HARVEY L. MOLOTCH
1987 *Urban Fortunes: The Political Economy of Place.* Berkeley: University of California Press.
MULKAY, MICHAEL
1991 *Sociology of Science: A Sociological Pilgrimage.* Bloomington, IN: Indiana University Press.
NATIONAL PARK SERVICE, UNITED STATES DEPARTMENT OF THE INTERIOR
1991 *National Park Service Administrative History: A Guide.* History Division. Washington, DC: National Park Service.
NATIONAL WILDLIFE FEDERATION
1991 *The Earth Care Annual.* Washington, DC: National Wildlife Federation.
OLSON, MANCUR
1965 *The Logic of Collection Action: Public Goods and the Theory of Groups.* Cambridge, MA: Harvard University Press.
ORGANIZATION OF ECONOMIC COOPERATION & DEVELOPMENT
1991 *Environmental Indicators.* Paris: OECD.
PHILLIPS, KEVIN
1989 *The Politics of Rich and Poor: Wealth and the American Electorate in the Reagan Aftermath.* New York: Random House.
REICH, ROBERT B.
1991 *The Wealth of Nations: Preparing Ourselves for 21st Century Capitalism.* New York: Alfred A. Knopf.
RUDEL, THOMAS K.
1989 *Situations and Strategies in American Land Use Planning.* London: Cambridge University Press.
RUDEL, THOMAS K. & B. HOROWITZ
1993 *Tropical Deforestation: Small Farmers and Land Clearing in the Ecuadorian Amazon.* New York: Columbia University Press.
SALTZMAN, AMY
1991 *Downshifting: Reinventing Success on a Slower Track.* New York: Harper Perennial.
SCHNAIBERG, ALLAN
1980 *The Environment: From Surplus to Scarcity.* New York: Oxford University Press.
1992 "Oppositions." *Science*, 255 (20 March): 1586–1587.
SCHNAIBERG, ALLAN, EDITOR
1993 "Social Equity and Environmental Activism: Utopias, Dystopias and Incrementalism." *Qualitative Sociology*, (special issue).
SCHOR, JULIET
1991 *The Overworked American: The Unexpected Decline of Leisure.* New York: Basic Books.
SPECTOR, MALCOLM AND J. I. KITSUSE
1987 *Constructing Social Problems.* New York: Aldine de Gruyter.
STAGGENBORG, SUZANNE
1991 *The Pro-Choice Movement: Organization and Activism in the Abortion Conflict.* New York: Oxford University Press.

SWANSON, STEVENSON
1992 "When in office, Gore may find it isn't easy thinking green." *Chicago Tribune,* November 8.
WORLD RESOURCES INSTITUTE
1992 *The Environmental Almanac.* Washington, DC: World Resources Institute.
WORLDWATCH INSTITUTE
1984ff *State of the World:* 1984–1991. Washington, DC: Worldwatch Institute.
WRIGHT, WILL
1992 *Wild Knowledge: Science, Language and Social Life in a Fragile Environment.* Minneapolis: University of Minnesota Press.

Index